To my dear friends R.

   With love and in hopes
that peace will finally come to
our people.

      Santa Fe, N. M.
   June 17, 1994

The Journey Home

From Poland
to the Promised Land

The Journey Home

From Poland
to the Promised Land
(A Family Saga)

By Sarah K. Heller

SHENGOLD PUBLISHERS, INC.
New York

ISBN 0-88400-167-9
Library of Congress Catalog Card Number: 93-08543
Copyright © 1993 by Sarah K. Heller
All rights reserved

Published by Shengold Publishers, Inc.
18 West 45th Street, New York, NY 10036

Printed in the United States of America

To my beloved sister
Celia S. Heller
Who has been a great inspiration to me throughout my life.
and
to my children and grandchildren, so they may know their heritage, and
be proud of their roots in the great Jewish community of Poland.

Chapter 1

THE PROMISED LAND

A bright cloudless Tel Aviv day came through the window slats. He lay there aware only of the reality of his dream. She was running toward him in the fields near his village, her long curly hair swept by the breeze, her body flexible and graceful. He moved toward her, caught her and was kissing her passionately when the noise of a military plane broke the sound barrier. Just a patrol, he thought. They flew that way daily, and he had gotten used to the vibrations of the house and the funny feeling in the pit of his stomach.

The other feeling, the nice feeling, was a dream of long ago. Now he was living in Tel Aviv, and she had died over a year ago in the spring. She had been an old lady when she died, not the young girl he had just seen in his dream, and he was an old man. Life was so hard, now that she was gone. It got harder each day.

He forced himself to get out of bed, washed and dressed meticulously, put on his panama hat, took his walking cane, and left the house. It was a fast day, the 9th of Av, and he must visit the Prayer House.

As he walked, he fell into a reverie. A few days before, he had gone to her grave. His daughter Surale, just arrived from the States, had gone with him. He hadn't been at Idisel's grave for a while, and it seemed to him that he was seeing it for the first time. A cement slab covered the place of her burial. The headstone was carved with flowers, and there was a quotation on it by a poet born in Spain. When he had been there before, he could only see Idisel as she had been in life, beautiful even in old age. Now he was beginning to accept her physical absence. Between the headstone and the cement slab, little flowers were pushing their way toward the sun, dancing in the breeze. He glanced at the other graves. There were no wild flowers on any of them. She had loved flowers. Surale, understanding his thoughts, smiled wistfully. Last spring, she had brought lilacs to her dying mother, lilacs from the land her parents had called home for many years, and Idisel was thrilled at the sight and fragrance of them. They had been her favorite flowers.

Mendale looked up at the blue cloudless sky. The perfect quiet was so strange. In this land, where every moment of existence had to be protected and the sound of planes traversing the narrow frontiers could often be heard, the stillness was comforting. He looked down again. Idisel had wanted her father's name on her grave: "Shaul HaKohen Rosenmann, a scholar, Kabbalist, and saintly man, died for the Sanctification of the Lord's Name, at the hands of the Nazi murderers, Skole, Poland, 1942." The yellow flowers trembled in the breeze.

Surale took his hand, and they both began crying quietly. How much like her mother she was, and yet untamed and searching, like himself, struggling and reaching for something elusive and not giving up. He looked at her carefully. She was no longer the tow-headed child he took with him when he went riding in the countryside, who sang and danced to the delight of all his friends. She was a middle-aged woman with three grown children of her own. After all these years of helping her, when his own strength was ebbing, she was his strength.

He lost track of time, until the sound of the patrol plane returning interrupted his transcendent meditation. "Idisel," he whispered, "I miss you. We'll be together soon, very soon."

Recalled to the present, he looked about him. Weizmann Boulevard. Yes, he was on his way to the House of Prayer, and had to cross over here. It was still very early in the morning, but traffic was already heavy. He crossed over carefully, and started up the hill toward Jan Smuts Boulevard. It suddenly seemed very steep, and he had to stop to catch his breath. A sharp pain went through his chest. His heart again. Funny, until a few years ago, Idisel had always been the stronger one. She was hardly ever sick, and always took care of him when he felt ill. He had never thought he would survive her and had worried about that. What would she do without him? He tried to make sure that she would be financially secure and comfortable after he died. Well, as sure as any human can possibly be these days. But, the Holy One, Blessed be He, decided to call her first.

Well, the pain had subsided. He could go on. Yes, today was Tisha b'Av, the 9th of Av, the anniversary of the dispersal and suffering of his people.

He recalled that, after visiting Idisel's grave, he and Surale decided to go up to Jerusalem, so he could pray at the Western Wall. It as the only part of the Temple that had survived the destruction of the city by the

Romans. Here the people came to pray and ask the Holy One for help. They wrote messages on small pieces of paper and stuck them in the crevices between the rocks. He had put notes there many times before, when he had come with Idisel. She had wanted him to. This time he wrote no request. In his heart he had only a prayer for peace and another one, to be reunited with her. He had stood for a long time in silent meditation.

The sound of the muezzin calling the faithful of Islam to prayer came from a minaret above the Dome of the Rock. He looked up. That's where the Temple had stood before its destruction. Now it was a Muslim shrine. The voice from above was melodic and sweet, and although he understood only the "Allah," Mendale prayed that the children of Ishmael be reconciled with the Children of Jacob, Israel.

He and Surale had had lunch in the deserted garden of the Rockefeller Museum, and then had gone to visit Golda Meir's grave in the national cemetery. She had been Prime Minister of the country, and had died the year before, like Idisel. Two valiant women, he thought. It had been the anniversary of Herzl's death some days before, and as they passed his grave, they saw a profusion of wreaths, flowers, and banners covering it. "Surale, when I die, I want no epitaphs, no writing on my tombstone, only my name and the dates. Remember that." She promised.

"Jerusalem, Jerusalem, the holy city," he hummed as he walked toward the House of Prayer. In his mind's eye he saw Jerusalem in golden tones, with that unique light that distinguishes it from all other cities of the world. But he wasn't in Jerusalem right now, he reminded himself, trying to keep his mind on the present. Ah, here was the House of Prayer now.

Many people were already there, waiting for services to start. He removed his shoes and sat down on the floor among the people, close to the friends with whom he daily studied the holy books. He saw them somehow differently today. In their readings and discussions on previous days, they had ascended together into a distinct reality, above the worldly concerns, somewhere there above, closer to the Holy One. There were just five of them out of this large assembly, but the bond was eternal. Soon they began chanting the lamentations of the prophet Jeremiah, and the Kinot, the elegy on the destruction of Jerusalem, its Temple, and its people by the Romans.

The service filled Mendale with sadness, and when it was over, he felt glad that his daughter was waiting for him at home. At least he wouldn't be returning to an empty apartment, full of memories of Idisel, and after a day of fasting, it would be good to have a tasty dinner.

He tried to explain some of this as he ate his daughter's good cooking. Surale smiled and told him not to be so sad. "There is a reborn Israel now, strong and proud," she said starting to clear the table. "Let's not think too much about the past, but about the bright future that awaits us."

"The past has a great deal to teach us, my dear," he said. "We must strive to be a better and more moral people, to love one another and to practice justice. We were destroyed as a nation because we went against these precepts. If we imitate the evil of the other nations, we're bound to fail."

"But remember last year in Hebron, how angry you got at the way we were treated?" Surale asked.

They had had to wait a long time to be admitted to the Machpelah Cave, where Abraham, Isaac, and Jacob were buried (Genesis 23 and 24). Mendale recalled his own anger at being treated in this manner. This was the West Bank, Israeli territory, and yet the Arabs seemed to be in full control. The burial place was occupied by a mosque, so Jews had to wait, whereas, Muslims could enter at any time.

"I feel like we're in exile again, in our own Land of Israel," Mendale recalled saying to the soldier who was guarding the group of Jewish tourists. The soldier was sympathetic. "When the Jordanians ran this place, no Jew was allowed in at all. We were cut off from visiting all our holy places, both here and in Jerusalem. They still retain a great deal of power."

The reservist fingered his Uzi and checked his watch. "Ah, now you can go in."

Mendale put his hand on the reservist's shoulder. "You probably know that Abraham our father, bought this plot and the Cave of machpelah from Ephron the Hittite for four hundred shekels of silver. Abraham needed it for a burial place for his wife Sara. It states clearly in Genesis. It is a legal contract and therefore, the Arabs have no right to treat it as their exclusive property."

A young soldier appeared at the entrance and signaled that the group could enter. The cave was dark but lighted by a number of candles. In one corner a pulpit was set up, and the people asked Mendale to lead in the prayer. His voice rose upward as he chanted. It seemed to reach up to heaven.

From the Cave, they had walked back quietly to the small restaurant where they had left Idisel, the climb and the long wait being too difficult for her. Now as they reentered the restaurant, Mendale realized for the first time that one corner of the ceiling was charred and burned.

"What happened here?" he asked the cashier.

"The Arabs tried to burn us out. For the third time. But we are still here and plan to stay." He helped Mendale to his seat.

"You're very brave, but is it worth it to endanger your life in this way?"

"My dear sir," said the cashier, "my ancestors have lived in Hebron from time immemorial. In 1929, my grandparents and eight of their children were slaughtered here by the Arabs. Their house is still standing, but an Arab family lives in it. My mother survived because she happened to be visiting relatives in Haifa at the time. My grandfather was a religious man, a peaceful man. He grew up with his Arab neighbors and spoke their language, and yet they did that to him.

"I have returned to this city never to leave it again. No one has a right to tell me that I can't live here. They can't treat me the way they did my grandfather. I'm armed and ready to defend myself."

Now back in the safety of his home in Tel Aviv, Mendale remembered vividly that day in Hebron.

"Both the Jews and the Arabs have a claim to this country," he told his son-in-law. "Yet I believe that, for the sake of peace, they must eventually establish some *modus vivendi*. I have great hopes for the future."

Just then, the doorbell rang, and it was Musa, an Arab neighbor and a friend. "I've come to say good-bye for a while," he said. "I'll be returning home tomorrow and didn't want to miss you."

Musa was from a village near Nablus. He'd been working in Tel Aviv for a year now as watchman for the new apartment building on the corner, and Mendale and he had gotten to know each other well. Musa owned a farm and an olive grove near his village. Before the Six Day War in 1967, he'd been a policeman in the Jordanian police force. He now worked with an Israeli construction company while his sons took care of the farm. The money was good, and he liked being in the big city. A pious man, Musa would perform his morning devotions on the construction site, before the rest of the crew arrived. Mendale would see him when he himself was on his way to six o'clock services at the House of Prayer. He would spread his prayer rug and turn toward Mecca, bowing and prostrating himself before God.

When Mendale and he began to talk to each other, they realized that they understood one another well on a religious and spiritual level. They had long discussions about the Koran and the Bible. Mendale told Musa about Maimonides, who had lived in Egypt and wrote many of his works in Arabic. He realized that Musa was not formally educated but was able to discuss many philosophical subjects. However, they didn't agree on the matter of the State of Israel. Mendale would try to avoid the subject, but it would inevitably crop up.

"You're not Israeli-born," Musa once said to him, "and that's why you can understand better how I feel about things. Daily, I'm subjected to indignities, because people assume that, being an Arab, I'm a terrorist and an evil person. I'm a believing person. Allah has willed it that we Arabs and Jews live in this land. We must find a way to live here in peace, respecting each other's ways and customs, and tolerating each other's differences."

"My dear Musa, I share your sentiments about peace, but you are mistaken about one thing: This is my land too. For countless generations, since the destruction of Jerusalem two thousand years ago, our people have lived here. My direct ancestors were among those scattered all over the world, but they never lost hope that they would return to this beautiful land and rebuild it. When I came here to live in 1971, I was a man coming *home*."

Musa was silent, and after a moment Mendale resumed awkwardly, "There are still many things wrong here that have to be corrected, but I think we're trying."

"You won your independence in 1948," Musa said in a strange voice, "but I lost mine in 1967, when the Israelis seized the West Bank. I could have fled and still can go to Jordan if I wish, but I will never leave my farm or sell the land that my father left me, and that I will leave one day, by the will of Allah, to my oldest son, when I pass on."

"But under Israeli law," Mendale argued, "you have equal rights as a citizen, social security, hospitalization, even the privilege of marrying more than one wife according to your own custom. Jews and Christians are only allowed one wife."

Musa would not look him in the eye. "Under Jordanian rule, I had my self-respect," he said slowly. "People honored me and my position. Now I'm just a second-class citizen."

"Well, I know how that feels. I was a second-class citizen myself for a long time. But surely there are compensations in your life now." Mendale wanted to hear his friend say something positive, but Musa was in a strange mood, apparently determined to make his feelings understood.

"Economically I'm better off, yes. I don't have to work at all if I don't want to. I've been able to build a big house on a hill overlooking the farm. It has all modern conveniences and is almost as nice as the village muhdar's. I have all my children and grandchildren close to me. I probably couldn't have afforded that kind of luxury in the old days. But again, in the old days I had my honor. . . ."

One couldn't very well argue with honor. Mendale clapped his friend on the shoulder and said, "Let's hope that other conditions will improve for you as well. Let us both pray for peace between our peoples—as we have made peace between ourselves." The two men shook hands warmly.

Since that day there had been a special bond between them. Musa would often come up in the afternoon, drink tea with Mendale, and play chess. From time to time Musa would go back to his village and bring back news of his family and the events in the area.

One day a neighbor of Musa's was arrested. He had killed a young man from the next village because the man had raped his sister; then he had come home and killed the girl as well. The man was arrested, and Musa was deeply upset.

"The Israeli judge will never understand that my neighbor killed to redeem the honor of his family. He is being treated by the authorities like a common criminal. There it is, your Israeli justice."

"Musa, the law has to be the same for everyone," Mendale said helplessly. He knew Musa could not understand the concept of Western law. He came from an older, different set of customs and thoughts. This was a basic problem in Israel bridging the yawning chasm between cultures.

Tonight they sat down together, and Mendale offered him tea. Musa, of course, spurned alcohol. The two men sat and talked and drank their tea. "You will come to my house in Nablus some day, and you will be a very welcome guest." said Musa. "In the meantime, may Allah watch over you."

As the day came to an end, he embraced Mendale. "God willing, we shall see each other soon." Mendale saw him to the door.

Mendale couldn't fall asleep that night. He got up to study, to find solace in the Torah and the commentaries. It was always a source of marvel to him, a revelation and strength, the Torah, "the tree of life." But his

his thoughts wandered far from the familiar page that he had studied and pondered over so many times.. He thought instead of his own destiny. H had been spared the martyrdom of his people during the Holocaust, and had finally returned to a free Land of Israel. Silently he mediated and thanked the Creator for that great privilege, for his children and grandchildren. . .

Mendale returned to his studies but a strange feeling overtook him, almost like weightlessness. He was outside his physical self and seeing himself as though he were another person. Suddenly he began to feel his body again and felt a sharp piercing pain in his heart. He pressed his hand against it as if to stop it. Now the pain went through his entire body, and he couldn't seem to hold up his head. . . .

Surale was there. Why was that? Hadn't she gone to bed? But he was too tired to explain her presence to himself or her voice saying, "Yes, an emergency. . ." Then he felt her hand in his, warm and alive, and he tried to squeeze it, but even his fingers seemed to have no strength in them. He knew the truth then.

"No need for them, Surale. . . . I'm dying." He stopped, exhausted, his blue eyes glowing with an intense unearthly light.

"Promise you will bury me next to Idisel."

"I promise. . . but no, you're not going to die now. You're going to live." She kissed his lips and lingered to make sure that he was breathing. "The ambulance will be here any minute," she said in a quivering voice.

He seemed to gather his strength now: "My time has come, Surale. I'm ready. Chipale, my child. . . . Chanale. . . ." his voice trailed away. Only his lips were moving as he whispered the "Shema Israel."

At the hospital, they did everything they could, but life had departed. Then they detached him from their machines and called his daughter into the small room where they had left him.

Surale turned down the sheet that covered his face and stared at her father. Death seemed to have stripped years away from him, so that he looked like a man of perhaps fifty, prematurely white-haired. The doctors who had tried to save him had bruised his lips, ruining their symmetry, but that was the only sign of his passing. She touched the crisp white curls and kissed his face, then found a pair of surgical scissors in a metal cabinet and with trembling hands, cut off a lock.

He was still a little warm. An unfamiliar sweet smell emanated from his body when she kissed his throat. It was the smell of death. She touched his hands, the long fingers and shapely nails that were so agile in life. Then she touched his face. A tremendous sense of pity overwhelmed her. How could this sharp and incisive mind, this beautiful body be dead? She felt inconsolable and totally alone.

She whispered, "Papa, do you remember the song you used to sing when I was small?"

> *"Come home little Israel, come home*
> *to your own beautiful land.*
> *Return, don't hesitate,*
> *to become a nation among nations.*
> *Little Israel, my brother, come home."*

She took his hand, feeling once again the long fingers with their shapely nails. "Your wish came true, Papa. You have returned. After years of striving, yearning, and wondering, you have come home. I promise you now that I will tell the story of your life, that through it others may learn of a world that was so brutally destroyed, the world of our people in Poland."

Chapter 2
THE BEGINNING

It was May, 1897.

An Austrian police wagon entered the courtyard of a small inn near the Galician village of Szwedy. A police officer and two of his deputies got out, went inside, and spoke to the tall red-headed man tending bar.

"Are you Symcha Heller?"

"Yes," answered the man.

"I arrest you in the name of Franz Josef, Emperor of Austria."

The official handed Symcha a paper.

"There must be some mistake, Herr Polizist. I've committed no crime."

"I must warn you that if you resist, we shall have to use force."

The two deputies put their hands on their guns.

"What are the charges against me, Herr Polizist?"

"Selling contraband liquor."

Symcha tried to think, to stall for time. He had indeed been selling contraband, but he had little choice. The "official" spirits, manufactured and sold by Prince Lubomirski, who was landlord to everyone for miles around, was rotgut and heavily watered at that. The peasants refused to drink it, and without their patronage, Symcha's little inn would have no income. One had to feed one's family.

But he thought of the prince. The prince would not want word to get out of his misuse of the liquor monopoly. Perhaps, if he were appealed to in the right way, he would intervene. These aristocrats were all-powerful.

"If you will be seated, Herr Polizist, I will send a message to Prince Lubomirski, my landlord. He will vouch for my honesty."

The prince's name evidently impressed the officer. "Very well. We will wait." But he ordered his aides to search the premises for evidence while they waited.

Symcha called Aron, his oldest son, and told him to saddle a horse and ride at top speed to the Lubomirski Palace. "Tell his excellency that he must send word immediately. It's a matter of extreme urgency.

Only he has the power to save me from going to prison."

Symcha scribbled a hasty message and handed it to the boy, who mounted and was off within minutes. Aron followed the main road for a while through the woods, then turned into a narrow tree-lined lane that led to the palace. The gatekeeper looked at the envelope and let him in, then showed Aron where to leave his horse and which door to enter by. In the kitchen, the boy was allowed to speak to the butler.

The butler gazed at him askance. "The prince is at breakfast and can't be disturbed."

"But, sir, this is a matter of life and death."

A maid in uniform now opened the door, and from inside Aron heard a commanding deep voice: "Let the boy enter."

Aron was about to go in, but the butler detained him. "In the prince's presence, you must behave properly, you know. You must remove your hat, and bow low. Don't get too close—the prince hates the smell of garlic. And address him as 'your excellency.' " He then admitted Aron to a large and ornate dining room, a dazzle of gold leaf, rich fabrics, and colorful paintings.

Prince Lubomirski and his wife, an elegantly dressed pair in early middle age, were drinking coffee and chatting in French. Suddenly, they both started laughing.

Aron couldn't collect his thoughts and only belatedly remembered to take off his hat and bow. He wondered if they were laughing at him. The butler took the letter from his hand and handed it to the prince on a small tray.

"Well, open it," the prince mumbled, then wiped his mouth and hands with a large linen napkin, and took the note. "It looks like the Jews are trying to cheat me again, and they've been caught red-handed. Yes, Symcha's been buying liquor from illegal sources." He slapped the note. "And look at *this*—now he wants me—me, his victim—to bail him out!"

Lubomirski's face turned a deep red, and his watery blue eyes bulged. He was breathing heavily.

"My dear, don't get yourself excited!" the princess cried in alarm. She stroked her husband's arm and then his face. "Remember what the doctor said. Those people aren't worth getting sick over." She handed him a glass of water and a pill, and gradually he calmed down.

After a minute the prince turned and glared at Aron. "Well? What have you got to say to all this, boy?"

Aron summoned up every ounce of resolution he could manage. "My name if Aron, suh—Your Excellency. Symcha is my father, and he's a very good man. All people around here respect him, both Christians and Jews. Ask anyone. Now he's in danger, and only you can help him. If you don't, they will put him in jail, and then what will become of us?"

The glare faded from the prince's face, and he glanced at his wife. "He speaks beautiful Polish, doesn't he?" Then, to Aron: "Where did you learn to speak Polish?"

"My father has a tutor for us," Aron replied proudly. Hoping to impress the prince, he added, "We are learning Polish and German and Hebrew, as well as mathematics, grammar, and literature."

"Who are 'we'?"

"My two sisters, my little brother, and I." Another child was on the way, Aron knew, but he didn't think he should mention that.

"Come closer, boy." When Aron, mindful of the garlic warning, had sidled timidly within reach, the prince touched his hair and side locks. "Pavel, bring a pair of scissors," he called to the butler.

Aron drew back. "We are not allowed to cut our payess, sir! It is forbidden."

But when the butler seized him, he let the prince snip off the side curls. Perhaps this sacrifice would induce the aristocrat to help.

The prince folded the red hair carefully into a tissue paper, and put it in his pocket. "I shall keep it because it's the most beautiful hair I've ever seen," he said. "Except yours, my dear, of course," he added, bowing toward his wife.

Was the prince won over? Aron decided he had to try again. "Your honor, will you come now? My father is waiting for your help."

"My dear boy, we just arrived from Paris yesterday. It is a long journey, and we are terribly tired. As a matter of fact, this entire conversation has exhausted me."

"But, your honor, please, he will be put in jail."

The prince shrugged. "Sorry, Aron. He should not have done what he did. He must now suffer the consequences."

Aron left the palace in a daze. Mounting his horse again, he got to a safe distance from the palace and then began to cry. He had failed his father. Maybe he hadn't said the right words to the prince. Maybe he shouldn't have protested when the prince was about to cut his side curls. But he must pull himself together before he got home. His father and mother mustn't see him cry—nor the policemen nor any of his father's customers. Now he would have to be the man in the family.

By the time Aron dismounted in the courtyard of the inn, he had himself under control. He walked in and talked directly to Symcha.:

"The prince refused to come, father. Forgive me that I couldn't bring him to help." Then his voice broke.

His father's face turned a shade paler, but all he said was "Thank you, my son. You've done everything you could."

His mother Golda, standing by his father's side, exclaimed in indignation over the missing side curls, and he stammeringly explained. Her heart ached. His hair, his beautiful payess, the mark of a Jewish boy, gone—and she was still livid with rage even as she was fetching his father's overcoat and the black velvet bag that contained his prayer shawl and phylacteries.

For this was the end. Symcha Heller would have to go to prison. If the prince would not vouch for him, then the income from his liquor monopoly must mean more to him than his honor or the welfare of an excellent tenant. He, Symcha, who always held his head high in Szwedy, would have to go to the imperial prison.

Resignedly, he called to the police officers and indicated his surrender. He donned the long black coat and hat that Golda held out to him and accepted the black velvet bag. Aron thought he looked wonderfully dignified as he walked to the police wagon. his red beard shining in the sun.

Golda followed her husband to the police wagon. She was very near her time now, so she waddled clumsily."Symcha, Symcha," she said, "the officers say it will be either six months in jail or a fine—a thousand gulden. I will find the money for the fine."

He bent over to embrace her. She was still in her twenties, this young woman he had married when his first wife died. He was close to 50 now, and she naturally had greater courage and faith in the future.

"May the Lord bless you, Golda, and strengthen you. My heart will be with you and the children." He held her close, and then gathered the two little girls and the little boy into his arms. Don't cry, my doves. Father will be back soon and bring you something special, and lots of candy."

He then turned to Aron and kissed him.

"You will look after your mother, and when her time comes, you will go for the midwife." The two policemen heaved two barrels of vodka into the wagon; one with the prince's seal and the other without. The little family watched as the police wagon disappeared from view.

That night when the children were asleep and Golda was alone in her bed, she cried as she remembered the evil that the prince had perpetrated against her family. When she was still a little girl, her father died suddenly. Her mother Hana, did her best to work the farm by herself, but needed money to plant in the spring. Prince Lubomirski lent her the money, but insisted that Hana return it before harvest time. When she couldn't do that, he put a claim on the land and took it away from her. Hana and the children suffered a great deal that winter. Many days they barely had enough to eat. But then Hana married the prince's innkeeper, Zisia Wald, and things were a great deal better. Zisia was a giant of a man, and very kind to Hana and her children. Soon Golda had a little half brother to care for, and she worked alongside her mother in the house and at the inn. Zisia, her stepfather, was admired by all who knew him.

Golda vowed to see to it that her unborn child's life would be happier than her own, because Prince Lubomirski was again trying to destroy her family. She thought of Symcha spending days in jail and her anger knew no bounds. She clenched her fist and shouted: "You will not succeed in your evil plan, Prince. This time Golda will defeat you with the help of the Almighty."

After a restless night, Golda sent Aron with a letter to her brother in Olszewice, a town much larger than Szwedy. Shmuel had recently returned from a five-year stay in America, where he had accumulated a bit of money, and Golda asked him to lend her the 1,000 gulden, which would obtain the release of her husband. But Shmuel could spare only 500 gulden. Well, they could only hope that would be enough to cover the fine.

The following week Golda embarked on her trip to Rzeszow, where Symcha's trial was to be held. Twelve-year-old Aron was left in charge of the inn, with the maid to do the cooking and take care of the children. The wagon was loaded with food and drink for the two-day journey. Jozef, the driver, helped Golda up to the seat, then took his place, and they set out.

As they plodded along, Golda made her plans. The first night of the trip they would stop at an inn, and then go on to the circuit court in Rzeszow. She had written ahead and asked for an audience with the judge, and she would do her best to plead Symcha's case.

They were only about sixteen kilometers from Rzeszow when the labor pains started. Golda had not planned on this. Fighting panic, she remembered that a distant cousin of her mother's lived in the village of Yasinka, only three kilometers from where they were. They turned the wagon and headed for Yasinka.

They arrived just in time. As her cousin Matel helped her to the bed, the water broke. Then Matel started a fire and put up some water to boil. She told Golda that there was no midwife in the village, and anyway, it was too late for that. She would help Golda and all would be well. The pains were coming strong, and very close now. Golda didn't cry out, but suffered through them. It was hot in the hut, and she was perspiring profusely. When the pains came again she tried to think of something pleasant and she longed to be under her favorite willow tree by the river, her fingers dug into her palms, as the pain grew stronger now. Jozef asked permission to stay in the hut and help. Golda muttered: "No, my friend, it isn't proper. Wait on the bench outside." She heard the door close behind him through a haze of almost unbearable pain. Matel, with her round, kind face was near her. She took hold of Golda's hands, and shouted "Push, push with all your strength. The baby is coming, Keep pushing, push, push." Golda pushed very hard, as hard as she could. She felt as though her body was being torn in two. Now she felt the head coming through. That was the hardest part, and the most painful. She couldn't control the scream that welled up inside her. And now it was all over. She heard Matel shout: "A son, you have another son." Golda repeated softly: "A son, a son." Matel continued surprised: "He has a little cap on his head. He will surely be a leader among our people. Blessed be the Creator." Matel was now cutting the cord, but Golda barely felt the sensation.

When the baby was put into Golda's arms, her pains left her, and an ecstatic glow suffused her face. She looked at him closely. He was unblemished and pink all over. He had blond ringlets that looked as though someone had especially curled them for this occasion. The baby began to nurse, and a pain went through her. But within a few minutes she felt a healing and calming effect in her womb. How she wished at this moment that Symcha were near her. He would hold her hand and kiss her, and be so proud of their fifth child. He would take the baby in his arms and be filled with awe and wonder at God's marvelous creation. As the baby nursed, she looked at him again closely.

"You are my most beautiful baby, and your daddy will be so proud of you. The One On High will give me the strength to rescue your father, so we'll be together again as one family."

Golda told Matel now to call Jozef, who'd been sitting outside on the bench as Golda had told him to do.

Time had passed very slowly for Jozef since Golda asked him to wait outside. It seemed like an eternity to him. When he heard Golda scream, he got up from the bench and began pacing back and forth outside the hut. He remembered his wife and how she suffered through the birth of their first child, but the other five came easy. The youngest, a boy, was born while she was working in the fields. She used to say that he just dropped out, and there he was. Now his children were grown and had their own families. They were all employed on the estate of the prince, except the youngest, who went to America. Irena, his wife, was dead for many years. She had been a good wife to him, always working alongside him, and never complaining. Jozef sighed, remembering her warmth and love. He was all alone and despondent, working the land that he rented from the prince, when Golda, a young bride, asked him to come and work at the inn. He had remembered her as a young girl in her stepfather's inn. He recalled their poverty after Zisia died, and how her mother Hana and the children suffered. Jozef was glad for Golda's good fortune in marrying the widower Symcha, who was prosperous and kind to her. Jozef knew how cruel the prince had been to her family. Well, he'd been pretty bad to him, too, although he, Jozef, was Polish like the prince. He worked the land for him all those years, and what did he have now? Nothing. Except for Golda, he would have become a beggar or something almost as bad, having to depend on his children. Matel's voice broke into his thoughts.

"Pan Jozef, you can come in now. We have a boy."

He followed Matel into the hut. The last rays of the afternoon sun were shining on Golda and the baby. They looked just like the Mother of God and baby Jesus on the altar of the church. Jozef stepped over to the bed and kissed Golda's hand, then got down on his knees.

"Thank you Jesus for bringing my lady through this ordeal. You, too, were born in a hut in Bethlehem. Mother of God, Virgin of Czestochowa, pray for this babe, and return his father to him." Jozef continued to pray silently for a while and Golda let him finish his devotion.

"Thank you for your prayers, Jozef. I too have prayed to our

Heavenly Father to help us. Matel is preparing supper, so please stay and eat with us. Tomorrow early in the morning I will be ready to continue the journey." Golda had now assumed a commanding tone, and Jozef knew that it was useless to contradict her. "My lady, your wish is my command."

Golda had been accustomed to getting out of bed the day after the birth of a child, so it did not seem unusual to wrap up her new little son and resume her place on the wagon. Jozef made a bed of straw for her in the back, and they continued on to Rzeszow.

Two days later, Golda appeared before the Austrian judge with her baby in her arms. The judge was an older man with gray hair and looked very stern. Golda realized how afraid she was when she felt her legs trembling.

"Well, young woman, what's this little baby doing in my court?"

Golda answered that he was only two days old, born on the way to Rzeszow, and that she dared not leave him even to appear before him. "Two days!" he exclaimed. He leaned down from his seat to peer curiously at the little face. "You have great courage, young woman. Now, what's this all about"

The judge listened as she told her story, and when she finished, he pondered for a moment.

"I'm moved by your efforts on behalf of your husband," he said, "but if he has broken the law, he must be punished." He paused, then added delicately, "Tell me, is Symcha Heller guilty as charged?"

"Your honor, he is guilty of trying to feed his family. The inn is our livelihood, but lately, people have stopped coming because the liquor supplied by Prince Lubomirski is of very poor quality." Golda gathered her courage and spoke out boldly: "Is it fair that my husband should be jailed because the prince is betraying the public trust?"

Suddenly a bearded man seated at a nearby table, leaped to his feet. "Your honor!" he cried. "This woman—is defaming the character of the illustrious Prince Lubomirski!"

The judge then ordered two barrels of vodka to be brought in—one containing the illegal liquor, the other with the prince's seal. Smilingly, he told the clerk to taste them. The expression on the clerk's face as he sampled the prince's product was ample proof of what Golda had said.

The judge then gave his decision: "It is quite obvious that Mrs. Heller is right about the quality of the liquor supplied by the prince under his official monopoly. However, this does not totally absolve Symcha Heller from breaking the law. He is fined two hundred and fifty gulden, and is to be released immediately."

Symcha was released that very day, and laughed and cried when he realized that he has a new little son. They returned home. The *Brit Milah* (circumcision ceremony and party) was celebrated with great joy in the courtyard and garden of the inn. They named the child Menachem Mendel (consolation), after the revered Rabbi Menachem Mendel of Kotzk.

Chapter 3
SYMCHA AND HIS SON

Symcha and his youngest son were riding home, in a hurry, because it was late and the Sabbath would soon be upon them. Unlike his brother, Mendale was a tow head, fair hair gleaming in the late afternoon sun.

As they approached the last bend in the road, they heard shouting. Symcha reined in and signaled to Mendale, mounted on a colt behind him, to be quiet. Almost without a sound they rode down the small path toward the noise. "Stay behind me," his father whispered. Soon they came to a clearing, where two men were standing over a bearded older one, whose hands and feet were tied. There was a rope around his neck, which one of them was tightening while the other fellow was trying to cut off the beard. "We'll fix you, you dirty Jew!" he shouted.

Symcha spurred up his horse and charged into the clearing. "Stop that! Let the man go!"

Taken by surprise, the ruffians paused, and Symcha recognized the one holding the rope. "Aren't you Stefan's son? Your father will not be pleased if they hang you for this crime."

Stefan's son looked for a moment at Symcha, then let go of the rope and took off into the woods, but the other man did not stir. "If you move, redhead, I'm going to let the Jew have it."

Symcha gazed grimly at him. "The law of Franz Josef, our emperor, deals swiftly and harshly with murderers, young man. If you stop now, I will not turn you in."

The man hesitated, and as he did, they heard someone coming. He let go of his victim and jumped up. One bitter glance at Symcha, and he was off into the woods.

The newcomer was Symcha's daughter Shainchi; she was carrying a stick and a basket of blueberries which she had been picking. Symcha, relaxed, beckoned to the girl, and bent over the men's victim. "This poor man seems to have fainted."

Mendale slid off his horse and helped his father and sister untie the man's and feet. He was beginning to move groggily and, after a few minutes, revived enough to be put aboard Symcha's horse. Symcha held onto him from one side and Shainchi from the other while Mendale walked behind leading his own mount.

He was puzzled by what had just happened. "Father, why were those two so bad to this man? He wasn't doing them any harm."

"They hurt him because they are evil. They do not have the Torah, which teaches man to distinguish between right and wrong."

That merely puzzled Mendale. "Is it hard to be a Jew?"

"Yes, Mendale, because we are strangers in a Christian land, and they hate us because our ways are different. But one day, my son, we will return to our own land where no one will be able to treat us like that. Then we will rejoice, because we Jews will be brought together from all corners of the earth to our land of Israel."

"When will that be, Father?"

"When the Messiah comes. We must pray for his coming and implore him to come soon, because our suffering in exile has been great, and the injustice of the nations is difficult to bear."

The stranger on the horse seemed to wake out of his stupor and began to recite: "When the Lord brought back the exiles of Zion, we were like dreamers. . . . Our mouth filled with laughter and our tongue was singing. . . ." His trembling voice broke off in choked sobs.

Mendale had begun his Hebrew studies with his father when he was three. Now, a year later, he could read the text well and his father decided to take him to Rozwadow, so the great Rebbe could bless him.

Symcha was not superstitious and didn't believe in old wives' tales. But he didn't reprimand Golda either, and allowed her freedom to practice her little incantations. It pleased her to do it, and there was no harm in it. At times he would joke and laugh about it, teasing her, but she didn't pay any attention.

Symcha was a proud follower and disciple of the Rebbe of Rozwadow, who was a holy and pure man of great powers to intercede with the Creator of behalf of his people, Israel. The Rebbe's realm was not only in heavenly matters, but included good practical sense. The Rebbe was a descendant of the Zaddik (righteous man) Naphtali Hurwic of Ropczyce, who was renowned throughout Poland and beyond its borders. Symcha decided to take Mendale along on his yearly visit to the Rebbe, so that the great man could bless his little son. In previous years, he had taken along his older boys. This year it would be just the two of them. The Rebbe knew Symcha well. He listened carefully and advised Symcha on all matters whether personal or business problems.

When Symcha's first wife died and he was left with two young children, he encouraged him to go on, and not to be despondent. "Be strong and of great courage. When the prescribed time will be over, you will marry again, for your own sake and the children's. Time will heal your wounds."

It happened exactly as the Rebbe had predicted. A few years later, Symcha found great happiness with Golda, who was devoted to him and gave him six lovely children to be proud of. The Creator had surely blessed Symcha, and certainly it had something to do with the Rebbe's intercession. But there was something that hurt him still, that he couldn't come to terms with. His two older children by his first wife, Sruel and Feigale, left home and went to America. They weren't happy that he took such a young bride, and didn't like his choice at all. With all his love for Golda's children, he still missed the children of his youth. They were both married now; his daughter living in Springfield, Massachusetts, and his son living in Willamantic, Connecticut. They had their families and were quite prosperous, but he hoped that they would come home and he would see them again one day. They wrote him regularly about that strange land, where people no longer observed the laws of the Torah, and desecrated the holy Sabbath. They had to do it, it was said, because otherwise they wouldn't be able to hold down a job. He never asked his children if they did the same. Symcha didn't want to know the answer. Certain things were better left as they were. The Rebbe explained to him that even in America there were observant Jews, and that there was a hope that his children and grandchildren would practice their Orthodox faith. The Rebbe knew how to make him feel better, but Symcha couldn't still his longing for those two "Americans." Now that he was going to see his Rebbe again, Symcha looked forward to hearing the latest news about the far away land. The Rebbe had followers even there, who corresponded with him, and even visited him in Poland. The Rebbe's Court was international. Symcha was glad that his children didn't live in that tremendous metropolis of New York, with its crowded tenements, but in the countryside and close to nature.

They traveled to Rozwadow by train and stayed in a rooming house, close to the rebbe's court. Symcha, dressed in his silk coat and round fur hat, walked to the rebbe's prayer house with Mendale at his side. Mendale was also wearing a new silk coat and a velvet cap. It was Friday just before sunset, and the sky was golden. Mendale had looked forward to this moment all day, but when they walked into the House of Prayer, he was afraid of all the people dressed in black. When the services were over, the Hasidim followed the rebbe to another room where the rebbe made the blessing over the wine and bread. The Hasidim vied with each other to get a morsel that the rebbe had touched.

Symcha was standing near the door with Mendale on his shoulders. The rebbe beckoned to him to come closer, and the usher made a passage through the group of disciples for them.

Mendale looked at the rebbe whose eyes were now closed, and then at all these people crowding around him, and he wanted to get away from there. He began to cry. Then the rebbe opened his eyes and fixed his gaze on the boy. He put his hands on Mendale's head, and his caressing voice blessed him: "Peace, health, and may you live to welcome the Messiah, the son of David, in the holy city of Jerusalem."

The boy stopped crying.

It was a sunny day, a few weeks after they had come back from the rebbe, and Mendale was playing with the inn puppy when he heard his mother calling Aron in an alarmed voice. He stood up to see what was the matter.

Aron appeared at the stable door. "What's the matter?"

"It's Father. He fell asleep in the sun and I can't get him to sit up."

Mendale saw his father lying under an elm tree, his mother bent over him. Aron tried to help her prop him up, but it was useless.

"Go get Jozef, and hitch up the wagon," she told Aron. "Mendale, get your sisters. Tell them to bring water, towels, blankets and pillows. We'll take your father to the doctor."

When the children got back, Symcha was still on the ground, but Jozef and Aron carried him between them to the wagon, and laid him on the blankets and pillows. Mendale climbed up and sat near his father, and Golda said that he could come along.

It took an hour and a half to get to Olszwewice. Mendale had to see that the compress on his father's head stayed in place, and dip it in cool water from time to time. He talked to his father, but got no answer.

In Olszwewice, the doctor had been called away on an emergency, so Golda decided to take Symcha to her brother's house nearby to await him. Symcha seemed to get worse after they put him to bed. Golda was trying to give him a drink of water, when he went limp in her arms. She screamed, and everyone came running.

Mendale, watching from the doorway, knew that his father was dead. Afterward, he was never certain how he knew, but he knew.

People were walking in the funeral procession. The day was cloudless and sunny, but it seemed gray, dreary, depressing. Perhaps it was all the tall men dressed in black. His sister Shainchi was holding his hand, and he felt safe walking next to her and his mother. A woman came up to Golda and cut and tore the front of her dress, as a sign of mourning.

Now they were putting his father into the ground, They had wrapped him in a prayer shawl. The prayer "*El Moleh Rahamim*" was being recited. "Receive into Paradise, oh Lord, under your sheltering wings, the pure soul of Symcha. . . ."

Mendale began to cry. He knew that the Lord had taken away his father to be in Paradise, but he needed him. He needed Symcha more than the Lord did. He wanted to talk to his father again, to go riding with him in the woods, and to listen to all the stories about the past. And of his father's soul was going to Paradise, why did they put his body into the earth?

The funeral was over. They returned home where the mirrors were covered, and the house seemed dark and cheerless. Mother cried all that day and the children with her. For seven days they all sat on low stools, and their relatives cooked and served their food. Each evening his brother Aron and the men who came from the neighboring villages recited the evening prayer, and his brothers and he said the special prayer for his father. Mendale didn't really want to do it, because he was angry at the Lord, but Aron made him pray. After the prayer, the men came up to each member of the family and said: "May you be comforted among the mourners of Zion." Mendale didn't want to be comforted. He wanted his father.

On Friday, the seventh day of mourning, Mother was allowed to get up from her bench early, in honor of the Sabbath. She bathed for the first time in those seven days, the mirrors were uncovered, and the Sabbath was ushered in as prescribed. After the prayers that night, Aron came in singing: "Come let us welcome the Sabbath Queen." Mother asked him to take his father's place at the head of the table. She tried to smile.

"Aron, make the prayer over the wine and *hallah.*"

Mendale didn't cry for his father anymore, either. There was a pain inside him always when he thought about him. He knew that he would see his father again when the Messiah came, and the righteous would be resurrected in the Land of Israel—but that seemed so far away. . . .

Chapter 4

MENDALE'S EDUCATION

Golda knew that, with Symcha gone, she had to make a new life for herself. The income from the inn was not enough to take care of herself and six children. Symcha had traded in cattle and in that way augmented their income, but Golda didn't know enough about that business. She did know about land, however, so she decided to try her hand at real estate. With some of the money Symcha had left her, she bought a farm and resold it a few months later at a profit. She realized that she had found a profession she liked a great deal.

The business forced her to travel about the countryside. The older children were able to take care of the inn and fend for themselves while she was gone. She was always home for the Sabbath.

In all the excitement of her new life, Golda didn't forget about Mendale's education. He had lost not only a father but also a teacher. He was four years old, and it was time for him to attend *heder* (Hebrew elementary school). There was none in the vicinity, but Golda had a cousin in Rzeszow who ran a *heder*, and although she hated to part from Mendale, she knew that it was necessary to send him away.

Mendale rode alongside his mother in the carriage. It was just after the Jewish New Year, and he didn't want to leave home.

"Mommy, why do I have to go away to *heder*? I already know how to read Hebrew and to pray."

"You know a lot for your age, but there is much more to learn. Education is one of the most important things in life. Once we have education, we keep it always, even though we may lose everything else. If you will study hard, I will be very proud of you, and so will your father. Remember, he is always watching over us."

Mendale wasn't happy, but there was no way to change things. Besides, if his father wanted him to study, he would do it.

Mendale didn't like Reb Chaim's house. He had to sleep in a room with four other boys. They didn't like horses, and knew nothing about the animals on a farm. They were always playing some kind of silly games, competing with each other all the time. But his mother, who had decided to remain a few days to get him started, was still there and that helped.

On his first day of school, Mendale was brought to the *heder* by Reb Chaim himself. About twenty children of all ages sat on benches alongside large tables. Each boy had a book in front of him. The class was noisy, but as soon as they saw Reb Chaim, total silence reigned.

The teacher cleared his throat and said loudly, "Today is a very happy day for me, because I have with me my cousin Golda's son, Menachem Mendel, named after that great sage of revered memory, Reb Menachem Mendel of Kotzk. He will be studying here." Reb Chaim then turned to Mendale. "May you walk in the great rebbe's footsteps and be a light on to Israel."

The teacher led Mendale to his seat and turned to the page in the book that he wanted the boy to read. He had tested him the day before, privately; now he would be tested in front of the class. Golda put some honey on the corner of the page, as was customary for the first day of *heder*. Mendale licked the page and began reading. Reb Chaim seemed pleased.

"Now translate the passage." The teacher nodded approvingly as the boy translated flawlessly. Mendale felt Symcha was watching him. With his father, it had been so easy to learn. Reb Chaim was very strict, but he would try to like him.

It was spring now. Mendale was learning a great deal, but he hated Reb Chaim's house and the dingy smelly *heder*, where he had to spend his days. He missed the open sky, his mother, and his brothers and sisters. And then one day his mother reappeared and announced that she was taking him home. But even as he was getting ready to scream with delight, she added her bad news: They weren't going back to their old home. The house and the inn had burned down, with everything in it. They were now living in Olszewice in a rented house. He had lost his father and now his home.

Prince Lubomirski had accused Aron of setting fire to the inn to spite him, but fortunately, the prince couldn't prove any of his allegations. Now, in Olszewice, they were finally free of this cruel man's domination. But nothing was the same anymore. Aron had gone to do advanced studies in Rozwadow, and taken along Meyer, who was now nine and very scholarly. Mother was very proud of Aron, who was the most brilliant student of Reb Moishe Vysotzki, a famous teacher and scholar from

Lithuania. Meyer was doing very well too. He wanted to be a doctor when he grew up. Golda hoped that Mendale too would continue to be a good student.

Mendale started *heder* in Olszewice. Again he was a stranger, and it took time to get used to the place. Soon his new rebbe moved, and Golda transferred him to a school in a nearby village. He had a long way to walk to *heder*, and there was little time for the fun of his earlier years.

Golda now decided to build a house of her own. She had bought a lot opposite her brother's property, and that summer, when Mendale's older brothers came back home on vacation, the whole family joined in building. It wasn't as nice as their former home, but this one was their own. They moved into it in the fall, and Golda started traveling again. She was developing a large clientele, and she became well-known as the only woman real estate broker in the area.

One day when Mendale was coming home from *heder*, he met Reb Faivel, the marriage broker, emerging from their house. When he went inside, he overheard his sisters talking about a very rich man who had come back from America and wanted to marry their mother. The girls refused to tell him anything about it. A few days later, Mendale found a stranger sitting in the dining room, drinking tea. Golda was away but was due home soon. The man was very big, and had dark hair and a Van Dyke beard, trimmed neatly. He was dressed in an elegant suit and bowler hat, and had been speaking German to Mendale's sister, Shainchi. But to Mendale he said, "I saw you carrying your brother on your back, young man. How far did you carry him?"

"Four kilometers, sir," said the seven-year-old boy with pride.

The man stretched out his hand and shook Mendale's. Congratulations. That's quite something. How would you like to come with me to America? We can certainly use clever people like you there."

Mendale shrank back. "Oh, no, sir. I wouldn't like it there at all!"

"What! Why not?"

"Well, sir, my father told me that America is the country where people have forgotten the Lord. They even work on the Sabbath, and eat food that is forbidden by the Torah. I couldn't do that."

"Don't be so hasty, young man. It's true that there are many godless people in America, but there are also others, like myself, who have not gone astray and follow the precepts of our religion."

"Besides, we have a democracy, and the president runs the country. People vote for him, and if we don't like him, we get rid of him after four years. It isn't like here, where Kaiser Franz Josef has ruled for so many years and will rule until he dies. In America, it's the people that count, and everyone is equal. They call that democracy." Mr. Jacob Stern paused to peer at the boy, questioningly.

But Mendale merely stared back, confused. What was he talking about? Demo—demo-something, what was that? In school he had heard of Rabbi Zvi Hirsch Kalisher, who preached that Jews should return to the Holy Land and settle on farms, and in that way hasten the coming of the Messiah. That sounded like what his father had always wanted, and besides he liked the idea of living on a farm.

"I want to go to the Holy Land, sir," he said.

"My boy, you're talking about dreams, fantasies. I'm talking to you about reality. I'm offering you a life of freedom and comfort. You'll get your education and grow up to be a worthy person, and *then* you will go to the Land of Israel."

Mendale shook his head, indicating that he wasn't convinced. He wished Mr. Stern would stop bothering him, and go away, but instead the man laughed. "Mendale, you would make a great American, because you think for yourself."

Just then he heard the wagon pull up. "It's Mother!" Mendale cried gratefully and hastened to meet her at the door.

His mother wore a dark blue dress, with a draped bodice and straight skirt. Her walk was graceful and bouncy. She was in her 30s but she carried herself like a young girl. Golda greeted the stranger cordially—it seemed that they had already met in Rozwadow— and taking off her blue hat, she asked Shainchi to give the children their dinner in the kitchen.

When the door closed behind him, Mendale began to worry. Would he have to leave his home again, and go with that man to that faraway country? He couldn't eat at all, although he was very hungry. His stomach clenched like a fist.

It was getting dark outside, almost time for the evening prayer. Suddenly the stranger opened the door of the dining room. "Please, Mrs. Heller, think about what I propose. When you have made your decision, you know where to reach me. I fervently hope that it will be yes." He held her hand for a moment, then kissed it and quickly walked out.

The children surrounded their mother. "Mother, are you going to marry that man? Are you, Mother? Are you going to America?"

Golda calmed them down as best she could. "Yes, Mr. Stern wants to marry me, but I haven't decided whether I will or not. I have to see Aron and Meyer, and get their opinion first."

Shainchi, the oldest one at home, wanted to make a fair decision. "But who *is* he, Mother? Tell us about him?"

Slowly Golda started explaining what she knew about her suitor. Jacob Stern was a very rich man in America, from a place called Brooklyn. He was a widower who had never had any children of his own and would be happy to have a ready-made family. Golda laughed ruefully. "He says I'll be a lady of leisure, never have to work again. But what is really important is that you children would get a very fine education and even be able to attend a university in New York. Well, what do you think of that?"

University! Mendale thought with concern. It sounded strange and scary. He wondered if his father would approve. His father loved the Torah, so naturally he would want him to go to a yeshivah. Mendale wasn't sure if they had any in America.

"Mother, you must do what you think is right," Shainchi said with a sweet smile. "We want you to be happy, and we'll be happy too."

Laichia was more practical. "I think I'd like it over there. You wouldn't have to work so hard and be away from home all the time."

Little Moishele had his own priorities: "I want to go on the big boat to America, Mother."

Only Mendale stood by, quietly and sad.

"What do you say, my dove? " Golda bent down and put her arm around his shoulder.

"Mother, there is only one place I want to go, and that's to the Land of Israel."

After the Sabbath, Golda went to Rozwadow to consult with Aron and Meyer. Her carriage drew up in front of the home of Reb Rachmile Araten, where the boys were staying, and Reb Rachmile welcomed her warmly. "You must have read my mind, Golda! I was going to write you about a matter of utmost importance to both of us." He ordered the maid to bring in refreshments and ushered her into his handsome parlor.

Golda was puzzled, but she assumed it must be good news because he was smiling. "Come now, what is it?" she said when they were settled.

"The best news, Golda. Your Aron has fallen in love with my Ester, and wants to marry her."

Golda felt herself reeling. Aron wanting to marry? Why, he was only eighteen! And the Araten girl must be—oh, years older. Oh, no, this wasn't what she wanted at all!

Apparently unaware of her reaction, Reb Rachmile went on talking:"I know that Ester is a few years older than Aron, but she is a gentle and talented girl, and an artistic spirit. She loves him to distraction. And I must admit that I'm very pleased about my future son-in-law. Aron is handsome, brilliant, and a true scholar. It's simply an excellent match."

Reb Rachmile stopped for a moment to give Golda a chance to respond, but she sat there staring at him. "If it is money that worries you, Golda, you can set your heart at rest. I will be happy to see that Aron continues his studies without financial worries. They can live right here like two doves, and everything will be taken care of for them. Aron will receive a big dowry in addition. Golda, you tell me how much you think would be a fair amount?"

Golda, now recovered, said coldly, "I've never heard anything so ridiculous. I'm surprised at you, Reb Rachmile. Why, Aron is only a boy."

"I realize it's a surprise, But—"

"I forbid it, I will never permit it. You have allowed your daughter to trap him. I want to speak to my son—right now." Golda was agitated and shouting loudly.

"Very well," he said calmly. "Aron should be back any minute. Perhaps you can talk to him out of it. But I warn you. He's your son, and he's stubborn. He's also madly in love with my Ester, and they are deeply committed to one another."

Golda walked out of the room and into the hall, slamming the door behind her. She tried to calm herself, but her mind was in a turmoil. She now reminded herself why she had come to this house—ironically, to obtain Aron's consent to her marriage. And instead—

Aron came in. Golda hadn't seen him in several months and she was struck by how tall he'd grown—taller even that his father. He stood towering over her for a moment, then bent down to kiss her hand and then her face. "Mother, what a wonderful surprise. I was about to write you—"

"Yes," she said shortly, "Reb Rachmile has told me about your plans."

"Well, did you tell him that you agree?"

She pulled herself together, cleared her throat, fighting to sound calm and reasonable. "No, Aron, I cannot approve of this. You're still too young for such a step. Perhaps in a few years when you finish your studies—"

Aron cut her off sharply: "I've made up my mind, Mother, and I've given my word to Ester and her father. I'm marrying her, with or without your approval." He turned and walked out the door again.

Golda was in a turmoil. She decided not to talk to her second son, Meyer, about her own plans, for the purpose of her trip had lost all meaning. She called to Meyer and spoke to him briefly. She brought him some jam and other goodies that she had prepared, then left the Rachmile Araten house in haste.

They rode home in silence. Finally Jozef asked Golda what had happened, and when she told him the news, he clucked in disapproval but added, "Don't worry, Pani Golda. Things have a way of working out for the best. Aron will have an easy life and won't have to struggle for a living. What would his father say?"

Golda grew quiet. Yes, what would Symcha say? There had been a great age difference between them too—he nearly forty with grown children by his first wife, she a girl of sixteen. Maybe it would be best to accept the inevitable. She couldn't keep Aron close to her forever. Suddenly she knew that the only way she could keep his love was to give him permission to marry Ester. She would write to him as soon as she returned home and tell him that she had changed her mind.

But what about her own suitor? No, she couldn't possibly consider him in view of what happened. The thought of sharing Mr. Stern's bed suddenly revolted her. Besides, she had grown used to her freedom since Symcha's death. She would be going to a new land where she would be totally dependent on this man. No, she liked her independence too much. She was still young and strong, and would take care of her own children. She would not give them a stepfather.

Golda didn't go to America. Aron and Ester were married that spring. They lived with Ester's father, and Aron continued his studies.

Golda resumed her work selling real estate, but it had lost its interest for her, and when a suitable property became available, she rented it and opened an inn.

Her new business was soon a great success—so much so that her brother Shmuel, who operated an inn just down the road, began to feel the competition. They quarreled. He wanted her to leave Olszewice, and when she refused, he and his friends broke all the windows of her inn and threatened to burn down the house. Golda closed the inn and started traveling in real estate again.

Things weren't going well for Mendale either. At the village *heder*, where he went every morning, the kids would try to fight him because he was not from their town. One day the students were playing tug-of-war with a large stick. Mendale's team was stronger at first, but then the tide began to turn. Mendale, at the head of his team, felt himself pulled across the line with such force that he let go of the stick, and the other leader, Schlomo, fell and got a nosebleed.

The rebbe rushed out of the *heder* when he heard the screaming, and asked what was going on. Schlomo, crying and bloody-faced, sobbed, "Menachem Mendel beat me up."

That was enough for the rebbe. He didn't ask Mendale any questions, but proceeded to give him a beating with a wooden board, until the boy was black and blue.

That day, he was too sore and trembling to carry his brother home from *heder*. Shainchi gave him supper and put him to bed, but he couldn't sleep. More that his physical pain, he hated the injustice of what the Rebbe had done.

When his mother got home and he told her what had happened, she was outraged. You will never go back to that Rebbe again. He's cruel, and doesn't deserve to have a student like you."

Golda was showing some property to a perspective customer, when she decided to buy it herself. The owners were ethnic Germans or *volksdeutsch*, who were emigrating to Argentina and were anxious to sell.

The farm was situated on the outskirts of a village named Zbora, whose inhabitants were called Lemkes, mountain people from the Carpathians. Although they claimed to be Ukrainians, other Ukrainians, who lived in the surrounding villages, disclaimed kinship with them. The Lemkes were extremely poor and lived under primitive conditions, and Herr Moser, who sold Golda the farm, advised her not to trust them or to allow them on the property. We have lived with these people all our lives," he warned, "and have learned through sad experience that they are lazy and will steal you blind if you give them a chance."

Golda was cautious but thought that she had no reason to worry. She suspected that jealousy was at work. The German farmers were considered to be the richest people in the area, while the Lemkes were the poorest, whereas she was merely a poor widow with young children. She decided to be fair to the Lemkes and help them whenever she could. She wouldn't employ them, but they soon found that if they were hungry, they could come to her for food.

For the first time since Symcha's death Golda felt secure. She had become a landowner by her own efforts. She was no longer part of that group they called *arendaren*, who rented from a landowner, like Prince Lubomirski, and were subject to his whims. This was her own land, and one day it would belong to her children.

But Mendale and Moishe had to continue their education, and there was no school in the vicinity. Meyer would have to come home from Rozwadow to help on the farm, and he must have an appropriate teacher so he could continue his studies. The girls too would need further education. So Golda made her way to Stryj, a nearby city and headed for a small square where the Teachers' Market was held every semester. Here teachers of every kind, looking for positions with wealthy landowners or rich city people, would assemble and offer their services.

It was not befitting for a woman to deal directly with a male teacher, so she went to a broker who was reputed to be knowledgeable. "I want the best that's available." she told him "Do you have someone appropriate for my children?"

"As a matter of fact," the man said, "I think I have just the teacher for you." He leafed through a large ledger and stopped at one of the pages. "Yes, this is the man. He is not a plain teacher, like you see outside. He's a rabbi and, what's more, the brother of the renowned Rabbi Rosenfeld of Lemberg." Reb Yankel stopped to catch his breath.

"I'm not here to find out the man's pedigree, Reb Yankel. Can he teach?"

"Mrs. Heller, it is most important that you understand the man's character." He rubbed his hands together. "Mr. Rosenfeld just came back recently from Vienna, where he studied philosophy, languages, history, music, and, of course, Hebrew. You will have to make a quick decision about him, Mrs. Heller, because a very rich landowner has interviewed him and wants him immediately. Rosenfeld only hesitated because the landowner is ignorant and uncouth.

Golda was skeptical. This Mr. Rosenfeld sounded too good to be true. "If he's a rabbi, why isn't he looking for a congregation? And, if he's such a great scholar, why doesn't he teach in the yeshiva, but chooses to teach small children?"

Reb Yankel shrugged. "These are hard times. Rosenfeld has had some reverses and couldn't finish his doctoral studies. He has been ill—not, god forbid, anything contagious—and he wants to work in the country where it's quiet and the air is fresh." Reb Yankel stood up. "Mrs. Heller, what's the use of talking? You must meet this fine young man in person. Shall I bring Rosenfeld to your hotel this afternoon?"

It was agreed, and that afternoon she found herself interviewing a thin dark young man. dressed Viennese style and in the latest fashion. He proceeded to outline the curriculum to her. Each school day would begin with a prayer, study of Rashi and other commentaries, then Jewish history and literature. The afternoon would be devoted to Latin, German, Polish, mathematics, geography, and penmanship. There would be time for music in the early evening, but he would want to be paid separately for that. He would help her purchase the texts and materials necessary if they agreed on his conditions.

Golda, uneducated herself, was overwhelmed by all this erudition. Almost timidly, she said, "Mr. Rosenfeld, we have a school house on our premises. I would be honored if you would come to instruct my children." Then she told Reb Yankel to draw up the contract.

"Excuse me, Mrs. Heller," Rosenfeld interjected, "there is another point we haven't covered. Without a positive answer from you I can't accept this job. I require meat every day for dinner."

This was a difficult request for people living on a farm. In a town they could visit the ritual slaughterer regularly, but for Jews who lived in the country it was an inconvenience, so they ate fish instead or vegetarian meals most of the week.

Rosenfeld must have guessed what was going through Golda's perplexed mind, because he added, "I am willing to go into town to fetch the meat myself if you agree."

Golda didn't know quite what to make of this strange request, but she did want this learned young man to teach her children. "Very well," she said. "Put that in the contract, Reb Yankel."

Rosenfeld held to his promised curriculum. All the subjects were covered each day, and the three boys worked very hard to meet his high standards. The girls would join them in some of the lessons in the afternoon. For Mendale, the most interesting lesson was the one in modern Jewish history. It was a lecture delivered in flawless German. Mr. Rosenfeld placed a picture of Theodor Herzl on the table and pointed to it dramatically. Herzl's handsome face, proud bearing, and most of all, his ideas would forever be an inspiration to Mendale.

The teacher first told about Herzl's early years, about his Austrian patriotism, and his assimilationist views. Then, in 1894, as a Paris newspaper correspondent for a prestigious Viennese paper, Herzl covered the infamous Dreyfus trial, in which a Jewish officer in the French army was convicted of treason, although he was innocent and later proved so. The anti-Semitism he witnessed as the trial progressed profoundly changed Herzl's thinking. That such a tragedy could happen in France, an enlightened and democratic country, traumatized him. He returned to Vienna, resolved to devote his life to freeing his dispersed compatriots. "This man," Mr. Rosenfeld said, pointing to Herzl's picture, "was now convinced that the Jews were a nation, and as such must return to their own land and form a true political entity. They must abandon the hostile environment of Europe, in which they live as strangers, under oppressive economic and social conditions, and resettle in the Land of Israel."

As his teacher looked out the window, it seemed to Mendale that Mr. Rosenfeld could see the Land of Israel itself in the distance. The teacher picked up a small book and pointed to the title: *Der Judenstaat (The Jewish State)*. "I want each of you to read this and know its contents thoroughly. Meyer, I would like you to help the younger ones through the most difficult passages. Well, children, you have a lot to do. Class dismissed."

That night Mendale dreamed that he was in the Land of Israel. It was full of flowers, vineyards, and palm trees, and he saw his father sitting in the shade of a fig tree. His father's hair wasn't red anymore. He had white hair and a long white beard, like Abraham our forefather.

"Mendale," Symcha said, "I told you that one day we would return to our land of milk and honey." He stretched out his arms, and Mendale felt his embrace.

"Father, father, you're alive, you're real."

"Mendale, the Messiah has come, and his name is Benjamin Ze'ev Herzl. He has redeemed our people from bondage and brought us back to the 'Old New Land'...."

When Mendale woke up, he resolved that he would do everything he could to make the dream come true.

His chance came a few months later. There was to be an election for the Austrian Parliament, and one of the men running was a Zionist. He and Meyer, thought they could help him get elected. They went to their mother and induced her to give them as many sacks of potatoes as she could spare, plus the loan of the wagon and Jozef's permission to drive it.

"I don't see how potatoes can get a man elected, boys," she said, "but if you want to try, all right."

The next day was spent campaigning and distributing the potatoes, and the boys returned home exhausted but proud of themselves. They had become Zionists. "If you will it, it is not a dream," Meyer quoted Herzl's words. That night when they were in bed, they heard Mr. Rosenfeld play a most beautiful melody on his violin. They had never heard such music before, and they knew he was playing it for them. The next day, he told them that it was his favorite piece, Beethoven's Concerto for Violin in D. That day he played for them the new Jewish national Anthem, "Hatikva [The Hope]," and they liked that even better than Beethoven's music. They soon learned all the words.

Some weeks later, Mr. Rosenfeld, who had been to Lemberg for the Sabbath, announced to them that their candidate for Parliament had lost. "But you must not despair, my boys. Never give up a cause that you believe to be right. In the end truth will prevail."

Chapter 5
MENDALE THE FIGHTER AND THE LEMKES

On a spring day Aron and Ester arrived with a lot of baggage. Aron had decided to help his mother on the farm. Aron helped Ester down from the wagon, heavy with child. He hugged his mother. "Soon you'll be a grandma. Isn't it unbelievable?" He spun her around playfully. Golda was delighted to have her son home again, and a grandchild would always be welcome because it was Aron's child. But she was less happy to see Ester, and her smile of greeting was restrained.

The three of them walked into the house, Aron in the middle, and each of the women holding his arm on either side.

A few weeks after their arrival, Ester gave birth to a boy, named Symcha after his grandfather and, like him, a redhead. Mendale loved the boy, and in his spare time would play with him and teach him many things.

But with Aron's arrival other things changed as well. It was decided that, in addition to their studies, the boys had to help on the farm. The harvest had to be brought in, and there was no money to hire extra workers. Golda began traveling about on real estate business, leaving Aron in charge of the family. He was a tough taskmaster, with no patience for excuses. If a task wasn't done the way he liked it, he would punish the delinquent—Mendale or his sister Laichia, especially.

Soon Ester bore Aron another little redhead, Srulik. With two children of his own, plus his two sisters and three brothers, Aron—still only in his early twenties—had to be father to a large brood. He tended to let out his frustrations on Mendale, for he considered the boy too willful. Mendale would always speak up when he thought that Aron was being unjust, and Aron resented that particularly. The slightest infraction of rules would result in a severe beating, which only made Mendale more rebellious. He tried to get his mother to make Aron ease up, but his brother behaved well toward him when Golda was around, so she didn't believe Mendale's stories.

And about then, trouble broke out with the Lemkes. They turned out to be exactly the way Herr Moser had predicted. They broke windows, stole chickens and geese, destroyed the vegetable patches, and in general were a menace and a nuisance. The Hellers realized that if they were to keep their property, they had to defend themselves. Once, when the children were in the school house at their studies, two young fellows attacked, and broke most of the windows. Luckily, no one was injured.

That evening, Aron called a meeting of the whole family, including Jozef. "We have tried to be understanding. We've tried to be peaceful. We used to think that this stealing and harassing were acts of a few, but now we have reason to believe that the elders of the village are egging on these young men. And today, they have gone too far—endangering our children's lives."

Aron gazed about him grimly. "There's only one way to deal with terrorism," he continued. "From a position of strength. For every attack, from now on there will be retaliation."

From that day on, when one—or more usually a gang—of Lemkes appeared at the farm intent on mischief, Mendale was after them like a shot. When he caught one, he fought. He took on boys older or bigger than himself, and often returned home bruised and scraped. But with tenacity and persistence, he learned to make the best use of his strength. After he became bar Mitzvah (thirteen), he took to pursuing them all the way back to the village. To the Lemke villagers he was *rozbojnik* (bandit) or the "blond menace," and as soon as the villagers saw him coming, they would retreat to their houses and call in their young children.

Aron respected him and was proud of him, and the beatings ceased for about a year. Then one day, Aron got angry at him and hit him. Mendale decided not to take any further abuse. He turned on Aron, employing some of his fighting skills, and he won. Aron never beat him again.

It was midmorning on the eve of Passover. Aron and Mendale were returning from Kalusz, a town about fourteen miles from the farm, where they had gone to some last-minute shopping for the holidays. They stopped at an inn to water their horses, continued on to the *mikvah* (ritual bath), and them home. Aron went up to chat with Reb Mehel, the innkeeper, while Mendale went to the well to draw some water. He had to wait his turn because there were a number of farmers ahead of him. Finally he drew the water and, as he turned to go, someone grabbed his pail from behind.

It was Vasil, a tall Lemke from his village, now spilling the water on the ground and laughing. Mendale saw that Vasil already had drawn water for his own horses, so he ran over to retaliate, but Vasil put himself hastily in front of him. "You son-of-a-bitch bandit, I'm going to teach you a lesson you'll never forget!" He struck Mendale in the face.

Mendale pushed him back, very hard, so that the tall boy fell down. He was soon up again and swinging at Mendale, but Mendale was ready for him and now easily blocked the taller boy's wild swings. A group of Vasil's cronies surrounded them, shouting, "Hit the bastard hard, harder—kill him!" Instead, Mendale knocked him down again.

Vasil could hardly get up this time. His nose was bleeding and his hair muddy, and as he was trying to climb to his feet, a short stocky man, much older than Mendale, ran forward and started punching Mendale in the back. Vasil was up by then, and they both tried to knock the boy down, but Mendale suddenly felt a surge of strength. He managed to grab both of them by their hair and brought their heads together with a loud crack.

The victor looked around, panting. Another man sat on the ground, bleeding and moaning, and a few steps away, Aron was fighting another Lemke. Reb Mehel, the innkeeper had an iron bar in his hands and was warding off Vasil's other friends, so Mendale helped him chase them off, while Aron finished off his adversary. The battle was over, and the Hellers were the winners.

Reb Mehel had some of the peaceful fellows carry Vasil and his three friends to the wagons, and drive them home. "They're a drunken lot of troublemakers, and I hope they never come back here again!" he said. He threw Vasil's hat onto the wagon, and asked the Hellers in to wash up and rest before continuing. He put his arms around the two boys and kissed them. "May the Almighty always give you strength to fight for justice and protect our persecuted people."

They were on their way now, tired but in excellent spirits. The ritual bath was a welcome relaxation. They changed into fresh clothing, and Aron decided to report the incident to the county police. Chief Landau was at his desk when Aron and his brother came in, and when they had related their story, he congratulated them. "It looks like you taught those people a lesson they won't easily forget."

Aron grinned appreciatively. "But the real hero of the day is my younger brother here. He fought like a lion." He put his arm around Mendale and gave him a prideful hug.

Landau called in his secretary to take down the information, then ordered two of his men to arrest the Lemkes immediately. After that, the villagers called Mendale the "blond killer," and most of them were afraid to start a fight with him.

For many months there were no further incidents, but one day when Zosia, the maid, went to the well near the village to fetch water, a group of young fellows surrounded her. One foul-smelling fellow drew her to him. "Give me a kiss, and I'll let you pass."

He tried to kiss her, but Zosia struggled out of his grip and slapped him across the face. He hit her back so hard that the girl fell down. Mendale was in the yard and, hearing the commotion, came to he rescue. "What's going on here, Zosia?" he said as he helped her up.

"Oh, nothing, nothing—they're just fooling around."

Mendale took her pail and went toward the well, but as he got closer, the fellow lifted the heavy wooden pail used for drawing water and tried to smash Mendale over the head. Mendale warded off the blow and grabbed the troublemaker by the waist, knocked him down, and hit him on the head with the same pail. As Mendale stood up, the other fellows attacked him. Two of them held him down while the others beat and kicked him. Meanwhile, Zosia ran to fetch Aron, who hurried to the scene of the fight. When he saw what was going on, he knew he had to do something very quickly, or the ruffians would kill his brother. There was a small bridge near the well. As Aron ran up, he shouted: "Let my brother go, you sons of bitches!"

They let go of Mendale for a moment. This was it. Aron bent down and, with all his strength, pulled the bridge supports right out of the ground.

They gaped at him, then started backing off, and finally broke into a run.

Aron let go of the bridge, and it fell back into place with a groan. He could not believe that he had been able to lift it at all. By then Mendale had gotten up, and they returned home to tell the story of their new adventure.

Chapter 6
THE STRANGER

It was a Friday afternoon in the summer. Aron and Mendale were in a nearby village on business. When they came back to their wagon, they saw a farmer they knew by the name of Reiter, arguing with a stranger. The man was dressed in what seemed to be a fashionable suit, but covered with dust of the road. His long beard, and sidelocks, gave him a wild look. He was taller than anyone they had ever seen, and had a commanding voice. He was shouting at Reiter, the two young men could hear him say: "I can't believe that you refuse me a place to stay, to observe the Sabbath." Reiter was trying to excuse himself but the man went on: "Have you forgotten that it is written: 'Be kind to the stranger, for you were a stranger in Egypt?' " And without letting Reiter say another word, he grabbed his arm and riveted his angry eyes on his speechless victim.

Aron realized that he had to step in or the stranger would strike his friend. He greeted him saying: "Peace be unto you (*Shalom Aleichem*). I'm Aron Heller." The stranger let go of Reiter's arm and shook Aron's hand, saying, "And unto you peace (*Aleichem Shalom*). Then Aron said: "Sir, I know Mr. Reiter very well, and understand that the circumstances do not permit him to take you home. But we would be honored to receive you in our house to celebrate the holy Sabbath." The stranger seemed thankful. He cast down his eyes and stood silently as though he couldn't make up his mind what to say. Then he looked directly into Aron's eyes, and the younger man was stunned by his gaze.

"So there is mercy and justice here," he blurted out. "The One On High will not destroy this place like He did Sodom and Gomorah." His face seemed to relax and he continued: "I'm on my way to Lemberg on very urgent business, but I had to make a stop at an estate nearby. I was detained and that's why I've found myself in this strange predicament."

"Well, sir, our wagon is waiting, and the Sabbath will be upon us if we don't hurry." Aron was now anxious to leave.

"Yes, I will go with you, Red Fox," he said, looking at Aron's red hair. "I like you. You're a man after my own heart." The stranger shook hands with Mendale and gave him a small, black leather bag, then suddenly grabbed it back from Mendale. The boy thought that the man was quite strange.

When they came to the farm house, the stranger walked right over to Aron's bedroom. Aron followed him quietly. The stranger lifted the mattress at the head of Aron's bed and put a package there. He seemed a bit startled when he turned around and saw that Aron had followed him. "Red Fox, you saw where I put the package. I'd like you to keep it for me until I return. I trust you only. Make certain that no one touches it until I come back." The stranger extended his hand: "Red Fox, give your hand as a promise." Aron shook his hand, amazed that the man knew where his bed was.

Now they washed and prepared for the Sabbath. Services were in the next village, where there were enough males for the required ten. They returned home singing the song that welcomed the Sabbath angels sent by the Lord. Then they recited "In Praise of Women," beginning with

"A woman of valor who can find?
Far beyond pearls is her price. . . ."

They ate dinner after blessing the wine and the bread. The stranger ate quickly, gulping down his food, as though he had not eaten in a long time. After he finished the main course, he asked each one at the table to let him have what was left on his plate. Each person complied smiling and joking except for Mendale. he refused, saying, "Sorry, sir, but I'm hungry too." The stranger looked surprised, but then began to laugh, and suddenly burst into song:

"Oh master of worlds and everything,
You are the ruler who rules over kings
Your wonderful deeds are marvelous ways,
Inspire our souls to sing your praise. . ."

They all knew the words, but the tune the stranger sang in a deep resonant voice was unusual, and they joined in on the second stanza. The meal was over, and they all recited "Grace After Meals." Again the stranger sang the introductory part of the Grace with a new tune. After Grace he began to preach. Around the table there was total quiet.

"Did you ever consider the treasure our Father in Heaven gave us when he blessed us with the Sabbath? For six days we work and there is no harmony between our physical and spiritual being. Body and soul strive toward opposite aims. But on the Sabbath body and soul are reunited to create a peaceful entity. The Holy One commanded us to rest on that day. Not only must you rest, but your servant, and even your animals must too. Some of the new social theorists talk about a day of rest as though they invented it for the benefit of humanity. But we know better. We spread the word of the Most High to all corners of the world, so most nations have legislated a day of rest for the 'working class,' as Karl Marx calls them. You, young people, try to remember when these devils of Socialists try to win you over to embrace their evil theories, that the Almighty gave us the Sabbath for the restoration of the body and soul."

The Sabbath was over. Early on Sunday morning the stranger could be heard praying. Then he thanked Golda for her welcome, blessed all the young ones, and took leave of Aron, embracing and kissing him. "Days of great tribulation are ahead of us. May the Holy One watch over you and save you from our enemies, Red Fox." Then he turned to Mendale. "And you, young man, be patient, and keep your independent spirit. You will one day see the Promised Land."

Weeks and months passed and turned into years. The stranger didn't return. Thinking that they might find a clue to the man's whereabouts, Golda and Aron decided to open the package. They found 500 gulden, a tremendous sum of money for that time, but no other information. Golda called a family conference and exhibited the treasure that the stranger had left. "We will wrap this money up and hide it in a secret place. I'm convinced that the stranger could be no other than Elijah the Prophet, in disguise, heralding the coming of the Messiah. Perhaps one day, it will be revealed to us why he left us the money. Only time will tell."

Ester and Golda didn't get along. Ester was a city girl and didn't know much about farm life, nor did she care to learn. She liked to sleep late, work on artistic embroidery projects, knit, take care of her children, and spend some time relaxing and singing. She had a beautiful soprano voice.

Golda thought that most of those activities were a waste of time. She wanted her daughter-in-law to help with the farm work and take over some of the tasks in the kitchen. She thought Ester was the laziest person she had ever met.

Ester complained to Aron about his mother's demands on her—and the name calling—but he refused to listen. He adored his mother, and he used the excuse that she needed his help to run the farm properly.

Ester was now in her early thirties and had four children, but she still felt like an outsider among the Hellers. She knew that the great love Aron had for her in their early years was wearing thin. He found all kinds of pretexts not to be with her. Ester could see how attractive her handsome husband was to the young women in the area. They flirted with him unashamedly, right in front of her, and some of them were married women. She told herself that these were only flirtations, but they still hurt and upset her. And one thing she couldn't dismiss from her mind.

In recent months Aron had begun to spend a great deal of time at the Teppers. Leizer Tepper was a mathematical genius and philosopher, and his home served as the intellectual center for the area, where young and old loved to congregate—some for the intellectual stimulation and others for a glimpse of Chanale, his beautiful young daughter. Chanale, charming, clever, and gracious to all, was a general favorite, and Ester was bitterly jealous of her.

She asked Aron not to go to the Teppers, but did not really explain her feelings. She simply stated that she wanted him at home. He refused. I need to be in a place where ideas are discussed, where I can meet with interesting people. To hear Tepper speak is like attending a lecture of a prominent professor. You would not deprive me of that pleasure, would you, Ester?" Ester didn't answer. She knew that his mind was made up.

It became harder for to take the taunts of her mother-in-law, and they quarreled more often. If Aron was present, he sided with his mother. Finally, after a fierce argument, in which Golda slapped her face, Ester took a small valise and her first-born, Symcha, and went home to her father.

Reb Rachmile was happy to see his daughter and his grandson, but distressed that Ester looked so tired and upset. Symcha was quickly dispatched to play with his cousin, so that father and daughter could talk.

Ester made herself comfortable in her favorite chair. It was good to be home, drinking tea that someone else had made. She didn't know how to tell her father what brought her there, and for now she wasn't going to try.

At last, Reb Rachmile could not contain himself any longer. "What has happened to you, Ester? You look so worn out."

Ester burst out crying, and it took her father a good ten minutes to induce her to stop. "Now tell me. What is wrong?"

Ester dried her tears and began to talk quietly. "No one cares about me anymore, Father. Aron is busy all the time, so I hardly see him. And my mother-in-law—she has destroyed our peaceful life. She's constantly after me, yells at me and finds fault in everything I do."

"Well, farm life is hard," he said neutrally, to which Ester reacted with passion:

"You didn't bring me up to be a farmer, and I hate the farm! I only tolerate it because it's Aron's wish. And now—now she has struck me across the face. I never want to see her again, and I'm not going back there for more abuse. Not even from Aron!" Ester began crying again.

Reb Rachmile let her cry for a while, then said: "Ester, my love, calm down. You can't solve this problem by running away. You're an adult woman and married to a good man. What does Aron say to all these abuses by Golda?"

"He takes her side. Always. As far as he's concerned, she can do no wrong. Sometimes when he hears us arguing, he just walks out, without saying a word. He doesn't seem to care about my feelings at all." She peered at her father through tears. "Father, I want to stay here with you."

"Of course you can stay with me, my girl. This is your home, and you'll always be welcome. But let me think a minute. You get a good rest here, and stop crying. Your father will find a solution."

Reb Rachmile woke up the next morning with a solution to his daughter's problem. As he went into the dining room for breakfast, he could hear Ester singing in her beautiful voice. She was in a better mood already, and she would be happier yet when she heard about his plan.

At breakfast he said, "My dear girl, you will stay here for at least a week without communicating with your husband. He will probably start to miss you and his son, and possibly Golda's conscience will begin to bother her, and she will realize the trouble she's caused. Then when you feel rested, you'll go back—but not to the same situation. It's clear that you can't go on living under the same roof with that woman, and I will not give her the opportunity to abuse you any further."

He took out a leather purse filled with money and emptied the kronen onto the table. "You can live in your own house and have your own cows. Take the money, but don't cry. I want to see you smiling and content." Ester kissed her father and hugged him.

Ester stayed at her father's house for three weeks. Then rested and self-confident, she took the train back to Kalusz. When she arrived at the train station, she was wearing a new dress and hat, and walked erect and proud. She had written to Aron to come pick her up later in the afternoon, but first she went to a cattle dealer she knew and purchased two milk cows. Then she walked back to the station with Symcha and stopped at a candy store to buy him some sweets, and some to take home to the other children. She felt wonderful. But as she approached the station, she saw Jozef waiting for them. Aron hadn't come. She felt like crying, but she remembered that she was to be strong and independent and fought back the tears.

When they arrived home, Aron greeted her warmly. He hugged and kissed his son first, and threw him up into the air. Then he hugged her. "But let me look at you. You look so different."

"I am different, Aron." This was it, the crucial moment. She had to be strong. "I've —made certain decisions about us and our relationship to your mother. If you agree to my plans, I will stay. If not, I'll return to my father's house." There, it was out. She stole a look at him.

Aron was rigid with shock. His first instinct was to get angry, but he controlled himself and waited for her to proceed.

"Father has given me enough money to be independent," she said. "I can afford to have a home of my own, even a maid. Will you help?"

He asked for a few days to think it over, but he agreed eventually to everything she proposed. He wanted her to stay and to have his children near him. He believed in the sanctity of the family, that nothing should ever break up a man's home. He suggested that they refurbish the old church on their property, and hired a carpenter, so that the task could be completed quickly.

Watching the renovation work proceed on the church, Ester couldn't help being grateful for her luck. Soon she would be out of Golda's house, which she now considered a jail. The day they moved in was the happiest for Ester since she moved to the farm.

Once they were settled in, Ester made up some rules. She would not go to Golda's house, nor would her mother-in-law be welcome in hers. They were no longer on speaking terms and thus no more quarrels. Soon she bore Aron another son, Herschel.

But the relationship between them deteriorated again. Aron spent very little time at home. He ate his meals there and slept there, but his world seemed to be way out somewhere where Ester couldn't reach him. She counted her blessings and decided to persevere. Maybe this too would pass. . . .

Chapter 7
SHAINCHI

Shainchi, Mendale's sister, dressed in her very best blue dress, was waiting for the marriage broker and his newest client. Reb Faivel had been to see Golda many times before about Shainchi. She was, after all, everyone's idea of a perfect daughter-in-law—slim, blue-eyed, and blond, a mother to her brothers and sister when Golda was away from home, able to run a household, cook, and supervise the help. Quite a few of the young men in the area wanted to marry her. Shainchi, however, had refused all the offers.

Lately, Golda had begun to worry. Her daughter was now eighteen, and something had to be done before she got much older and, God forbid, became an old maid. She went to see Reb Faivel and ask for his advice.

"Maybe the young men around here are too familiar to her," he suggested. "We must go farther afield." He took out a small file box and started rummaging through it. "There!" he said, producing a card and a picture. "Isn't he the most handsome young man you ever saw?"

The young man in the photograph was good looking enough, but Golda was not impressed. "What about his character, his family, his health, his prospects?" she demanded.

Reb Faivel launched into a long speech about the prospective groom's illustrious antecedents, about his kindness, about his intelligence. Golda broke into this sales talk by saying all right, she would see what Shainchi said. The girl had agreed, and now she sat waiting to meet Nehemiah from Bukaczowce, a town some distance away.

Shainchi was not expecting much. In her heart, she had always hoped for a romantic meeting, out of the blue, not prearranged. But for now, she would conform to custom and tolerate this experience, hoping it wouldn't turn out to be too unpleasant.

But to her surprise, when she saw Nehemiah, he took her breath away. When he shook her hand in greeting, she trembled. He was poised and handsome and had a wonderful smile. She was suddenly self-conscious, something she had not been with other suitors. Did he like her?

Was he disappointed? She became very quiet and serious, and Nehemiah started telling a humorous story. It made her laugh, and that broke the ice, and they talked as though they had known each other for a long time.

After lunch, they took a walk in the woods. He talked to her about life in Bukaczowce, his town, and about his hopes for the future. He seemed to have a way with words, like no one she had ever met before. Suddenly he walked away from her, picked some flowers, and came back with a bouquet.

"Shainchi," he said, offering it to her. "I know this is unusual for a first meeting, but will you consent to marry me?"

She was stunned. She liked him, yes, but. . .

He took her hand and kissed it. "I don't want to rush you. Maybe you need time to think about it?"

Her heart was suddenly so light it seemed to float. "You didn't ask me if I cared for you," she said teasingly, and then, before he could protest, she turned serious: "I've never been in love before, Nehemiah, but I think I am now. I feel—well, I don't k now what I feel, except that it's different from anything I've ever felt before."

"Then do you promise to marry me?" and when Shainchi swallowed and said yes, Nehemiah burst into a song. It was a love song, and Shainchi soon joined in.

Golda was delighted when she saw that her daughter for once had been pleased by a prospective suitor, but she was a little taken aback that Shainchi, usually so quiet and sensible, should bubble over with excitement. "Infatuation is one thing, and marriage is another," she warned. She wanted to make sure that Shainchi understood the deep seriousness of this commitment. "Remember, you are entrusting your entire life to this man."

"Oh, yes, that's exactly what I want—to spend the rest of my life with Nehemiah!"

Golda kissed her daughter, profoundly relieved and thankful. Then she called Nehemiah, who declared his affection for Shainchi and formally asked permission to marry her. And so it was settled.

The following day Nehemiah returned with a scribe to write the engagement contract. The dowry and conditions were decided upon and written in, after which both parties signed the contract. The wedding was planned for the following summer. The vodka and cake were passed around, and they all drank "L'Chaim" (to life).

Shainchi couldn't believe her good luck. She floated through life on a golden cloud. She longed to see Nehemiah, to be close to him, to experience the strange and wonderful feelings his nearness awakened in her. All around her wedding preparations were going on. A dressmaker was employed, fabrics had to be bought for the trousseau, and patterns for the wedding dress and veil had to be selected. A caterer was hired, a menu decided upon, and musicians hired. For Golda the weeks sped by in a blur, but for the bride they dragged. She missed Nehemiah. She wished that they had set an earlier date for the wedding. She longed to be with him or at least to get a letter.

On a dreary, rainy afternoon a letter did come from him. She tore it open and began to read voraciously. But her smile soon faded.

Mendale, who had brought the letter from the village, noted the changes. "What's happened?" he asked, alarmed. "Did he change his mind?"

"No, he didn't. But maybe I will." Indignantly, she showed the letter to her brother. "Just look at his handwriting. It's terrible, And his grammar—practically illiterate. This isn't the way he spoke."

Indeed, it did not read like the letter of an educated man. Mendale did not know what to say. "If this is the real Nehemiah, I can't marry him," Shainchi said. "I fell in love with his looks and pleasant disposition, not the man." She began to cry.

Golda heard her daughter sobbing and came in to find out what bad news the letter contained.

"I'm not going to marry that man, Mother. Never, never."

Golda put her arm around the sobbing girl and tried to quiet her down while she got the story out of her. But when she heard Shainchi's reasons for wanting to cancel the wedding, she couldn't believe it. "My dear girl, so he's not a scholar—what's the difference? He's a wonderful person. You were so in love. How could such a change come upon you all of a sudden?

When her daughter continued to cry without answering, Golda changed her tone. "Shainchi, you have made a commitment, and I have given my word. We signed a contract. The family's honor and good name are at stake. The wedding *must* take place."

Shainchi cast a terrified glance at her mother, and Golda softened. "When you see him once more, you will realize how much you care for him. Believe me, once Nehemiah is here in person, you will see how little this whole subject matters."

Golda wasn't going to allow her daughter to ruin everything, but she realized how much Shainchi needed reassuring. "Remember, my dear, that perfection doesn't exist in the world, except for the perfection of the Holy One. We are all imperfect. Writing letters is an art, and Nehemiah is obviously not good at it. May that be his worst fault! Think of those other qualities that pleased you so much."

In the end Golda won out. There was no breaking of the engagement contract, and the wedding took place as planned in July. Once Shainchi saw Nehemiah again, she was glad that things had worked out all right. He was so handsome, and it was obvious that he adored her.

The wedding began with a procession, headed by a master of ceremonies (badchan dressed in a colorful costume and holding a large red handkerchief. then came the bride and groom and the wedding party, followed by the musicians (klezmerim), playing and dancing as they walked along. The marriage vows were made under a velvet canopy in the courtyard, and a wedding feast was spread out for 200 people. Each day, for seven days, the seven blessings were sung at a sumptuous meal, and the bride and groom presided over the festivities.

Chapter 8

MEYER

The wedding was over, and the season of dance parties was on. It was quite fashionable for landowners with eligible daughters to give dances in the girls' honor. Mendale was only sixteen, but the party givers began inviting him along with his older brother Meyer. Mendale was the gregarious one and the best dancer among the young men, the swiftest and most agile. When the musicians struck up the polka or the mazurka, the girls vied with each other to dance with him. Meyer, the scholarly and quiet type, preferred the graceful waltz.

At one of those Saturday night dances, Meyer met Miriam. As they twirled to the "Emperor Waltz," he thought her the most beautiful girl he had ever seen. She wasn't very tall but perfectly shaped, slender and yet curvy. Her strawberry blond hair framed a lovely face, and large green eyes seemed to look right into his soul. She was shy and didn't say very much, but he wasn't much of a talker either, so they danced and were oblivious to everyone else in the room. She had told him that her favorite waltz was "Tales from the Vienna Woods," so he requested that the musicians play it, and they danced again.

"Why haven't I ever met you before?" he asked when the music stopped. He pulled her into a little alcove off the dancing room. They sat down on the bench while she caught her breath.

"Well, you might not have noticed me, but I've seen you before."

At his urging, she explained that she had been sent to live with her wealthy uncle for four years and helped with his children. She had only recently returned. "I come from a poor family," she added shyly. "I probably don't fit in with the people at this party."

"Don't fit in? What a ridiculous thing for you to say! You are the most beautiful girl here. I like you more than anyone I've ever met before, and I want to get to know you better."

He took her hand and kissed it with a great deal of feeling, and she tried to pull it away. "Aren't you rushing things a bit? We have just met. We have to be more cautious of—"

Just then, Mendale burst in. "Meyer, I've been looking for you all over! They're going—" He broke off, realizing belatedly that he had interrupted their flirtation. "Excuse me, but they're going to drink a toast to Matis, and they want you to compose it."

Matis was a friend of theirs who—to Mendale's great envy—was leaving soon for a kibbutz in Palestine, and Meyer didn't want to miss the toast.

"Miriam, I'd like you to meet my younger brother, Mendale. He's not only the best dancer here, but also my shadow."

The two greeted each other, and Meyer conducted Miriam into the next room, where dancing had stopped, and someone had pushed a table into the middle of the room. Hiil, a muscular young man, jumped up on the table. "Quiet, everybody. We're about to begin. You boys," he pointed to his friends, "bring Matis up here." Mendale and two other fellows picked up their hero and then heaved him onto the table beside Hiil, and they all raised their glasses. "All right, Meyer," Hiil prompted.

Meyer said, "On this most important day in our lives, we drink to you, Matis, the bravest man among us. You will help redeem the Land of Israel for all of us. L'Chaim."

Everyone answered "L'Chaim," and drank to Matis. He accepted their good wishes with a happy smile and tears in his eyes. Then he shouted to the musicians, "A hora!" and everyone linked arms in spirited singing and dancing.

Meyer began to visit Miriam very often, looking for any excuse. He was soon quite besotted, and she seemed to reciprocate his feelings. At dances now, they danced only with each other. Before he had met her, he had some very definite plans for his life. Once he had turned eighteen, he would be called up to military service, and after he had served his time, he would go to Vienna and study to be a medical doctor. Now, his only desire was to be near her.

One day, walking in the woods not far from her home, it all came bursting out of him: His feelings, how he couldn't stand being away from her, that the only solution was for them to get married.

"How can we marry now, Meyer?" she said in distress. "You have no profession or trade, yet. What will we live on?"

"My mother would allow us to live with her until I'm able to support you. I work on the farm anyway—I'd just work harder. I love you more than anyone in the world, and you've got to say yes."

"Meyer, Meyer, I love you too. Don't you think that I want to marry you? It would be the happiest, most wonderful thing if it were possible. But it isn't." Miriam fought back her tears.

"Why? Why isn't it possible?"

"Oh, Meyer, don't make it difficult! I have no dowry—I have nothing to bring to our marriage. We'd have to live with your mother for a long time, and that would not be easy." Miriam had heard plenty of stories about the strong-willed Golda. "And then, you have to consider your career. What would happen to your studies? I know how much you want to be a doctor. I would only be a burden to you."

"You would come with me wherever I go. I would take care of you always and keep you close to me."

Miriam, more practical than he, recognized the romantic vagueness of that. "No, Meyer. I can't live on love alone. Let's wait a while and hope that the situation will change."

"Has your stepfather been after you again?" It was common knowledge that he had picked out a fat widower to be her husband. She would have stepchildren older than she was.

"My stepfather wants me to get married, so he will get rid of one more mouth to feed, but he thinks you're too young and financially insecure."

"We don't need his consent," Meyer said hotly. "We can run away to America. There I can get a job, and go to school at night."

"America! What are you thinking of?" Miriam stared at him aghast. "No one in my family has ever been to America!"

They decided that things were too unsettled just then and that they had better wait a while before deciding.

The next days were very busy ones for Meyer. He was notified that he was to begin his military service in two months. He knew that he was to escape conscription, he would have to leave for America immediately.

His first free evening, he went to Miriam's house to speak to her stepfather, and as he approached the sagging hovel where they lived, he saw Reb Faivel slip out and head down the street. The marriage broker! What was he doing there?

Inside, he found the girl and her parents sitting at a table, talking in low tones. They broke off at the sight of him.

"May I speak to your daughter privately for a moment?" Meyer asked, but when Miriam's parents hesitated, he just took her hand and led her outside.

"What's going on? We're apart for a few days, and already you receive proposals from suitors behind my back?" It was a clear, starry night, and Miriam was more beautiful than ever. But he had a sinking feeling that he was about to lose her.

"Oh, Meyer, please don't be angry with me. I just don't know what to do. My stepfather wants me to marry Avrum the bookkeeper, and he won't take no for an answer. He's after me all day, and I'm at my wit's end."

"Tell me now, and be done with it," Meyer demanded. "Which one do you love?"

"I love only you, Meyer. You know that. But what am I to do? I must listen to my stepfather." She began to weep helplessly.

"You must consent to your marriage. He cannot force you. So what are you planning to do?"

She licked her trembling lips. "I told Reb Moishe that I would consider Avrum's proposal—just consider. . . ."

"How could you do that? Meyer cried. "How could you even think about leaving me? You told me you would wait." With an effort he got control of himself and began to plead feverishly. "Let me take you away from here, come with me to America. We have relatives there—my cousin and his family. They will take care of us. Please, darling Miriam. . . ."

"No, no. I can't run away like a fugitive. Forgive me, my love, for hurting you so. It hurts me too." He wasn't listening to her anymore. He was crying, and so was she. They clung to each other like two lost children. She wiped his tears and he hers, and they were kissing now.

"We'll find a way, Miriam. Don't leave me. I'll let you go now, but remember I love you more than anyone in this world. To Avrum, you're just a beautiful girl he would like to possess. To me, you're my very life. We'll find a way."

Meyer slept very little that night. In the afternoon a boy came with a letter from Miriam. He opened it with trebling hands. After a long argument with her stepfather and mother, she had given in to their wishes. Word had been sent to Avrum that she would marry him.

Meyer didn't try to see her again, but he heard that the wedding was to take place within a month. He wrote her a long letter, but he never received an answer, and in due course, Miriam married Avrum.

Meyer could no longer stay in Zbora. He would go to America without her, and become a successful doctor. Golda tried to talk him out of it, but once she realized that he was going to leave with or without her consent, she gave in. She supplied him with enough money to take the train to Antwerp and from there the steamship to New York. Meyer was to go to his cousin, who lived on Fifth Avenue in a very luxurious apartment. The cousin would help him get settled and begin his studies in medicine.

Chapter 9
WORLD WAR I—THE GREAT WAR

On July 29, 1914, Mendale was working in the fields. He was thinking about the events which had shaken the Austro-Hungarian Empire, and wondering what was going to happen next. He felt so helpless about world politics and diplomacy. There was nothing to do but try to carry on normally, during these difficult times. Just a month before, on June 28, in Sarajevo, a Serbian had assassinated Archduke Francis Ferdinand, the heir apparent to the throne of Austria, and his wife, Countess Sofie Chotek. War seemed imminent, although as far as the Austrian people were concerned, the Archduke was very unpopular, and certainly not worth fighting over. Count Leopold von Berchtold, the Austrian Foreign Minister, felt differently. He had advocated sending in the army immediately to punish the Serbians. That idea was met with opposition by the entire government, including the Kaiser. They wanted passionately to avert any step that might lead to war. Von Berchtold, however, didn't give up. He continued agitating and winning over important people to his cause. He was also putting subtle pressure on the Kaiser, aiming to change the monarch's mind concerning Serbia.

Russia, on the other hand, was preaching pan-Slavism, the uniting of all Slavic peoples under her leadership.. She would probably support the Serbians in case of war, and at the same time gain the sympathy of all the Slavs within the Austro-Hungarian Empire. What would happen next was anybody's guess.

At a distance he could see his sister Laichia approaching, her red hair glistening in the sun. It was braided and fell down below her waist. The family was worried about her lately. She was over twenty now and not married yet. She would make someone a good wife. She was strong, full of energy, could do a man's work in the field and a woman's work in the kitchen. She was tall, thin, nicely built, and not bad looking at all. She seemed very attractive to him, but in Galicia, red-headed women were generally considered undesirable and bad-tempered. Why didn't some decent man see her good qualities and marry her?

As Laichia came closer, he saw that she was waving a newspaper, and when she got within earshot, she screamed, "It's war!"

Mendale took the paper from her and scanned it hastily. "At 11 A.M., on July 28, 1914," he read, "one month after the infamous murders in Sarajevo, Austria-Hungary notified Serbia by telegram that a state of war exists between the two countries." He ran his eye down the columns of newsprint: mobilizations. . . war measures. . . statement by this one and that. . . .

Mendale looked at his sister, and then at the sky. Not far from this peaceful setting, other young men like himself were getting ready to fight and to kill and to die. It didn't seem possible.

"What are you going to do, Mendale?" Laichia asked him. "You're of military age."

"I really don't know. If Russia stays out of it, it may blow over. If not—if the German Kaiser gets into it. . ." He spread his hands.

"We should have gone to America when Mr. Stern gave us the chance. Maybe you can still go there, Mendale, before the army gets you. I don't want you to go to war."

"I'm not going anywhere yet. We'll talk about it when I get home tonight." Laichia returned to the house at a slower pace.

He wanted to be alone for a while, to think about himself and his future. Would there be a future for him at all, now that he would be drafted into the army? Could he leave his mother and the family and travel to the United States? What about his dream of going to the Land of Israel? His mind was in a turmoil. Tomorrow things may become clearer. He was grateful for the peace of the moment.

The following day, when Aron had joined them for dinner, Jozef returned from town with a newspaper. He handed it to Aron to read, saying:"It looks like we're in for trouble. The damned Russians are coming," he cried, "and they'll brink the Cossacks. May Jesus protect us from those beasts." He crossed himself and became silent. Aron began to read aloud: "Today Russia mobilized her armies. Nicholas II, Czar of all Russias, has blamed our country for the Serbian trouble. In a telegram to his cousin, Wilhelm II of Germany, he wrote, 'An ignoble war has been declared on a weak country. . . ' He concluded the telegram with a threat: 'I shall be forced to take extreme measures that will lead to war!' " Aron stopped reading. No one said a word. Fear filled their hearts. They were so near the border and within reach of the Cossacks. Through the years they had heard about Russian pogroms and massacres. Even the smallest child knew what Bogdan Chmielnicki had done to their people, many years before. As the leader of a Cossack uprising against Polish rule, he and his hordes massacred 100,000 Jews in a bloody holocaust in the Ukraine. The Lemberg area where their home was, was the scene of one of those massacres. Could this happen again in the civilized world of the 20th century? Aron seemed to be the only one not afraid. He folded the paper and put in down on the table. "As the head of this family, I advise everyone to remain calm. Austria is a strong country, and the Hungarian Magyars are its fiercest fighters. Don't be afraid. The Russians will not dare attack us."

Aron was right, Russia did not attack Austria. But Germany, Austria's ally, declared war on Russia the next day, The event was followed by an order from General Conrad von Hotzendorf, the Commander of the Austro-Hungarian Army, for a full mobilization of the country.

A family consultation was now in order. The task was to discuss a strategy for survival. Aron spread a map on the table. Their village wasn't even on it. Even Lemberg, the capital of Galicia, was only a speck on the large map. Mendale thought about the insignificance of the human being in face of the terrible events which seemed to be engulfing them. He made a vow to himself, right then, to stay, and try to protect his mother and his family.

Golda broke the silence. "What chance is there that the Russians will attack this area? They have, after all, a very large frontier with Germany, which declared war on them first."

Aron answered her question: "I would say that there is still very little chance that the Russians will attack here. General Hotzendorf is reputed to be one of the most brilliant soldiers in the world. They would be afraid to cross swords with him at the very beginning.

"I agree with Aron," Mendale spoke up. "And besides that, Austria has a powerful artillery. They have the most advanced guns in existence, the 'Austrian 88!' The Skoda Works will produce as many of the as ill be necessary to defeat the Russians." Mendale pointed to the Czech area on the map to indicate the location of the munitions factory.

"It seems to me that an attack here is very likely." They were all surprised at Moishe, the youngest of the children, but they all listened as he continued: "The Cossacks are poised here, ready to strike." He pointed to the border. "Who's the closest to them? We are. I think I see something terrible will happen to the Empire. It will fall apart because of internal strife. The Ukrainians in Galicia will join the Cossacks, once they attack. They want their own country, and like the Serbians, they would rather be with their fellow Slavs. The Poles want their independence, and would easily turn against the Austrians who have occupied this land. If it came to Polish independence, we as Polish Jews would fight for Poland. Then there are the Czechs and the Slovaks. They want to be free too. How about the fact that only one of four of the minorities speaks German? How are the Austrians going to form a coherent force to protect the Empire? Most of the minority soldiers wouldn't even understand the orders in German. We're in for trouble. That's all I can say."

Golda was listening carefully to her youngest son, and shook her head in total disagreement. "What is this talk about the breaking up of the Empire? We have more rights in Galicia than any of our brothers in Europe. In Russia our people aren't even allowed to go to public schools, and are excluded from the universities. They can't live in the cities without special permission. Here everyone has a right to an education, and they teach Polish and Ukrainian as well as German. Our people can run for public office, and even the senate. They can be officers in the army. Kaiser Franz Josef, may he live long years, has been just to our people. We can trust him. And as for fighting for Poland, you're too young to be fighting anybody. I pray to our Heavenly Father, that he should protect us from all our enemies, and that he should preserve the empire."

She suddenly thought of Aron and Mendale. They weren't too young to go to war. "Mendale, will they call you up right away? And you, Aron?"

"Well, Mother, they'll probably call up the youngest ones first," Aron said with an uneasy glance as Mendale. "I'm twenty-nine now and have a family. By the time they get around to calling me, the war will be over. But Mendale. . ." Now they were all looking at him.

"Have you thought about what you want to do?" Golda asked—for her, uncertainly.

"I'm staying right here until they call me up. You need me."

"What if they call you up tomorrow?" she cried. "What help will you be to us when you are at the front? I'd rather see you in America, like Meyer."

"Mother, I've told you. I will not desert you, and I will not go to America. When I leave my home here, it will be because I've been conscripted or because I will be going to the Land of Israel."

Golda was not finished protesting, but Aron considered the matter settled and managed finally to quiet her. "All right," he said. "Now we have to leave to make plans for the farm. The spring wheat isn't ripe, but let's get the oats in, and begin putting other food aside. Perhaps we should erect a new storage shed. . ." Everyone listened and promised to cooperate.

In the weeks that followed, neither Aron nor Mendale was called up, nor did the Russians attack Galicia. They were waiting for the outcome of a battle that was shaping up in Serbia, in the southern part of the Austro-Hungarian Empire. And the unexpected happened. The Serbian General Putnik defeated the Austro-Hungarian army in a bloody battle on Serbian soil, and at the end of August, the Austrians withdrew from Serbia. They had lost 40,000 men, and the entire Austro-Hungarian Empire trembled with defeat. General Hotzendorf now moved north, passed through the heartland of the Empire and on to Galicia to make contact with the Russians.

Now the tide seemed to turn. The Austrians were finally victorious against their most powerful enemy, the Russians. The Hellers managed to get most of the harvest in. Flour was milled, wood collected, and sauerkraut, beets, and pickles were being prepared in barrels, to last through the winter.

There were daily reports about General Hotzendorf's armies going north, but Zbora was not in their path, and the family didn't see any Austrian soldiers. The General successfully pushed into Russian controlled territory without much resistance, and was aiming for Warsaw, the Polish capital occupied by the Russians. He realized only too late that the Russians, under General Ivanov had fooled him. They purposely drew him north, to distract him from their planned attack on Galicia. Hotzendorf had been caught off guard. Now General Ivanov sent General Brusilov and his army into Galicia. Brusilov advanced slowly and cautiously at first to make sure that he would not be entrapped.

Events in the rest of Europe were moving at a tremendous pace. It seemed like a spreading fire, which was about to consume the entire continent. Convinced that France was about to attack her, Germany now declared war on her neighbor on August 3. The following week, Great Britain joined her allies Belgium, France and Russia in the fight against Germany, Austro-Hungary and the Ottoman Empire.

For the Hellers this meant that anything could happen now, and they had to find a way to survive in a world gone mad. They drew closer and became very attuned to any sign of danger.

Chapter 10
THE RESCUE

At the inn in Zbora, business was booming. The Ukrainian peasants who came from the East to sell their produce at the market, were telling of battles and skirmishes. The Russian General Aleksei Brusilov was their hero, and soon they said he would smash the Austro-Hungarian army to pieces, like in Serbia, they said.

Andrei, a tall powerful man, put his arm around Aron and said excitedly, "Now we will get our own independence, under the Little Father, Tsar Nicoli. And we'll be rid of the damned Austrians and Polish princes with their superior airs."

Aron tired to move away, but the man held him so tightly that he couldn't.

"Well, what do you say to that, Brother Aron?" Andrei said tipsily.

"I believe in freedom for all people and am against the oppression of any nation," he rattled off woodenly, and this time Andrei released him.

"I knew you'd be on our side. You're the smartest Hebrew I know, and we all respect you, because you're also an honest man."

Andrei now joined his friends at one of the tables, and they began singing songs and telling more stories about the towns and villages that had fallen to Brusilov. Aron listened carefully, and it sounded to him as if Lemberg would soon be surrounded—and Bukaczowce was directly in the Russians' path. Bukaczowce, where Shainchi lived.

He took alarm. His sister and her three boys were alone there, since Nehemiah, her husband, had gone to Germany on business. The thought of Cossacks descending on gentle Shainchi—

Aron went home early and explained to his mother that he was going to Bukaczowce to fetch his sister and her children. Golda instantly agreed. Then he took Mendale aside.

"You'll have to be the one to protect the family, Mendale. Be on the alert every minute. Some of these Russians may have already infiltrated these parts. Be watchful especially at night." Aron got out his gun and bullets, and handed them to Mendale. "I'll take only a knife. In case I'm searched a gun might incriminate me."

"I understand. I'll be careful."

Mendale put away the gun and went out with Moishe to help Jozef get the horses and wagon ready. Golda and Laichia got busy packing a basket of food for Aron to take along.

When Aron was about to start off, Jozef said: "I'd like to come with you, my boy. I don't want you to go alone into a war zone." Aron was amazed at the old man's offer, but it was Golda who answered for her son: "I can't let you go, Jozef. We need you here. Aron will be safer alone. The Holy One, Blessed be He, will protect you, my son." She kissed Aron and added in Hebrew: "Go in peace, and return in peace." Ester and the children crowded around him, and he was hugging and kissing them all.

Aron had no time to be sentimental, however. He had to start out immediately if he was to reach his sister before nightfall.

Aron followed the main road through Shivka. As he approached the Dniester River, which he had to cross, all he saw was devastation. He heard shooting and cannon fire in the distance. He thought of the possibility of being captured by the Cossacks, but felt safe in this respect. He would pretend to be a Ukrainian. His command of the language was flawless, and besides that, he had his official papers with him, which identified him as a Greek Orthodox. He smiled as he recalled the mistake that had been made by the priest when Golda registered him at birth. That error of religious affiliation was left on all of the official papers, and became somewhat of a joke in the family. Now it might help him save his sister and himself.

He headed for the main bridge, but saw that it had been blown up. There was a smaller bridge nearby, so he headed that way, but he was stopped by a unit of the Austrian Army. They spoke an unfamiliar language—Hungarian, he suspected—so they took him to their captain, who questioned him in German.

After examining Aron's papers and hearing his explanation for his presence, the captain said, "Mr. Heller, Bukaczowce may already be in Russian hands—Brusilov is advancing very fast now. I'm in sympathy with your mission, but I can't let you cross the river."

"Then at least let me stay here in this vicinity for a few days, Captain. Perhaps I can still find a way to rescue her.

The officer looked dubious. "We're in a very precarious situation here, Mr. Heller—blowing up the bridges to delay the Russian advance. But I'll give you permission to stay for two days." He took a little notebook out of his pocket, tore out a page, wrote down a few words, signed it, and handed it to Aron. "If you want to chance it, you might still find someone to take you across in a boat. But do be careful."

"Thank you very much, Captain. I won't get in your way."

Aron spent the night in a nearby inn, and the next morning he went out to reconnoiter. Everywhere, the bridges had been blown up, and although he did find a man with a boat, two Hungarian soldiers stopped him from closing a deal with him. Aron showed them the pass, but they told him new orders had come, and all civilians would have to clear out. Aron could do nothing but go home.

When he got back to the farm, gloom reigned. What now? What could they do but hope and pray Shainchi was still safe? Mendale, however, had a plan.

The following morning, Mendale, dressed like a Ukrainian peasant, started out on foot. He traversed the 40 kilometers through the back roads and woods with little difficulty. But then he came to the Dniester. He knew from Aron that he had to find a boat to take him across. He asked around a little village for somebody who owned a boat. Several people had fishing skiffs, but no one was willing to let him have one. They had sighted Cossack scouts on the other side and expected to be liberated any day now. Mendale finally found an old man who agreed to take him across for a considerable sum of money.

"I'm not afraid to die," he said, grinning. "Besides, our little brothers on the other side will never shoot this old Ukrainian."

The crossing was uneventful, as the old man had predicted, and when they arrived at a quiet cove on the eastern bank, they heard only the birds in the willow trees. The old man was to wait there for Mendale until the next morning.

Mendale again avoided the main road and got to Shainchi's house by way of winding paths in the woods. It was quiet here too. The door was open, but there was no one inside. He was beginning to imagine all kinds of terrible things when he heard children's voices outside. He ran out and saw his sister and the boys in the courtyard.

Shainchi explained breathlessly what had happened. "We were warned last night that a Cossack patrol was coming through this area, so we and the other village people hid in the woods. They passed a while ago. We waited for about an hour and then decided to come back. But how did you get here, Mendale? It's so dangerous."

Mendale then told her of Aron's attempt to rescue her, and his own adventure. He ended by saying, "All right, now get a few things ready—whatever we can carry—and let's get out of here before dark. There's no time to lose."

"Now?" his sister said, surprised. "We have to have something to eat first—the children are starved and you—"

"Shainchi, there's a war going on out there! All the bridges have been blown up. If we don't hurry, we may miss our boatman."

"Let's not get panicky. We all have to eat, don't we?"

He tried to shake her out of her complacency, instill a little of his own sense of urgency, but she refused to listen.

"You don't fully understand the situation here, Mendale. It's not as dangerous as it seems. We don't need your boatman—there's a shallow part of the river where we could wade across. Besides, you have to go get the horses and wagon, because I'm not leaving without our bedding and our valuables."

"Shainchi, will you please listen! To go home and come back will take me at least three days. Your life is on the line here, and you're worried about possessions? The Cossacks may be back here any minute!"

Shainchi put her arms around her brother's neck. "Nothing will happen to us, Mendale." She told him that when the advance Russian patrol arrived—Cossacks, obviously—she had been terrified. But their sergeant had been very polite to her, kept the others away, and when he heard her name, immediately figured out that she was Jewish. He told her not to be afraid, and spoke to her in Yiddish, saying his name was Berl and that no harm would come to her or the children.

Mendale was astounded. "And you believed him?"

"I didn't at first, but listen to what happened next. He came back alone, a few hours later. He asked me if my husband was hiding in the woods, and I told him the truth—that Nehemiah was in Germany. He seemed to believe me. He asked for some tea, and fortunately, I still had some in the cupboard. He drank it and then he left."

"You were lucky, Shainchi. Don't stretch it."

"I haven't finished. He came back the next day and told me that other patrols had arrived in the area, but that he would warn me if we were in danger. I fed him a good lunch and he said that it tasted just like his mother's cooking. Then he started asking me questions—what was it like for our people to live in the Austro-Hungarian Empire."

Shainchi told Berl although there was some anti-Semitism in high places, the law protected all minorities. He seemed very impressed by that, and said that he would like living under the Austrian system. He even hinted that he might desert the Russian army and help her and the children to rejoin her family.

He stayed and played with the children for a while, then left, but early that morning, he came back again to warn her to hide, because one of the newer patrols was going to come that way.

"We were to go into the woods until nightfall—he showed me where on a map—and that's exactly what we did. We also managed to warn Nehemiah's relatives, so they fled as well. He's going to come back tomorrow to give me the latest news." Shainchi smiles brightly at Mendale. "So you see—there's no danger."

"By the time he gets here tomorrow," he retorted grimly, "we'll be gone. We'll hide your valuables, and take only what we can carry. I must get you out of here!"

"But Berl—"

"Look, Shainchi, this Berl might have the best intentions in the world, but he's only a sergeant—a Jewish sergeant in a Cossack unit. You're playing with fire if you think that he has any control of the situation."

"No, Mendale. I'm going on foot. He will protect us. He's a good man."

They wrangled some more and Mendale was finally convinced that he could do nothing to make his stubborn sister see good sense.

"If you insist on staying," he said in defeat, "play along with Berl, but don't tell him of our plans. I'll go back to Zbora to get the horses and wagon. Now explain to me where to find this ford."

She drew the details of the area on a piece of paper, and Mendale left. He could only pray that the Blessed One would watch over her and save her in spite of herself.

Chapter 11

THE ENEMY IS HERE

When Mendale returned home and told his story, Golda was furious at Shainchi.

"This foolish girl is going to get herself killed! What is the promise of a Russian soldier worth?"

Mendale and Moishe got out the big wagon and hitched up the horses. Golda thought it best this time for Moishe to go along to help with the crossing. The boys traveled along country roads, avoiding villages and inhabited places. Using Shainchi's rough map, they located the shallow ford and drove the horses into the river.

It began shallow enough, but after a short distance it grew progressively deeper. Now only the horses' heads could be seen above the water. and soon they had to swim, as they pulled the wagon along.

Suddenly the boys felt something loosen. They looked back and saw that the back wheels were mired in the river. The front wheels still moved along behind the horses.

There was nothing to do, but go all the way across first. When they got to the shore, Mendale unhitched one of the horses and, mounting it, went back in the river to pull out the wheels. He had taken a heavy rope from the wagon. When he got to the spot, he found that the wheels had completely sunk under water, leaving only a board sticking up.

He dismounted and dived, swimming underwater, he managed to find the axle and tie the rope around it. Then he tied the other side of the rope to the horse and mounted. The horse pulled again and again, but was unable to extract the wheels. Then the rope came loose at the horse's end, and Mendale had to grab and hold it so as not to lose track of the wheels.

"Moishe," he called, "bring the other horse." When he caught sight of a shepherd watching them, he added, "Bring him with you." The shepherd jumped up on the horse in back of Moishe, and in they went. After a long struggle, the three of them managed to get the wheels to shore.

It took a good two hours to repair the wagon and secure the wheels, and when they finished, they paid the shepherd for his work and they started off toward Shainchi's house.

It was getting dark when they arrived at their destination, and they were exhausted, but they wanted to start loading the wagon immediately. Shainchi wouldn't hear of it. "First you will rest. At dawn, before Berl gets here, we'll leave."

They objected, but to no avail. She told them that Nehemiah's uncle was coming with them, and it would be hard for the old man to travel at night. The brothers were too tired to argue with her and were glad just to throw themselves on the floor and sleep.

Next morning it was still dark when they started loading the wagon. They carried the still sleeping children to the wagon and laid them down on the bedding. Shainchi insisted on bringing her cow along, to make sure that the little ones would have milk and the plodding animal slowed them down every step of the way.

They had reached the Dniester just as the sun was rising. To their surprise, their shepherd was waiting for them with a boat. Mendale put Shainchi and the children in the boat with the shepherd. Then Moishe and Nehemiah's uncle mounted the horses, while Mendale stayed in the wagon and guided it across, the cow floundering and lowing pathetically behind. There was a moment when they thought that she had drowned, but they pulled her out.

With the crossing behind them, they put Shainchi and the children back in the wagon, and paid off the helpful shepherd. They had just started off, when they heard shooting in the distance and began to see houses burning on the horizon. Mendale took the reins and hurried the horses as fast as they could go with the poor cow slowing them down. He didn't stop until they put some twenty kilometers between them and the river.

There was an inn there, where they stopped to rest and get something to eat. The innkeeper's wife was just taking some freshly baked cornbread out of the oven, and offered it to them, with butter and herring. They ate their meal quickly, while they gave the innkeeper what they knew of the news.

"Brusilov is on the move again," Mendale concluded.

The innkeeper jumped up in alarm. "Then we will have to leave too." He started giving orders to his son and wife to get everything ready. By the time Mendale pulled out of the courtyard, he was locking his front door and preparing to join his wife and son in a small wagon full of their belongings.

"Have a safe journey, and may the Lord protect us all," the innkeeper shouted at the young people rode out the gate.

They continued as fast as they could, until they saw their own house in the distance. The sound of artillery became fainter now, and they felt somewhat safer, but as they approached the main gate of the farm, they saw many people streaming toward it down the road. And when they turned the wagon in, they were amazed at the number of people camping in their yard, some of them cooking food on small fires, some just milling around. Mendale could hardly get through to the stable.

These tired and miserable people must be the refugees, he thought, fleeing before Brusilov's advance.

Golda and Laichia were so busy distributing bread, tea and milk that they seemed unaware of Shainchi's arrival. But when she and the boys got off the wagon and ran toward them, Golda woke up and was thrilled and happy to see them safe at last.

The house was full of people as well. Many of their relatives had fled their homes. But Mendale did not see his older brother.

"Where is Aron?"

"He left for Kalusz this morning with a wagonload of oats," Golda said. "He'll sell it, so that we'll have some money handy. We've decided to leave too. As soon as Aron comes home, we'll be on our way."

"I'm not sure that this is a good idea, Mother," Mendale objected in dismay. He didn't want to see her and his sisters in the same plight as those homeless refugees.

"After what we've heard from the people out there," Golda replied, "we don't have much choice."

They had told terrible stories of murder and rape, of houses burned over people's heads. It wasn't just the Cossacks who were acting like beasts, but their Ukrainian neighbors as well. Even Golda was gripped by a sense of helplessness and despair when she thought of what was heading their way.

Aron drove the horses hard, and arrived in Kalusz with hopes that he could sell the grain quickly. But the town was deserted—the stores closed and bolted, the streets empty of people. Only in the yards and alleyways was there activity. People were feverishly packing carts with food, bedding and other household items, in a panic to get away from the coming Russians. Aron stopped in a few of the alleys and tried to sell the oats, but people just waved him away. He finally drove to the other side of town, where a friend of his, a grain dealer, lived.

Like everyone else, Shloimo was outside his house completing his preparations to flee. His wife, children, and in-laws were in one wagon. He was loading the other wagon with food and bedding.

"Aron, you won't find a human being in this town to buy your oats. Go home as fast as you can, get your family, and get going west before the Russians get here."

Aron could see that that made sense, but he wanted to get rid of the oats, so he could get back more quickly to Zbora. "Put them down in the cellar, and if you're lucky, you'll get them back when the war is over." Shloimo helped Aron put the grain away. Then he locked everything up, kissed the *mezuzah* on the front door, and was off.

By now the main road leading into the town was filled with refugees, some in wagons, others pushing carts, and still others walking. They were going west. Aron was trying to go the opposite way. As he waited in his wagon to decide how to proceed, he heard a murmur that came from the multitude. It was like a sad humming. A young boy sitting on a wagon full of people started singing in a beautiful voice:

> *Oh Creator of the world,*
> *All Israel sings to You.*
> *Let our redemption come speedily.*
> *Let the Messiah come soon.*

Aron realized that it was impossible for him to go against this stream of people. He turned into the alleyway and continued on some of the side streets until he reached the road home. Even here on the back roads, the sound of the fleeing people came to him. Soon he could hear the shooting and the *whump. . . whump. . . whump. . .* of the big guns. He entered the woods and drove through the narrow roads for what seemed an eternity. At last the gate of the farm loomed up.

Everyone crowded around him in the courtyard, asking questions. All he could tell them was that the Brusilov offensive seemed to be on again.

As he was headed for the house, he saw that some of the refugees were already pouring out through the gate, and others were packing to leave.

Aron was happy to see Shainchi and the children, safe at least for now. Ester and his own children crowded around him. Somehow the women didn't seem to realize the danger he had just gone through, and he didn't want to alarm them. He looked out of the window and saw the refugees flooding like a stream down the road. Already the yard was empty, except for litter.

Now he and his family would be refugees too. Worst of all, they had little cash. He tried to figure how much food they could take with them and still be able to travel at a quick pace. It would take a good part of the night to load the two wagons. The animals would have to be fed, then taken along. They would go like gypsies, with the horses and cows tied to the wagons.

With Golda to supervise the loading and many hands to help, the worked fast. Even the children helped out. It was an adventure for them. They knew that there was something called "a war," but so far all they had experienced was excitement. After a while, they got tired and one by one dropped off to sleep.

By morning they were loaded up, and Golda started to prepare their last good meal at home.

Aron came in and grabbed some bread. "Mother," he said to Golda, "I'm going to see Vashta, to ask him to keep an eye on our property. I'll be back in fifteen minutes at the latest. See that everybody is ready to go."

Vashta, their nearest neighbor, had been a good friend. He was the richest Ukrainian in those parts, owning a vast expanse of land, including part of a forest. He was a short powerful man, who liked to say that Aron was the only Jew who had ever beaten him in wrestling. Aron had also helped him with farming advice: how to increase his crop yield, improve his livestock, where and when to market his produce. Aron's knowledge of farming was famed far and wide.

"Vashta, I came to say good-bye, because we're leaving," Aron said as he walked in.

Vashta jumped up. "Leaving? Are you out of your mind?"

"No, but—"

"Are you going to America, like Meyer?"

"Vashta, we have no thoughts about America now. We have to flee for our lives. You must realize that the Russians and the Cossacks are all around us. All the Jewish people are running west to escape from them.

"Look, I came to ask you, as a favor, to keep an eye on our property. You can kill and eat all the chickens and geese you want. We can't take them with us."

"Aron, my friend, you're confused." Vashta put his arm around Aron. "You can't compare yourself to the other Hebrews. You're different. You're one of us. You speak our language, you know how to be a friend, and even how to win a fight. No one will do you any harm. I can vouch for that."

"Vashta, our family took a vote, and we all agree that we must go. We'll be homeless for a while, but the Lord will restore us to our home again."

"Stay and you won't need to be restored. Look, Aron, the Russians are our little brothers. They promised the Ukrainians an independent country, one they win the war. What reason would they have to hurt you? Don't go away. We need people like you on our side, people who have knowledge of science and the advanced techniques of farming. Then we can build up a new country and be strong." Vashta walked over to the wall where a large wooden crucifix was hanging. He took it off the wall and, holding it in his left hand, crossed himself with his right.

"Aron, I swear by our Saviour, Jesus Christ, that I will help you and protect you and your family from the Russians and the Cossacks—if you need protection. Whatever happens to you will happen to me." Vashta had tears in his eyes as he embraced Aron. "Don't refuse me, brother Aron. Stay."

Aron was very moved. Vashta was really a friend. Perhaps the Creator didn't want them to leave their home and land. Maybe it was ordained that they stay and live.

"Say that you will stay. I know that you'll be satisfied if you do."

"Well," Aron said slowly, "if I can get my family to agree. . . ." He took a deep breath. "We will send word to you of our decision."

The family decided to stay. A few days later, on September 3, 1914, Vashta came to visit them with news: Brusilov took Lemberg that morning. It is now called Lvov again. Do you realize what a victory means to us Ukrainians? We are finally free."

When he saw Aron's expression, he tried to console him: "Don't worry, my friend, I have a feeling that they're not going to come to Zbora at all. It's of no importance to them, and it's quite out of the way of their offensive."

Somehow, nothing did happen in Zbora. The Russian army went somewhere else and life on the farm soon took on its habitual routine. The family milled the grain and put food away for the winter. Weeks passed, and slowly some of their friends began returning to the other villages nearby. They all had stories to tell of their suffering on the road and in hiding. The Hellers were grateful that they stayed.

But nothing was the same anymore. No one dared go into town. Their only communication with the outside world was through Vashta, who came to visit Aron often, and seemed to know about everything that was going on. He was always cheerful, but the Hellers could not fight off a constant fear that the worst was yet to come. Sometimes during the night they would hear shooting in the distance, but eventually that stopped too. The Hellers felt as though they were on a peaceful island, while the war raged all about them and in time would swamp them.

It was a beautiful Sabbath morning in November, and the three brothers decided to walk to the next village to pray with their coreligionists. It was the first time they had done that since the war had started. Their friends were overjoyed too see them, and the service proceeded peacefully, in all its beauty. The Hellers walked back home through the woods.

It was one o'clock when they got home and found the house fragrant with delicious smells. A long table was set for the Sabbath meal: two hallahs, covered with a pretty hand-embroidered cloth—two lions of Judah holding a crown of gold—and a carafe of wine and a silver goblet by Aron's place. The family gathered and took their places, and Aron blessed the wine. He had just finished when they heard the clatter of hooves in the courtyard.

Aron glanced out quickly and saw three Cossacks riding toward the front door. Aron closed the drape and snapped out orders. Golda snatched up the silver goblet and silverware and ran to the bedroom to hide them. Moishe cleared off the food. Mendale hustled the young women and children to the cellar entrance, told them to keep quite, lowered the trap door, and pushed a chest over it. He wanted his mother to go down to the cellar too, but she refused.

"They will think it strange to find no woman," she said calmly. Aron went to get out his gun, but she said, "Leave it," and when the pounding started on the front door, she managed a normal-sounding "Who's there?"

"Open to the soldiers of Brusilov's Army!"

Mendale went to the door and opened it, and they pushed in. The Cossack sergeant was stocky and had short bowed legs and the slanted dark eyes of a Tartar. The two others were somewhat younger, but looked wild and disheveled.

"Who owns this farm?" they demanded of Mendale.

"I do," Golda answered. "My name is Golda Heller, a widow, and this is my son, Mendale." When the soldier directed his angry gaze at Aron and Moishe, she added, "My other sons."

Golda now stretched out her hand to the cossack, but he ignored her gesture of civility.

"I don't understand what's going on here. You all look like Ukrainians and talk like Ukrainians, and yet you seem to be observing the Sabbath of the accursed Jews." He looked at the white tablecloth and their Sabbath clothing. "Are you telling me the truth? Is this really your own land?"

"My dear sir, in Austria it is permitted. This is our farm. We're just people, farmers, working the land with our own hands. Surely that is not so hard to understand." At a gesture from her, the three brothers displayed their callused hands.

"You look tired," she said. "Perhaps we can offer you something to eat?" and before the sergeant had a chance to answer, she said: "Boys, bring some fresh milk and butter for these gentlemen." She took out two large hallahs from the cupboard, and began to slice them, while the boys went into the kitchen to get the rest of the food.

"Is there anyone else here?" the leader asked, and when he got a negative reply ordered the other two to search the house. He himself sat down to eat right away. The two young Cossacks came back quickly and told their leader that there was no one else there. They seemed in a hurry to eat too, but the sergeant told them to search the three Heller boys first.

Aron was glad that his mother had stopped him from getting his gun. The Cossacks searched him carefully, and then went on to Mendale and Moishe.

The three men ate wildly, using soup spoons to eat the butter, stuffing large slabs of cheese into their mouths, slurping sour cream from the bowls in large noisy gulps, and stuffing their mouths with hallah.

"You sit here next to me, little mother, and let your little Jew boys serve us," the leader shouted. "And you, redhead, get us some more of that nice Jew-bread." He looked at Golda again. "Don't worry, little mother, we're not going to harm your boys as long as they behave. That's because I have a feeling that you're really one of us."

Golda still outwardly self-possessed, was trembling inside, afraid for the safety of her sons, afraid that one of the children in the cellar might cry out, and they'd all be in mortal danger. To keep the ruffians in good humor, she replied lightly,"It does my heart good to see you men eat so heartily. Have some more sour cream."

It was the right note to strike. His hunger sated, the sergeant leaned back. "Your food is delicious, little mother. We haven't eaten so well since we left Tsaritsyn. In fact, we like your butter and cheese so much that we decided to take the cow." He stood up and so did the two soldiers. "You, redhead," he ordered, "and you two blond ones, don't move. My brother here will watch you very carefully." He ordered one of the soldiers to guard the Hellers. "And you, little mother," he turned to Golda, "will lead me to the stable."

They all followed orders. Golda knew that she had to sacrifice the cow, but she wondered if the Cossacks also intended to rape or kill her or both.

But as she led the sergeant and his follower to the barn, he said to her in a reasonable tone—not apologizing, just explaining—"I'm a very peaceful man, myself, but we were attacked by the Germans, so naturally we had to fight back."

He didn't try to harm her, but he changed his mind about the cow and took the bull instead. They tied a rope through the ring in its nose and then to the leader's horse and led it toward the front of the house.

Meanwhile the boys were thinking that it might be easy enough to overpower their single guard. Aron had seized the chance, while he was waiting on the Cossacks, to slip his pistol out of hiding and under his shirt. They would wait for the right moment and then go into action.

The sergeant called the soldier out of the house, and the three men mounted and headed for the main road.

The Hellers watched from the window. The three Cossacks could only advance very slowly. They had trouble getting the stubborn bull to move at all.

"Mendale and Moishe," Aron said, "follow those bandits, and see where they are taking the bull. Maybe they'll abandon it. But make sure that you don't encourage the Cossacks to come back."

The boys caught up with the Cossacks not far from the farm. They were still struggling with the bull, who was young and willful, and Mendale thought they might be sufficiently tired of the struggle to let the animal go—for a price. But the soldiers took the money and continued to drag the bull after them. Later the Hellers saw the animal again—in the possession of the Lemkes.

It was a cold, clear February night. Although it was Friday, no one had gone to pray in the neighboring village. Things seemed to be getting worse. After the incident with the bull, the family kept the doors shut and didn't allow anyone in the house. They were careful not to go out at night. The Russians and Cossacks were out there somewhere, and no one knew what they would do.

That evening as the men were praying, they heard the sound of hooves. They snuffed out the candles and peeked out the window. Vashta, their friend, had just dismounted from his horse and was walking alongside a Russian officer, showing him around. A soldier followed them. They walked into the stable, while the family watched silently from behind a curtain. After a minute, Vashta and the soldier emerged, leading their two horses. The Hellers stared at one another in shock. Vashta their friend? The one who "respected" Aron, who had sworn on the crucifix to protect them? As the three men passed the front door, one turned and fired his pistol. Two of the windows were shattered but no one was hurt. "Vashta, you liar," Aron muttered. "I will live to avenge this deed." But the thieves were already out the front gate.

By the end of March things had gotten progressively worse. The Russian army had slowly depleted the rest of the Hellers' livestock. All the horses and cows were gone now, except for Shainchi's cow, which she had brought with her across the river. One day some Cossacks came and took that cow too. The family no longer tried to intervene with marauders; they simply hid. The animals the Russians stole would often end up with the Lemkes.

Spring came, and the fields had to be plowed. Aron scoured the countryside and finally found a man with three horses. The owner, one Ivan Hutera, wanted to sell him a horse, but Aron didn't have enough money to buy it outright. Instead, he said that if Hutera trusted him and waited until after harvest time, he would pay him the price he was asking for the horse. Aron gave a deposit, and they shook hands on the deal.

The plowing was almost finished. The family had only one more day's work to do, and the young men were in the barn putting away their implements, when they heard someone calling Aron in Ukrainian. Aron went out to see who it was. It was Hutera with a Russian soldier.

Aron took alarm. "Moishe, go inside quickly and warn the women. Lock all the doors, and stay in the house." Moishe slipped out the side door just as the two ominous figures, Hutera and the Russian, appeared at the main door, outlined against the setting sun.

Good evening, Hutera. What seems to be the problem?" Aron stretched out his hand to greet the villager, but Hutera looked away.

"Is this the man we're looking for?" the soldier asked.

"Yes, that's him— Aron Heller."

The soldier handed Aron a paper with an official army stamp. "The commander of this district was informed today by this good Ukrainian brother that you Jews stole his horse."

"What!"

"He said that you pretended to buy it, but refused to give him any money. When he asked you to return the horse, you ignored him."

Aron tried to say that it wasn't true, but the soldier didn't want to hear. "You're lucky that our commander is a good man and didn't order me to shoot you."

Aron was forced to put a halter on the animal and lead him outside. As they waited, Mendale beckoned to Hutera. "Come over here," he said. "I have something to tell you." He led the man to a far corner of the barn, where they weren't visible to the soldier. There Mendale whispered into his ear:

"You lying son of a bitch. You're trying to get us killed. Remember, Russians or no Russians, we Hellers always get even with people who wrong us."

Hutera went pale with rage and took a swing at the boy, but Mendale knocked his arm aside and brought his right in a bone-cracking punch under the chin. Then he grabbed the villager by the neck and started choking him.

"If you tell the commander or anybody else any more lies," he whispered, "I will come at night and personally finish you off." Mendale then slammed the man against the wall and ducked out.

Aron came out of the barn, leading the horse and turned him over to the soldier, and just then Hutera came lurching out, his teeth red with blood.

"Hey," said the startled soldier. "Who did this to you, little brother?"

Hutera pointed toward the wooded area where Mendale's figure was disappearing between leafy trees.

The soldier hefted his rifle and got off a shot. Then he lowered it. "It's useless. He's out of my range, and it's too dark to see anyway." He slung his rifle. Go home, little brother, and take your horse with you. I have done my duty." He helped Hutera get on his horse and walked after him toward the main road.

Chapter 12
THE HOSTAGE

Somehow they finished the plowing, using Moishe and Mendale to take the place of the horse. They were ready to start sowing when an official commission arrived on horseback one morning. The Hellers expected trouble again, but for once the soldiers were polite and well behaved. Only one of the Russians carried a gun, the officer. They said that they'd been sent by their colonel to buy hay. The villagers said the Hellers had a lot of it.

Aron was surprised. "Well, yes, but that's because our livestock has all been confiscated." He added, "You do realize that it's last year's hay?"

"We understand. Let's see what you have."

The commission was satisfied with the quality of the hay and made Aron a fair offer. They even lent him two horses to haul it to their cavalry headquarters. Aron was to deliver it the next day.

Mendale was in the fields sowing when Laichia came running. "They took Aron!" she shouted. "They came for hay and they took him." She seemed totally hysterical. "Mendale, hide in the woods. They're taking hostages, only Jews."

"Laichia, who took him? What's going on?"

"The Russians came just a while ago and took him away. Who knows what they'll do to him."

"Calm down, Laichia. Maybe there is something I can do."

"All you can do is hide because if you don't they'll get you, too. Mother sent me. Here." She gave him a sweater, a blanket, and some food in a basket. "I'm off to Zawadka to see her friend Malafi."

Malafi was now a *radnik*, or councilman of the Ukrainian Council set up by the Russians. Golda thought that he might help get Aron out of the clutches of the Russians.

"Come into the woods with me and rest a bit," Mendale said. "You're all out of breath."

"No, Mendale, I have to hurry. Time is on their side. You go and find yourself a good place to hide. When you come back home at night, don't forget our signal. Just whistle and I'll whistle back if the coast is clear."

Radnik Malafi came into the hall when he heard his housekeeper arguing with Laichia. The girl was shouting that there was no time to lose, that her brother had to be saved.

"What's all this commotion? Oh, it's you Laichia. What's this about your brother? Come in, come in." The councilman ushered her into his living quarters.

"Your Excellency, Aron was taken this morning by the Russians. He's a hostage. Can you help get him out?"

"Hostages—no one is taking hostages. Sit down here and rest, my girl." Malafi called to the housekeeper for some refreshments.

"Now, my dear, I would like very much to help your brother, and I would do anything for Golda. But this is different. My hands are tied." He took a document from the table. "This is an order from the General Staff that all Jews over the age of eighteen are to be enlisted into work brigades."

Laichia couldn't contain herself. "How can that be? Aron hasn't done anything against the Russians."

"I know that he hasn't, and if necessary, I'll vouch for him in this respect. But he is not in danger. In fact, he's safer where he is than if they drafted him into the army. The labor brigades dig trenches, build gun emplacements—not much different from farm work and they will probably release him within a few weeks. Go home now, Laichia, and tell your mother not to worry." This time Malafi was firm. He ushered her out into the hall.

Laichia walked home through the woods very dejected. She wasn't sure that Malafi was telling the truth about not being able to help, but even if he was, the result was the same: Aron was a hostage, and no one would come to his rescue. When she got home and told Golda and Ester what had happened, they both began to cry with fright, and the children with them.

Mendale returned home that night, reassured by Laichia's all-clear signal. Now that they knew that only men over eighteen were being taken, maybe Mendale would be safe. He would have to carry his identification papers at all times. Besides, with Aron gone, he would have to deliver the hay to the Russian commission the next day—they had to meet their commitments or worse things could happen to them.

The next morning Mendale and Moishe hitched the commission's horses to two wagons loaded up with hay, and were on their way. As they were driving past one of the villages, they saw lines of men, young and old, being led into the courtyard of the inn by Russian soldiers. The boys looked for Aron among them, but couldn't find him. Mendale decided to do a little more investigating. He turned into the courtyard of the inn. The soldiers guarding the gate stopped the wagons, but Mendale had the requisition bill with the commission stamp on it and showed it to the guard.

"So what are you doing here, boy? You're supposed to be on your way to the weighing station."

"We're thirsty, and so are the horses. We'll water them, get something to drink inside, and be on our way."

"Well, don't take too long. We've got a serious job to do here, guarding all these prisoners." The guard let them through.

When Mendale and Moishe walked into the inn, they immediately spotted Aron's red head. He was sitting at a big table surrounded by other men, talking quietly. The two Russian guards must have assumed that the boys were Ukrainians since Mendale greeted them in that language. They didn't even ask them for identification. Mendale went right up to the counter and, still speaking Ukrainian, asked the old innkeeper for two vodkas. The old man looked at him, surprised. He knew the Hellers very well. But Mendale paid him and whispered in Yiddish to pretend not to know him. The innkeeper got the message.

Mendale now edged over to where Aron was sitting, followed by Moishe. Mendale whispered to his brother:

"We're going out the door. You follow us into the courtyard. I'll tell the soldiers that we need your help to write out a bill because we don't know how to write."

Once in the courtyard, they were able to talk freely. "What's really happening, Aron?" Moishe asked.

"So far, nothing. They aren't treating us too badly. There are rumors that they're taking us to work in Russia. Some people believe they'll release us soon. Nobody really knows."

"Mother tried to get you out through Malafi, but he claimed that he couldn't do anything because the orders came from high up." Now Mendale got closer to Aron and whispered, "But I can get you out of here. I'll hide you in the hay and nobody will know the difference. I'll take you home and then go on to the weighing station."

"Don't be stupid, Mendale. I'd be a fugitive. Where would I go? The Russians are all around us, and our neighbors, the Lemkes, would have fun hounding me out."

"Aron, please listen to me. You'll be safer in hiding than in their clutches. Don't trust them."

"Forget it, Mendale. If you get caught hiding me in the hay, we'll all be killed. At least this way you two are safe for now." He turned and walked back into the inn.

As the boys were driving out of the courtyard, they could hear the hostages singing, "Avinu Malkeinu:"

"Our Father, our King,
Be gracious to us. . .
Take pity on us and redeem us."

They drove for quite a distance. Part of the commission was quartered at a nearby estate, where they was a big scale. The Polish count who owned the estate had fled in the wake of the Russian advance.

The boys drove up to the weighing station and got in line. Other people were ahead of them, all Ukrainians. After their hay had been weighed, they were given an official receipt and were told that they would get paid in Kalusz. The officer in charge sent two soldiers with them so there would be no mix-up; the soldiers would then return with them to Zbora and take the two horses back.

The boys, each accompanied by a soldier, arrived at the commission headquarters in Kalusz. They presented their receipt and were paid 250 rubles, the amount agreed on.

As they were leaving town, they passed by the railway station, where a long column of men was filing into the entrance. They were Jewish hostages, guarded by armed Russian soldiers. They saw a neighbor, Reiter, walking toward the gate. He was limping a bit and being helped by his teenaged son. Mendale wanted to help them get away, but the soldier next to him brought him out of his dreaming and told him to keep moving. Soon they were on the way to Zbora.

All the time it took them to get home, he thought about his brother. The words of Psalm 137 ran through his head: "By the waters of Babylon, there we sat and we wept remembering Zion. . . ." He remembered the entire passage, but wouldn't weep. He wouldn't let the Russians get him. If they tried to make him a hostage, he would either run off to the woods or die fighting.

Chapter 13
A SOLDIER IN THE WAR

The Austrian forces reoccupied Lemberg in the summer of 1915. The Russians had been pushed back beyond their former border. Mendale turned eighteen in May of that year, but somehow escaped being taken by the Russians before they withdrew. Aron had disappeared with the other hostages, no one knew where. There were rumors that they had been taken to Siberia and that many of them would not survive the hardships of that terrible climate.

Jozef had gone to visit his children in the western part of Galicia when the war started, and he had not come back yet. The family had endured a great deal that year, but somehow managed to survive and avoid hunger. They had even found two scraggy horses for sale. Now there was hope again that the war would end shortly and that Austria would be the winner.

Mendale heard that he was to go to sign up in Rzeszow, where the Austrian Military Commission was enlisting everyone over eighteen, but since he hadn't been called up officially, he certainly wasn't going to volunteer. With Aron gone, he was in charge of protecting the women and children.

And that meant keeping them fed. When they realized that their stockpiles were almost depleted—and that included money—Mendale and Moishe cut down some of their trees, sawed the wood into stove-lengths, and drove to Kalusz to sell it for firewood.

In town, they avoided all official-looking buildings and headed for the Jewish quarter. But before they got there, a man stopped them, speaking in Yiddish. He looked at the wood and said that he liked the quality and he wanted to buy the whole wagon load. This struck Mendale as a piece of good fortune, since he had expected to have to hawk the wood all over town. They agreed on a price and shook hands, and the man asked him to take the wood to his house and unload it, which was done.

The man took out a large purse from his pocket and gave Mendale a coin. "Here's a deposit for the wood. Come back tomorrow, and I'll give you the rest of the money."

"That wasn't our agreement," Mendale said hotly. "I came a long way to sell this wood, and we can't stay here another day."

"If that's the case, then take it back." The man started walking away, toward his house, but Mendale grabbed his arm and spun him around.

"You bastard, pay me what you owe."

The man tried to get away, but Mendale was too strong. " Take that purse out of your pocket again and let's see how much money you have right now."

Reluctantly, the man pulled out the purse and, as Mendale had suspected, there was ample money there to pay for the whole load. He helped himself to the amount that they had agreed on and threw the purse back.

Mendale climbed up on the wagon and cracked his whip loudly, and as he was pulling out of the yard, the man suddenly seemed to lose his fear. "I'll get even with you, you dirty crook!" he shouted, shaking a fist. "I'm going to the commission right now to denounce you as a draft dodger!"

When they were out of earshot, Moishe looked at his brother curiously. "Do you think he'll do it?"

"Probably, but—"he turned the horses down a side street—"we'll forestall him." Mendale was heading for the enlistment office. It would be best to get there before the man did and volunteer.

The officer in charge of recruiting saw the papers that Mendale had filled out and was impressed by his knowledge of German. He called the young man into his office and questioned him further about his background and the time he had spent under Russian rule. Mendale told him about Aron having been taken hostage and the hardships that the family had endured during the Russian occupation.

"Barbarians!" the officer said in disgust. "We Austrians are civilized. Let's hope that your brother will survive this ordeal." The officer filled out a form, signed it, and handed it to Mendale. "Since you have to help your family with the harvest, I will defer you for three months. If anyone should question you, this paper is your proof, so don't travel without it."

When they got home to Zbora, Mendale found that loyal old Jozef had returned. The boys embraced him joyously, and Mendale felt a slight easing of his anxiety. Now there would be someone to help the family when he got called up.

In October, Mendale was called up. He was assigned to a basic training unit, stationed in Przemysl, a town west of Lemberg. Two boys from his village, also about to begin army training, traveled with him, Nikita and Bohdan. They were Lemkes who spoke no German and were traveling by train, so Mendale took them under his wing. Despite their background, Mendale liked these two very much. They bombarded him with questions, but he didn't mind, because they were bright and learned fast.

Przemysl had just been liberated from the Russians. Parts of the town, pockmarked with shrapnel and some buildings in ruin, looked deserted, and there was a shortage of food. For Mendale and his two friends, training intensively, being hungry all the time was an especial hardship. Soon the rains started and with them came unseasonably cold weather. There was no wood to heat the barracks, and the boys, although all of them strong and healthy, were cold and uncomfortable.

In spite of the hunger and hardships, Mendale passed his training with high honors and received a medal for sharpshooting. Nikita and Bohdan both passed everything as well, and thanked Mendale for helping them out. The three stayed together as much as they could, and hoped that they'd be sent together to the front.

On Saturday, the three boys went to the canteen for a few beers. A strange sergeant blocked their way at the door.

"We're cold, sergeant, and we'd like to get something hot to drink," Mendale said to him politely.

"Too bad, We don't want you dirty swine in our canteen."

"Sergeant, I know the rules, and we are allowed in, so please step aside."

Mendale tried to push his way in, and the furious noncom slapped him in the face. Mendale was beside himself, but he controlled his temper enough to ask in a low voice, "Sergeant, is it permitted to strike people in the Austrian army?"

"Certainly it's permitted, you numskull!"

Mendale then punched the man right in the throat and knocked him down. He and his friends continued unhindered into the canteen. Soon there was a whistling and a great deal of commotion, and the sergeant walked in with two military policemen. Mendale was taken to jail.

The next day he was brought up before his captain, who seemed a fair man. He asked Mendale to tell his side of the story, and the young soldier explained everything that had occurred. When he got to the part about the question that he had asked the sergeant, the captain had to smother a laugh. But then he said in a very serious tone:

"As a matter of fact, it is forbidden to strike anyone in our army, especially a superior. However, if the sergeant struck you, it was incumbent upon you, Soldat Heller, to report this infraction to me. Without discipline we are lost." He then shuffled some papers, cleared his throat, and said, "Five days in solitary confinement."

That was mild punishment enough, but even so Mendale stayed in solitary for only a day. On the second day, he came down with a rash and was immediately transferred to a military hospital for treatment.

The stay in the hospital was unpleasant, but at least there was enough to eat. After he was cured, Mendale was given two weeks leave to recuperate at home.

Things seemed to be going better at the farm. There was more food, and with an absence of enemy raids, it was possible to start recouping their losses. Their worst fear was for Aron. They had still heard nothing of his fate.

In the late afternoons, Jozef would join Mendale on the porch, and they would talk about their adventures while each of them was away from Zbora. Jozef's son and grandson had both joined the "Legiony" (The Polish Legion) under the leadership of Jozef Pilsudski. The old man explained to Mendale that his son Yan, had originally been a member of a rifle club headed by Pilsudski. By 1914, a few of these rifle clubs had joined forces and, with the approval of the Austrian authorities, they formed the Polish Legion. When the war broke out, Pilsudski got a promise from the Austrian government that if the legion fought against the Russians, Austria would grant Poland its independence after the war.

When the Polish Legion marched north to the city of Kielce and defeated the Russians, it was one of the most patriotic events in Polish history. Jozef said that this victory over their traditional enemy, brought great awakening to the Polish people, and young and old flocked to the banners of Pilsudski. His own son and grandson had participated in the fighting and in the great victory march into Kielce. Now, the old man told Mendale, Pilsudski formed The Supreme national Command, which would lead the people in the struggle for an independent Poland.

"After a hundred and twenty years in bondage, we will finally have our own country," Jozef said and crossed himself. "May Jesus bring Poland victory over her oppressors, and may the Mother of God protect our sons who are fighting heroically for our freedom and yours." With tears in his eyes, he began to sing the new song of freedom:" We the First Brigade." It was a catchy tune and Mendale whistled along as Jozef sang the second stanza. Then he joined the old man in the last refrain:

"We, the First brigade,
Just a group of riflemen,
Have united our lives and future
together...."

Mendale too felt a surge of emotion and patriotism.

"I too hope for a Polish victory, Jozef. If Austria had her way, Poland would get her freedom, but Hungary seems to be opposed to the idea. They argue that if Poland receives its independence, all the other nationalities within the Empire will demand freedom as well. And that, according to the Hungarians, would mean the end of the Austro-Hungarian Empire."

"We're not afraid of the Hungarians," Jozef said emphatically. "Why, I myself am ready to fight and give my life for this great cause. We will redeem our country with our own blood. We ask no one to do it for us. Would you believe it, Mendale," Jozef went on sheepishly, "this old man also tried to join the legion, but they wouldn't accept me. Too old, they said. But they told me that there would come a time when everyone would be allowed to help. I want to be ready for that great day."

"Then you must train, Jozef," Mendale said enthusiastically. "come on. Right now. Up, up!"

The two men went into the woods. They had only one rifle between them, Mendale's, but Aron's pistol also came in handy. Jozef had been a soldier in the Austrian Army when he was young and fortunately had not forgotten everything he had learned. He listened to Mendale's instructions and improved daily.

At the end of his leave, Mendale felt strong and well rested, ready for the hardships that lay ahead. He was also less anxious about those he left behind. Moishe and Jozef between them were a strong bulwark.

Back in the army, he found that his two Lemke friends, Nikita and Bohdan, had been sent off to the front, no one seemed to know where. He missed his two comrades.

On the second day after his return, he was having dinner in the mess hall. A boisterous fellow sitting opposite him was boasting about the bravery of his people, the Slovaks. Then he addressed Mendale:

"Are you one of us Slovaks, too?" Mendale didn't answer him.

"Well, speak up. At least tell me your name." When Mendale finally told him, the man shouted gleefully: "So you're a dirty, coward Jew. What is your kind doing in the army?"

Mendale jumped up and shouted furiously, "You better apologize for what you said about my people—or you'll be sorry."

The man began to laugh. "Look at the Jew. He suddenly found his tongue. What are you going to do about it?"

Everyone at the table froze, wondering what would happen next. Like a flash, Mendale bent over the table and drove the fork he'd been eating with into the man's chest. He then jumped over the table and started battering the Slovak, who fought back, despite the fork still in his chest.

The soldiers formed a circle around the two combatants, but they were rooting for Mendale, who was the shorter of the two. "Come on, fork man. Teach the clown a lesson. . . . Get the fat slob. . . . That's the way to fight, Heller. . . ."

Encouraged by them, Mendale had the man down on the floor. he grabbed him by the throat and made him apologize so all could hear. Then he let him go.

The soldiers were just helping the loser to his feet when an officer appeared and called for the medics. While the injured man was being bandaged, the officer began questioning the witnesses. One and all declared that there had been an accident and they had no idea how it happened. But the wounded man, patched up, accused Mendale of starting a fight and deliberately stabbing him.

"With a fork?" the officer said, unable to conceal his amusement.

But again Mendale was given a light jail sentence—three days in solitary confinement.

On November 15, 1915, after his release, the commander called the troops together and told the regiment that an emergency situation had developed in Szoprun, Hungary. He asked for volunteers for the artillery to leave that very day. Mendale was not eligible because he hadn't completed his basic training, but when the volunteers had assembled, he fell in with them and marched off. He would rather take his chances at the front than suffer the hunger, cold, filth, boredom, and humiliation that he had been subjected to at Prszemysl.

They were all put aboard a train bound for Hungary, and when it stopped at the first station inside Hungarian territory, the soldiers were amazed at the number of vendors selling all kinds of food. None of the boys had seen anything like it since before the war. Some bought as much as ten loaves of bread and then stuffed their empty stomachs. At their destination too, there was an abundance of everything. The field kitchen served good meat, vegetables, coffee with milk, and even doughnuts and fruit. The best news of all was that they didn't have to fight. The danger of battle had passed, and they were assembled and told that they would be staying in Hungary to defend it in case of a renewed Russian offensive.

Chapter 14
FROM HUNGARY TO VIENNA

In December, Mendale was tested for further training. Because of his agility and knowledge of languages, his captain recommended him for the signal corps. His training would take until the end of March. Now, he thanked his lucky stars for his decision to leave Przemysl.

At Christmas, the outstanding signal corps students were invited to wealthy homes for Christmas dinner. Mendale was dazzled by the splendor and elegance of the lovely house he entered. He danced with the pretty brunette daughter of the house, Magda, and enjoyed the glitter of the decorations and the magnificence of the dinner. But it was all too strange for him, and he was glad when the evening ended.

He had gained some weight from the good Hungarian food he'd been eating, and his uniform tunic was getting pretty snug. On his first free day off he headed for another part of town, where a tailor recommended to him lived. A lovely girl with black curly hair opened the door. She told him that her father was out, fitting a suit. If Corporal Heller would wait for about half an hour, her father would be back. Mendale decided to wait, and they began to talk.

She told him that her name was Hana and that her mother had died when she was small. She lived with her father in this one room, the corner of which was his workshop. Her green eyes twinkled as she talked, and she had a very beautiful smile. Hana asked him many questions about his home, the war, and his family. She wanted to know if the Jewish people were persecuted by the Russians during the invasion, and Mendale told her a little about his adventures.

"When this war is over," she said, "I'm going to Vienna, where my mother's sister lives. Her husband is a doctor. I'm going to be a doctor too."

Mendale was a bit startled. He'd never met a woman who had a profession—although, of course, he had read about Marie Skoldowska

Curie, the great Polish chemist. She was twice recipient of the Nobel Prize, the first woman so honored.

"I certainly admire your ambition, Fraulein Hana. I hope your plans will be fulfilled."

"And what do you plan to do when this war is over?" Hana asked.

"Well, when I was small, I dreamed of building up the Land of Israel. But this war has made me doubt that I'll live to accomplish that dream."

Hana's eyes seemed to grow bigger and greener. "Don't say such sad things. It's unlucky. Promise me that you will do everything to survive this evil war and recapture your dream."

She took his hand and said again: "Promise."

He did.

Her father arrived just then. He was such a happy man, whistling a tune as he walked into the house. He seemed to be pleased that the two young people had met, and promised the jacket for the following week.

Mendale thought about Hana all the time, but weeks passed before he got his next leave. When he went back to get his jacket, the tailor answered the door. Hana had gone to Vienna to look after her aunt who was ill. She had left him a letter with her address.

He did not write—he wasn't sure it was proper. But he kept the letter in his trousers pocket. Then—what astonishing luck—at the end of March, he was transferred to Vienna, for a special course in decoding.

Vienna, the storied capital of the Austro-Hungarian Empire, was a beautiful and exciting city to be stationed in. Music seemed to be everywhere, and in spite of the war, both men and women were dressed very elegantly. Officers and soldiers alike were welcomed everywhere as heroes.

From time to time Mendale saw civilians wearing black armbands and was reminded of the many casualties at the front. And yet the outdoor cafés were doing tremendous business. Be gay while you can, the Viennese seemed to say, because tomorrow might bring bad news and disaster.

His first afternoon off, a Sunday, he went to see Hana. Her uncle lived on a tree-lined street in a large apartment house with a doorman and a gilded elevator. A neatly uniformed servant girl opened the door and said that Miss Hana wasn't expecting anyone today, but she would inquire. Within minutes, Hana came running into the room. Mendale! How marvelous!"

She seemed thinner and paler than she had been in Szoprun. He explained about his transfer and that he would be in the city for some weeks. Her face lighted up. "What a surprise," she whispered. "You didn't write, and I never thought we'd see each other!"

"I thought the same thing. Then when I knew I was coming here. . . ."

She took his arm. "Let's talk in the living room, but very quietly—my aunt is resting."

She rang a bell and asked for tea to be served, and when they were seated at the table with the teapot between them, she told him her good news: Her uncle had enrolled her at the university, to enter in the fall. He had already engaged a tutor to prepare her for the examinations. She studied all morning, but her afternoons were generally free.

"Then you must show me Vienna," Mendale said excitedly. "Perhaps this very afternoon?"

"I have to get permission from my uncle. Do you mind waiting until he gets home?"

Permission was granted, and Mendale began to look forward to the afternoons with Hana, whenever he had a pass. They promenaded in the Prater, the largest park in the city. They went on rides in the amusement park, and Hana arranged tickets to concerts and introduced him to the music of Mozart, Haydn, and Brahms. She took him to see *The Merry Widow* at the opera house. They sat in her uncle's box and after the performance danced most of the way home, Hana humming the music of the show. They walked in the Vienna woods and went rowing on the Danube. They made special excursions to look at the palaces of the emperor: Hofburg, the principal imperial residence, and Schönbrunn, the summer home of Franz Josef.

On evenings when Hana couldn't accompany him, Mendale and his buddies would go to the cinema. His closest friend was Stash, whom he had met for the first time in Vienna. Stash came from a village not far from Zbora. His mother was Polish and his father Ukrainian, and he had suffered a great deal in his village because of his Polish background. Like the Hellers, he'd had to defend himself from bullying youngsters.

Both Mendale and Stash had heard about movies, but this was their first experience of sitting in a darkened theater and seeing a story unfold before their eyes. It was like magic, and they could never get enough of it. They liked American movies best of all, and went as often as they could.

The course was ending soon. They were told that within a short time they would be going to the front, where they were needed. Fighting had intensified in the Carpathians in recent weeks. The Russians were on the move again.

Hana was becoming more precious to him. He was tempted to ask her to marry him, but how could he? Suppose he was killed. It didn't seem fair. Anyway, she had other ambitions and would probably refuse him.

His orders came in June: He was to report to a position in the Carpathian Mountains. He went to say good-bye to Hana, and they took a walk in a quiet park near her house. She was wearing a white summer frock of Swiss eyelet, trimmed with light blue ribbons and looked graceful and lovely. He took her hand, and they walked in silence.

He was trying to get up the nerve to tell her about his being sent to the front when she suddenly started talking about the future. She had had a marriage proposal, a colleague of her uncle's a physician. If she accepted, he would pay for her studies, and she would be able to become a doctor.

"What should I do, Mendale?" she asked innocently.

He knew what she wanted him to say—that she shouldn't marry the doctor, that she should marry him, but he had already decided not to ask her.

He took a deep breath. "Before I answer your question, I must tell you that I'm leaving tomorrow."

Hana started crying. Mendale's heart sank. He didn't want to hurt her, but even more he didn't want to make a bad mistake for both of them.

"Don't cry, Hana," he begged. "We've had some wonderful times together, haven't we? I know I'll always treasure them." He wiped her tears and kissed her eyes. When she quieted down, he said, "Do you care about this doctor?"

"Of course not. It's you I care about. But you know the family all after me to accept the proposal. He said that when I finish my studies, he will make me his partner. Isn't that fantastic"

"It sounds like a wonderful proposition to me. Your studies and your work are very important to you, and here you could combine them with marriage."

Hana began to cry again. It hurt him to think that she was to belong to another man, but he couldn't tie her to his own uncertain future. He tried to comfort her, but she continued crying.

Chapter 15
BAPTISM OF FIRE

Czernowitz, the capital of Bucovina in the Western Ukraine, had suffered great privations. Invaded by the Russians in the early days of the war, it had been regained by the Austrians some weeks later, and then changed hands several times more before the Austrian army finally liberated it. The city and the surrounding area had suffered great destruction and disruption, and when Mendale arrived, he could not help but contrast conditions there with Vienna. He was only in Czernowitz a few days; then he received orders to move into the mountains, where troops of the Ninth Austrian Army were battling the Russians.

It was night by the time he and the other men arrived at their destination. Mendale was ordered to lay the telephone lines immediately. There had been a battle the day before, but it was quiet now. As he began to work, he thought of the extreme danger he was in, how easily his life could be snuffed out. The Russians were entrenched just a few yards away. He hadn't been issued a gun, because his equipment was so bulky and heavy, that a rifle would have hindered his work. But the job had to be done.

Mendale was soon absorbed in the technical aspects of his work and forgot to be afraid for minutes at a time. He worked all night laying the telephone lines and using fir trees as posts. When the morning sun came up, accentuating the beauty of the mountains, he rested for a few minutes in the thick wooded area. He was thirsty and had nothing left in his canteen, but he remembered that during the night he had come across a small mountain stream. He walked back there and bent down, and as he did so, the shooting started.

Mendale dived behind a tree for protection and looked around for a way he could escape. He spotted Stash about twenty meters off, waving to him frantically. He crawled toward his friend, dodging the bullets. When he reached Stash, the two continued crawling together, up toward the Austrian side of the mountain. When they saw their comrades, they hugged each other.

"We made it," Mendale said, smiling.

"Yes, but you have more luck than brains, Heller," Stash said. "You were on the Russian side and they could have picked you off easily if they'd been better shots."

This was Mendale's baptism of fire.

The shooting stopped temporarily, but started a few hours later. The Austrians would capture a hillside, then the Russians would get it back. There was fierce fighting and many casualties on both sides. In addition, there was also a lack of food. The field kitchen served only a thin broth, plus a small piece of bread. The soldiers had to forage for their own food. Sometimes they found berries and nuts, but not often.

Finally the Austrian army began to gain ground, though paying a tremendous price in lives. One morning after they had captured a hill, one of the soldiers spotted a dead horse.

"Heller," he called, "and all you other guys, come over here. Let's eat."

About ten soldiers rushed over. Within minutes, they had cut up the horse with their knives and were eating the raw meat.

"Heller, taste some of this. Don't be shy. It's good."

Mendale refused. He was hungry too, but he knew instinctively that he shouldn't eat carrion. Now they were cutting up the liver and drinking the blood. It was gross, and he couldn't believe they could behave so much like animals.

As their unit continued to move forward, the boys who had eaten the dead horse became ill, one by one. They had to be left behind, with no one to attend them, because the medics could not be spared.

They kept advancing north, until they came into Galicia, in the area east of Lemberg. It was then that they heard the news that Emperor Franz Josef had died. The old man had ruled for fifty-eight years; no one in the unit could remember an Austria without him.

But Mendale felt little. The slaughter had been going on for two years now. Austria and Germany had lost 600,000 soldiers, and the Russians a good million men. How could anyone grieve over the death of an old man of 86, when millions of young people were being killed and maimed each day.

Archduke Karl, the great-nephew of Franz Josef, was now the new Emperor. The new Kaiser wanted the Germans out of his country, so he could conclude a peace treaty with Russia, which was also war-weary. The slaughter on the battlefields of Europe in 1916 was unparalleled in history, and even some of the German generals has second thoughts about continuing the war. Yet, neither Kaiser Karl, nor they prevailed, and the war dragged on fired by discord and lack of proper communication among the leaders of the combatant countries.

The war, which was now being called The Great War, was becoming even more treacherous. The Germans, Austria's partners, had introduced poison gas in the Battle of Verdun, in France, with the most devastating effects. Of 2,000,000 soldiers engaged in this longest and bloodiest battle of the war, 1,000,000 men lost their lives. Soon the Allies retaliated on the Western Front. Poison gas had not yet been used against the Russians. But before long, the Germans were beginning to use it on the Eastern Front as well.

Mendale's regiment, being Austrian, had not received any gas masks. In many of the battles, when the Germans used gas, and the wind turned unexpectedly, it proved devastating to the German and Austrian armies in the area, killing and injuring their own soldiers. But the Germans continued to use this new weapon, as they claimed it would shorten the war.

Prince Leopold of Bavaria, an outstanding soldier, was given the command of the Ninth German Army, which would spearhead a new offensive. Field Marshall Mackensen was to coordinate the drive. These were two of the most effective leaders who would assure a speedy victory. Now along a 250 mile front, they mounted an attack to defeat the Russians, under the command of Grand Duke Nicholas. The Ninth Austrian Army, in which Mendale was serving, was part of that great offensive. They would smash the Russians within days, they said.

Chapter 16
THE VISIT

A long awaited letter arrived from Mendale, and Golda opened it with trembling hands. He was alive, on the Russian front and only 35 miles from Zbora. She kissed the letter. She'd been sick with worry about him. The daily reports from the front were getting more horrible each day. Many of the neighbors hadn't heard at all from their sons, and assumed the worst.

She thought about Aron. The Russians must have killed him by now, because no one had seen him or heard of him in two years. Now they were going to kill her Mendale too, in this bestial, senseless war.

"Jozef, get the horse and wagon ready immediately," Golda called. "I'm going to see Mendale."

When Jozef found out where the boy was, he threw up his hands in horror. "Pani Golda, I will not let you go to the front lines. You'll get killed there, and what will happen to your family then?"

"Since when are you giving orders around here?" Golda snapped. Then seeing his crestfallen face, she softened.

"Jozef, my old friend, Mendale may be hungry and cold. I may never get a chance to see him alive. I *must* go to him."

Jozef pleaded some more, but he soon realized it was a lost cause and went reluctantly to get everything ready. Golda meanwhile packed most of what she had in her cupboard: a few loaves of bread, a couple of cheeses, and a sausage she had been saving for a special occasion. She dressed quickly in peasant clothes and was on her way.

As she traveled the road, she was undistinguishable from the other peasant women who greeted her in Ukrainian: "May Jesus Christ be praised."

She knew the formula perfectly well: "For ever and ever, amen."

She continued riding for hours without a stop, until she began hearing the boom of the big guns. She asked an old peasant where the army headquarters was situated, and he pointed to a farmhouse in a distant clearing.

As she approached the farmhouse, the shelling got more severe. Now she could actually see the shells landing, the burst of the explosion, debris flying high. A soldier took her to the captain in charge, a tall Hungarian, dressed in an impeccable uniform.

He gazed at her in consternation. "My dear lady, how did you ever get through the front lines? Can't you see that this place is within shellfire of the Russian lines?"

"Your Excellency, forgive me. I came because I am desperate. The Russians took my oldest son, and I never saw him again. Now my younger son Mendale—Emanuel in German—is here facing death. I plead with you to let me see him, before it's too late."

The tall officer looked her over in perplexity, then apparently decided that the quickest way to get rid of her was to let her have her way. "Please sit down, madam, I'll see what I can do." He called the sergeant and told him to locate Corporal Heller, and bring him here.

Then to Golda, he added, "Your son is an excellent soldier, madam. He has kept our communications open under the most dangerous conditions. We have awarded him a medal for bravery under fire. I hope you will find him in good condition. Good luck to both of you."

Golda thanked him profusely as he ushered her out. Half an hour later, the sergeant returned with Mendale in tow. "Mother!" he cried. "What—?" They fell into each other's arms. He couldn't believe that she had come to see him here. "Mother, this is no place for a woman! You could be killed—you could be blown up!"

She hushed him up and led him over to a nearby bench, where she gave him a basket of food and made him eat some, which he did in a kind of daze.

"I'll save the rest for later," he said, and they began to pour out their troubles to one another, asking hasty questions—no, no word of Aron, this friend had fallen in Italy, that one was missing near Lemberg. . . .

"Mendale, I pray for you each day, and I plead with the Holy One that he return you safely to me soon. Here, I brought you this to wear under your uniform."

She gave him a fringed shirt, and he promised to wear it at all times. He gave her his medal and asked her to keep it for him.

All too soon, the sergeant interrupted their conversation, insisting Golda would have to leave. One last desperate embrace of her son, and she did.

Chapter 17
ALTONA

Shainchi had been in Germany for over a year. As soon as she was able, Nehemiah had brought her and the children from Zbora and out of the war zone. Nehemiah was doing well. He was traveling to the small villages to sell his wares. They lived in a small apartment in Altona, a suburb of Hamburg. Most important of all, they didn't have to worry about invading enemies. The German heartland felt little of the terror of the war. Although losses had been appalling, especially during 1916, there was still an unswerving belief in a German victory.

Altona was a port city, and everything was available—if you could afford the price. There certainly was no shortage of food.

Shainchi felt guilty about her relatively comfortable life. She was now receiving regular mail from Zbora, and she worried about the family—Aron, still missing, Mendale at the Russian front, her mother and sister and Moishe still in danger of being invaded, and Ester and her five fatherless children. She wanted to go and visit them and see for herself how things were. Nehemiah tried to talk her out of it, but stubborn Shainchi had made up her mind.

She arrived at the farm with many boxes and baskets, bringing food and clothing that were scarce in Zbora. She was elegantly dressed and had on a hat of the latest fashion with a large brim.

Golda was thrilled to see her looking so well and prosperous.

"My dear child," she said after Shainchi had poured out some of her worries, "things are not as bad here as all that. I gather all kinds of herbs, we have some vegetables and fruit, and we also have milk and cheese, which we make ourselves. No one goes hungry."

The children surrounded their aunt when she unpacked one of her boxes and gave them candy. There was chocolate, coffee, and real tea from Ceylon, and all kinds of dried fruit and raisins. Ester put the new clothes on the children, and to everyone it seemed like a holiday.

At night when all was quiet, the four women sat at a table reminiscing about the good old days before the war. They laughed a lot and, when they remembered Aron, cried a little. Golda didn't want any crying.

"I have complete faith in the Holy One, blessed be He. He will send me back my boy one day." Then she abruptly changed the subject.

"Shainchi, we have to talk about little Symcha. He's ten years old now and still hasn't had any formal schooling. Normally, his father would take charge of his studies. But. . . " She sighed. We've tried to find him a teacher around here, but all the men are at war."

"You want me to take him back to Germany, is that it?" said Shainchi, guessing. Well, they said, yes, that was the idea. The German schools were still functioning in the normal way—or almost normal—and Symcha could at least get a start on his education. Ester especially looked at her with a plea on her face.

Shainchi smiled and got up to kiss her sister-in-law. "I'd be delighted. Nehemiah will be a wonderful substitute father, and when the war is over and Aron is home, little Symcha can come back."

There was general relief and rejoicing. Golda still only tolerated Ester, but at this point she got up and kissed her and Shainchi, too. "That solves a big problem for us. Thank you, my daughters."

On the second day of Shainchi's visit, a letter arrived from Aron, by way of the International Red Cross. Screams of joy echoed through the house, and everyone pushed and shoved to get close to Ester as she opened it. As a gesture, she handed it to Golda. "You read. I can't see too well." And, indeed, her eyes were swimming.

Aron was well, but couldn't tell them when he would be released, nor could he give them an address where he could be reached. But he assured them that he would do everything in his power to come home.

Golda said a special prayer, thanking God for preserving her son's life, and all joined in saying "Amen."

A week later, Shainchi left to return to Altona. Ester was crying as Symcha got onto the wagon, and the other four children looked anxious and uncertain. But Symcha was bursting with excitement. He was wearing a new suit that his aunt had brought him and sporting a German student's hat with a visor. "Good-bye!" he called gaily to the others as Jozef drove the wagon out of the yard. "I'll write soon!"

Altona held many fascinations for Symcha. Ships from all over the world came to its harbor, some with strange names, written in characters he couldn't decipher. He saw black people for the first time, and Chinese as well. There were many tunnels in the city, which became his special playgrounds once he had made some friends. When he had a little money, he loved to ride the trolleys, clanging and gliding through the streets.

His Uncle Nehemiah took him to the Talmud Torah Science School, where he had to take an entrance exam. He passed and was accepted, and soon started classes. The school was part of the Jewish Community Center, which housed different organizations. His aunt and uncle wouldn't have to pay for his education, because he was considered a refugee from the war zone.

In class, Symcha soon found himself the object of ridicule. He understood everything that was said, but when he answered the teacher, all the boys started to snicker. Since he knew that his answer was correct, he finally realized that they were laughing at his Polish accent.

When recess came, Shimon Schultz, the tallest and strongest boy in the class, came up to him in the schoolyard and gave him a push. Symcha ignored that, but when the boy punched him, he punched back, and soon they were scrapping. It was a close fight at first, but Schultz soon got tired when Symcha, who had learned rough-and-tumble from the Lemkes, was just getting his second wind. A circle of boys had formed around them, screaming and egging them on. Soon Shimon gave up, and Symcha was victorious. He became the leader of Schultz's gang, with his former rival as his assistant.

Within six months, Symcha was second in the class in scholarship, the orator of his class, and the star of the soccer team. Soccer was generally played in a tremendous gym, which was equipped with all kinds of athletic apparatus. Sports were an important part of the boys' education.

He spent most afternoons playing soccer. Some days he and his buddies would meet their newly acquired girlfriends, who would be coming from a girls' school nearby on Weber Strasse. They would walk to one of the tunnels and spend some time there.

One day, Symcha, Schultz, and a few boys from the gang went to explore a new tunnel they had heard about. They saw a group of light-skinned blacks coming toward them. Symcha had heard about this group. They were children of German colonists, who had brought their African wives with them when they returned home to Germany. They were reputed to be ferocious fighters, and Symcha's friends were scared. But Symcha told each one what to do and worked out a strategy, and when the black youths attacked, the boys were ready. They didn't have it easy, however. In the end, exhausted, the two groups called it a draw.

As they were walking home, bruised and battered, Symcha said, "I guess we'd better leave that tunnel for the Africans. We've got plenty of other tunnels." The others, groaning, fervently agreed.

Symcha became so accustomed to his new environment that it soon seemed as if he had been there always. He didn't think much about home, except to worry sometimes about his father. Aron still had not returned.

Chapter 18
THE WAR CONTINUES, LATVIA

In the late fall of 1916 Mendale's regiment was transferred to the northern front, near Riga, in the area of Düneburg. Conditions here were as bad as they had been in the Carpathians. It was extremely cold, and again the soldiers were hungry most of the time.

The Russians had retreated from the region almost two years before. While they occupied it, they had expelled most of the people who formed the economic base of the city—that is, Jews—who were mercilessly exiled to the interior of Russia. That plus many battles fought in the area had turned this farming region into a desolate wasteland. Now the Russians mounted a new offensive, and the Austrians were busy entrenching. The shelling was incessant, and there was constant damage to the telephone lines.

Each evening, as the sun was setting, Mendale would start out to find breaks in the line and repair them. He would return at dawn, hungry, cold, and bone-weary, and find nothing to eat. One morning, he finished his work early, and it was still dark when he returned. Exhausted, he fell asleep in spite of the heavy shelling all around him. He only woke when a shell landed close enough to rain debris directly on him. He cleared it off him and was about to go back to sleep when he spied a large mushroom growing in the corner of the trench. He cooked it, and had his best meal in days. Each day after that, for a period of two weeks, the mushroom regrew every night. For that long, he wasn't hungry.

One early morning, a heavy shelling barrage began. A shell landed so close that the concussion knocked him down. He got to his knees and crawled lickety-split to the nearest trench. There were three soldiers in it, two familiar to him, but the third, a stranger.

Mendale asked the newcomer his name. The boy didn't answer. He just stood in the corner and began to shake. The other boys said that he was from Vienna and had never been under shellfire before. As the barrage intensified, the boy threw himself on the ground, covered his ears with his hands, and began to howl like a dog. Mendale tried to help him, but the fellow pushed him away and started to climb out of the trench. It took the three of them to keep him down. He was only subdued when they knocked him out.

At night, when the shelling stopped, Mendale called the medics and explained that the youngster was suffering from shellshock. They took him away and Mendale never did learn what happened to him.

The Austrians and Germans had the advantage now. they were moving forward, while the Russians retreated. It was winter by then and there was a lull in the fighting. The Austrians established their head-quarters in a Latvian village, and for the first time in months, the troops had enough to eat. From time to time, Mendale could buy eggs and other items from the farmers. The Latvians didn't much like the Austrians, but fortunately for Mendale and his comrades, they hated the Russians even more.

Chapter 19
THEY DREAM OF FREEDOM

The Russian Revolution
The Balfour Declaration
Ukrainian Independence

The new year of 1917 was to be an eventful one. Russia had been defeated again in numerous battles. Tsar Nicolas II, a weak and ineffectual leader, tried to take over the command of his disintegrating army. In February, when he was at the Supreme Army Headquarters in the Ukraine, the revolution against him began.

A provisional government was immediately set up by the revolutionaries, and when the tsar sought help from the army, he found that they had joined the uprising themselves. The tsar, realizing his serious predicament, abdicated for himself and his son.

The people, fed up with the autocratic regime, which had brought them nothing but misery and continuous defeats, paraded through Petrograd carrying signs that declared, "Down with the Imperialistic War." Everyone thought that with the tsar gone, the war would quickly end.

Now the Russian armed forces were beginning to disintegrate. The fighting at the front almost came to a standstill. Some tsarist officers were killed, others deserted, and many soldiers just decided to go home. Then came a wave of peasant disorders, and the Ukrainians demanded their independence.

Alexander Kerensky, the socialist Minister of War and later head of the Provisional Government, was able to rally the remaining Russian troops for a short period of time, but by June, the Bolsheviks under Lenin were calling upon the soldiers and the people to rise against his government and demand immediate peace.

On October 25, 1917, the Bolshevik Revolution began, having as its slogan, "Bread and Peace." It was to be followed by one of the most bloody civil wars in history.

Earlier that year, on April 6, 1917, the United States had declared war on Germany. They had joined their allies by sending troops to fight in France. Mendale was hoping that they wouldn't make him fight the Americans. His brother, Meyer, would probably be drafted into the American Army. He prayed that they would never have to face each other in battle.

In November, he received a letter and a newspaper clipping from his youngest brother in Zbora. The clipping, dated November 2, 1917, contained information about a letter from Arthur James Balfour, foreign secretary of Lloyd George, then prime minister of England. Lord Balfour's letter was addressed to Lord Rothschild. It read:

> *"His Majesty's Government views with favour the establishment in Palestine of a national home for the Jewish people, and will use their best endeavours to facilitate the achievement of this object. . ."*

After reading this momentous news, Mendale felt elated. He wished that the bloody war would end so that he could help his people. But after considering the matter for a while, he began to doubt England's motives. Palestine belonged to the Turkish Empire, England's arch-foe. It was the expressed desire of the British to dismember that empire. By declaring its intention to create a Jewish Commonwealth, the English were simply playing politics, and trying to enlist Jewish support for their cause.

Mendale decided that England's motives didn't really matter in the long run. So many of the Jews of Europe were now homeless. If the British government kept its promise, they would find a haven in the Land of Israel. The Balfour Declaration was a positive step toward his people's freedom.

Later that month, on November 20, 1917, news came that the Ukrainians had declared their independence. Their newly elected president, V.K. Vininchenko, formed a socialist government, which soon issued a proclamation: "All lands which had previously belonged to the royal family, the church, and large proprietors, would be distributed to the working people." It also emphasized that the minorities in the Ukraine: the Russians, the Jews, and the Poles, would be granted freedom and autonomy.

Austria was happy about the turn of events and made peace with the

Ukrainians, but the Bolsheviks in Moscow were angry. They declared war on the newly formed Ukrainian Republic.

In spite of their harsh actions against their "brother Slavs," the Bolsheviks wanted an end to the war with Germany and Austria. On March 3, 1918, Lenin, pressured his delegation to sign the Treaty of Brest Litovsk. All his advisors were against signing the treaty, but he prevailed. His main reason, to save the Bolshevik Revolution, and his government.

It marked the end of negotiations which had started on December 9, 1917. The harsh terms of that treaty were spelled out by Foreign Minister Baron von Kulmann of Germany, and supported by Austro-Hungary's Count Czernin. When Trotsky, the chief negotiator for the Soviets, and his contingent heard the terms, they were shocked. The Bolsheviks felt that it was a shameful treaty, which would force them to give up all their European possessions. Trotsky, in a fit of anger, walked out of the conference, declaring the end of the war. The Germans then attacked again and occupied more Soviet territory. After seeing the consequences of their action, the Bolsheviks finally agreed to sign the treaty. Russia was now a defeated country. She had to agree to the independence of Poland, the Ukraine, Finland, Lithuania, and the Baltic Provinces.

If the Bolsheviks were unhappy with the treaty, the war-weary people of the area breathed a sigh of relief. Kaiser Karl of Austro-Hungary voiced their sentiments in an address in Vienna:

"In common with my hard-tried people, I trust that after the first conclusion of peace, which is so gratifying an event for us, a general peace will soon be granted suffering humanity."*

---

* Kaiser Karl's Address of February 14, 1918.

Chapter 20
FIGHTING THE REDS

In the spring of 1918, portions of the Austrian Ninth Army were invited by Hetman Pavel Petrovich Skoropadski to fight the Bolsheviks, who were trying to destroy the newly established Ukrainian Republic.

Skoropadski had been a general in the tsar's army. He owned large tracts of land and estates in the Ukraine, and he wasn't ready to give up anything to the Reds. He considered himself a nationalist, who was fighting to free the Ukraine from the Bolsheviks. Soon Skoropadski was to fight both the Bolsheviks and Simon Petlura, a rival Ukrainian nationalist, in a protracted and bloody civil war. The Jewish population of the Ukraine was the chief victim of the constant disorder, mistreated by all sides.

In May 1918, Mendale arrived near the city of Yuzefov, with a contingent of the ninth Army. There was great disorder and destruction in the region, guerilla bands constantly roaming the countryside. It was sometimes difficult to know who occupied the next hill, let alone the next town. Were they Bolsheviks or the hetman's people? Often they just wore tattered uniforms, which were unidentifiable.

Mendale was out one day putting down telephone lines on a hill, when he saw a cloud of dust moving toward them. Into the clearing below came a Cossack, galloping at a swift pace, and dragging behind his horse a prisoner with a rope tied around his neck. He was followed by another Cossack with another prisoner, and then yet another—Mendale counted twelve in all. At a command from the first Cossack, the prisoners were cut loose and ordered to stand up.

"Get on your feet, you Bolshevik swine!" they shouted.

Some of the prisoners just lay there, unable to move. At an other order from the chief, each was dropped to his feet and tied to a tree. By then a group of people—apparently relatives of the prisoners—came running into the clearing. Some threw themselves at the feet of the Cossacks, begging and pleading, but the Cossacks just kicked them aside. Then they raised their rifles, and the prisoners were all mowed down.

The civilians ran toward their loved ones, hugging and kissing the limp bodies. Terrible cries of anguish came up from the clearing below.

Mendale looked on in state of shock. He had heard that the Cossacks in this area were killing people indiscriminately—usually out of mere suspicion that the victim was a Bolshevik—but he had never personally witnessed such behavior. These murderers were part of Skoropadski's army, friends of the Austrians, and he was here to facilitate their barbarism. His sense of outrage and disgust could no longer be hidden. He heard himself shouting, "Savages, Cossack pigs," while he started ripping up the lines he had just laid. The Cossacks heard him and looked up, but were unable to locate the origin of the sound.

Finally, Hans, his assistant, put a hand over his mouth and pulled him behind a tree.

"Are you trying to get us killed, Heller? Let's get out of here."

They began running away while bullets began to ricochet against the trees. It was only the shelter of the woods that saved their lives.

Some days later, Mendale received a letter from home, with the news that Aron was now free and in Moscow. Elated, he wrote his brother a letter and saw to it that the dispatcher would hand-deliver it to Aron in person.

Later, Mendale learned the whole story of his brother's sufferings. When Aron had first been taken as a hostage in 1915, he and the others traveled for many weeks, undergoing hardships and hunger, until they reached the city of Penza, in central Russia. There they were interned in a camp. Some months later, without previous warning, they were suddenly set free. Aron had no money, but after many months of travel and living hand to mouth, he got as far as Tarnopol in Galicia. The city was still under Russian occupation, and fierce fighting going on. He heard that Zbora had been recaptured by the Austrians some time before, and thought of making a break for home, but with two large armies fighting between him and Zbora, he didn't dare risk it.

He stayed on in Tarnopol, hoping that the Russians would soon be driven out. Meanwhile he had to find a way to make a living. At prayer, one day, he met a man who was delivering provisions to the Russian Army. The man was impressed by Aron and agreed to employ him for a small wage. In this new job, Aron met a colonel, who took a liking to him. Over a game of chess, the colonel proposed a business partnership. He would give Aron surplus food and clothing which the younger man would sell to civilians, and then they would share in the profit. It was an illegal, risky and dangerous venture, but Aron agreed. He had been living from hand to mouth. This would be a chance to make some money to bring back to his family.

Late in 1916, the colonel sent his partner to Moscow to make some purchases. He wanted Aron to visit his family and bring them gifts which he had purchased for them.

After a strenuous journey, Aron finally arrived at the colonel's apartment. The footman showed him to the living room, and helped him with his packages. The colonel's wife, Natasha, was a tall slim brunette. She was elegantly dressed, but looked distressed, as though she'd been crying.

"My husband wrote me that he was sending you here, Mr. Heller." She said looking him up and down in an imperious way. "But I didn't realize that you were so young. . . . You don't look like a foreigner from the provinces." She smiled and extended her hand.

Aron kissed her hand, as was the custom.

"But I am both a foreigner and from the provinces, your excellency. I bring you gifts and a letter from the colonel."

He paused and gave her the letter.

"Please sit, Mr. Heller, and allow me to read the letter."

She began reading and he had a chance to observe her closely. She was smiling now and her sad expression had vanished. Aron waited for her to finish. He remembered the colonel telling him that his wife came from an aristocratic family, and was terribly spoiled. He thought her very attractive, with that certain poise and elegance which befitted her class in society. She finally finished reading, and called for her maid to take the packages.

"The children will want to open their own gifts when they get up from their nap, so I will open mine at that time, too."

Now she moved over next to Aron, on the sofa.

"Forgive me, Mr. Heller, I'm not myself today. Since this terrible war started, and Nicky left for the front, I get these terrible head-aches and crying spells. Each day we hear about the slaughter out there. Today we found out that the son of a very dear friend was killed. He was only nineteen, and such a gentle boy. When will peace come to our suffering country? I was crying when you arrived, Mr. Heller, but now I must stop. This letter from my husband lifted my spirits. We have to enjoy life while there is still time. Tomorrow evening you will accompany me to the ballet." She wasn't asking him to come with her, she was commanding, but Aron was pleased to accept the invitation.

Aron was now busy every morning, attending to his purchases and making business contacts. He entertained these people at his hotel and was making excellent progress. Each afternoon he was a guest at Natasha's for tea. The children adored him. Natasha was now a friend, and not the distant aristocrat he had met on his first day in Moscow. Evenings were spent at the theater, and private parties. Aron became part of society life, since Natasha, by virtue of her birth, was invited to the homes of the most prestigious families in the city. He also accompanied her to Petersburg, the capital, for a number of social functions.

Life was splendid for Aron. He wished that he could continue living in this somewhat euphoric atmosphere, away from the war, but the time had come to return to Tarnopol. It was February, 1917, and he was making preparations for his trip, when the Revolution broke out. It became impossible for him to get out of Moscow. He felt responsible for Natasha's safety. Soon all her servants had left her, except for the old nurse. But on the positive side, Prince Lvov, who was now the leader of the new government, was a friend of the colonel's. He assured Natasha that she and her family would be protected. Then when Kerensky took over the reigns of the government, Natasha was honored and respected as the wife of a hero in the patriotic war.

Although Aron thought it best to move out of the hotel he'd been living in, to a more modest establishment, he continued doing business, and helped Natasha by handing over half of his profits to her.

All this changed when in October, the Bolsheviks staged their Revolution. Aron was trapped in his hotel for day. The streets were full of marauding groups. He tried to telephone Natasha, but communications were down. When he was finally able to get out of his hotel, he hurried to her apartment, but she, the children, and the nurse were gone. The concierge was new, and claimed she knew nothing about Natasha's whereabouts. Aron imagined the worst.

In the days that followed, he tried to find out about what happened to her but all her friends had disappeared as well. The Bolsheviks were waging war against the aristocracy.

Aron fared much better then his new friends in Moscow. The Bolsheviks needed some normalcy in trade, and Aron was in a position to supply them with some food and clothing. As a foreigner, representing a country allied to Germany, he was tolerated. After all, had not Germany facilitated their leader, Lenin's, return to Russia from exile in Switzerland? Most of the Soviet officials whom Aron knew, needed him, and used him as a neutral messenger to the White Russians* on a few occasions. Aron realized that he was again in a precarious situation, but had no alternative. He hoped to survive this too. He had witnessed the cruelty of the new regime, daily. It was difficult for him to comprehend how the Bolsheviks, who claimed to be humanitarians, could perpetrate such bestial and terrorist acts.

When he had lost all hope of ever finding Natasha, he saw her old nurse on the street, one day. She pretended not to recognize him and tried to pass unnoticed, but Aron grabbed her arm, and didn't let her go.

"Is Madam Natasha alive?" he asked anxiously.

"Yes, Comrade Heller," she answered quietly.

"But where is she?"

"I can't tell you that." She looked around to see if anyone had overheard their conversation. "There are spies everywhere." Her face was filled with terror.

"Don't talk any more nurse. Just come with me to a safe place. You can trust me."

He put his arm around her and gently led her to his hotel. The nurse still didn't know if she could trust Aron. She sat silently in his room, until he served her some tea, and bread and jam. She ate very quickly, as though she hadn't eaten in days. With a great deal of prompting from Aron, she slowly began telling her story.

When the Bolsheviks began to arrest aristocrats, Natasha decided that the safest place to be would be her parents' dacha** in the countryside. She had no one to help her, so Natasha made her own plan. In the morning she dressed in her maid's clothes. The nurse was to pretend to be her mother. Natasha gave the nurse all her jewelry, and silverware to hide

---

* Those who fought against the Bolsheviks who were called Reds. On March 8, 1918, Lenin changed the name of his party to the Communist Party.

** Country home and estate to which aristocrats generally used to go in the summer.

under her clothing. Since the nurse was quite corpulent, the extra weight didn't show at all. Their journey seemed unending until 10 miles from the dacha, they found out that the peasants had looted and burned her property. There was no alternative but to stay on in town.

Natasha doubted that anyone here would recognize her. Since her marriage fifteen years before, she had seldom been in town and besides at the age of 32, and within a period of a month, her hair had turned totally gray. She knew that a former lieutenant under her husband's command lived in town. He had been gravely wounded the year before, and had come back home. He had been totally devoted to the colonel, and Natasha decided to enlist his help. He agreed immediately. They would stay in a room in his modest house. He would claim that they were relatives from the provinces, who had fled from the Germans.

"In these tragic times, it's convenient to be the son of a poor shoemaker, like I am, Comrade Natasha." Lieutenant Bolochov said, with a sad look at her. "The Bolsheviks are after me to join their party and help them spread propaganda, to the common people. I've told them that I don't know anything about politics I've been a soldier since the age of twelve, and hardly even knew my own family. Now, they're gone, and I have this little house." He pointed to his missing left leg. "I gave that part of my body for my country. That's enough for me. I'm sick of war and fighting, and don't even understand what this new religion of Marxism is all about."

Natasha was grateful, and thanked him for saving them. The lieutenant gave them some food. They ate quickly and all fell asleep without undressing.

Next morning, Bolochov told them that he was going out to see if he could get those false identity papers, he had told them about. If the Bolshevik officials came to check they were to say that they were his relatives. Under no circumstances were any of them to go out into the street. There was talk that the servants from the dacha were in town, trying to sell some of the looted treasures. Natasha might be recognized by them.

They didn't go out for a few weeks. The Bolsheviks never came to the house. By then they had their new identity papers, for which Natasha had to pay with her most valuable jewels.

"Things are quiet in the town now," the old nurse told Aron, "but there is a scarcity of food, and Natasha had given the lieutenant all the jewelry, one by one, to buy food for her and the children."

"Natasha sent me to Moscow to sell this." The nurse reached in under her skirt and took out a sizeable linen bag. Then she emptied it on the table. It was a set of sterling silverware, engraved with the family coat of arms.

"We have very little food now, and no money. Lieutenant Bolochov is doing the best for us, with his meager pension. We are desperate, Mr. Heller. What will become of my Natasha, and those innocent little children?" The nurse was beside herself.

Aron calmed her down. He took the silverware from the table, then gave the nurse a sizeable sum of money. "Go back to Natasha, granny, give her this, and tell her that there is more to come." The money quickly disappeared in the nurse's ample skirt. When she stood up to leave, he added:

"Tell Natalia that I will come to see her soon. Take good care of them, granny." Aron shook her hand. She crossed herself and said a prayer for him.

But when the letter from Mendale was put into his hand, crushed and smudged from a long journey in a wagoner's pocket, he decided instantly to travel to the Ukraine and be reunited with his brother.

Chapter 21
THE BROTHERS MEET

It took weeks for Mendale to get an answer from Aron. The letter was brief and had very few details in it. Mendale understood. His brother was on the Bolshevik side, and his letter might have been intercepted. The good news was that Aron was planning to be in his area shortly, and hoped to be reunited with him.

Some days later, Captain Huzicki, Mendale's immediate superior, was sitting at his desk. His black pomaded hair was pasted to his head, his blue beady eyes squinted over his cheeks. His German had a marked Polish accent. Aron stood before him and tried to obtain permission to see his brother. He handed the captain his papers, which included his identification as a foreigner and Austrian citizen, and a letter of introduction.

The captain smiled as he looked over the papers. "So you're from my neck of the woods," he said. "How I wish I could be back in Lvov. I miss the beautiful women, especially. Instead, I'm stuck in this God-forsaken country, fighting a war I care nothing about. What does it matter to me if that son-of-a-bitch Skoropadski wins or the dog's blood Bolsheviks get the upper hand?" He glanced up. "I'm ready to give my life for my beloved Poland. What about you, Mr. Heller?"

Aron didn't quite understand what that had to do with his request, but he answered frankly:

"Our people have always fought alongside our brother Poles, in time of danger. We will fight again, if we must. We want an independent free Poland, with equal rights for the minorities—the kind favored by the great Polish patriot, Ignacy Paderewski."

Huzicki seemed pleased with the answer.

"You're a man after my own heart, Heller. As to your request—well, what the hell, why not?" He shouted, "Sergeant, call Corporal Heller here immediately."

The captain was about to dismiss Aron when the latter took out a silver cigarette case and offered him one. Both men lighted up, and Aron left the case on the captain's desk.

While waiting, Aron started telling Huzicki some of the newest off-color jokes from Moscow. When the captain was in a good mood, he posed a request.

"I'm staying at a hotel nearby, and would appreciate if you would let my brother stay with me for a few days. I haven't seen him in three years. Our father died when he was a little boy, and I helped raise him."

Captain Huzicki thought for a minute, and then shrugged.

"Well, Heller, if you promise to come back and tell more of those jokes, you can have him." He put the cigarette case in his pocket. Then he called his sergeant to write out the furlough papers, which he signed with great ceremony. When Mendale finally entered the room, he first saluted the captain. Then sighting Aron, he gave a cry of surprise and delight, and they fell into each other's arms.

Aron took his brother to a hotel on the outskirts of town. It had been a luxury resort hotel before the revolution. It was springtime, and the garden was in bloom. There were tables covered with white tablecloths, with bouquets of roses in the center of each. Mendale hadn't seen anything like this since his stay in Vienna. They sat down at a table under a tree, and had their afternoon meal. The food was superb. A gypsy was playing *"Wien, Wien, nur du allein"* (Vienna, Vienna, you alone are the city of my dreams). The war seemed far away.

In the days that followed, Mendale had a new uniform made to order. Aron and he went to an American movie starring Charlie Chaplin. The two brothers played chess and spoke of the future.

Aron told about the hunger, terror, and deprivation in Moscow. Things seemed to be getting worse, especially for the aristocrats, and he had a plan to get Natasha and the children out of the country. The arrangements, however, were not completed as yet. She hadn't heard from her husband, the colonel, since the Bolsheviks took over. Aron had tried to find out through his contacts, about the colonel's whereabouts, but got no information.

Aron, too, was worried about his own wife and the family. The Ukrainian revolt may have spilled over to their area. He hoped that they would find someone to protect them, like he was doing for the colonel's family.

Mendale wanted to know what was really going on in the north. Here in the south, things were very chaotic, and one seemed to hear a great deal of propaganda. He wanted to know more about Lenin, the leader of the Bolsheviks.

Aron explained that when Lenin returned to Russia on April 16, 1917, after his exile in Switzerland, he did so with the help of the Germans. He was being accused by his enemies of being in the service of the Kaiser. Mendale thought how ironic it was, that the Germans, through the Austrians, were now helping Lenin's arch enemy, Hetman Skoropadski. They were playing both sides against the other. Aron then told his brother about Lenin's principles. He had been to Petrograd when Lenin addressed the people at the station there. Lenin had called for an end to the imperialistic war, he rejected the provisional government, which Aron believed to be truly democratic. The Bolshevik leader called for all private land to be confiscated and transferred to committees of poor peasants. The following month, Trotsky, who had been his adversary, arrived from Canada and joined him in the struggle. Trotsky was an outstanding speaker, and knew how to use propaganda. Within one year, he helped Lenin to consolidate his power. Now that they had overthrown the legal government, Lenin gave his political party a new name, the Communist Party.

"Their ideals are good for the most part, but they enforce them ruthlessly," Aron finally said.

Mendale was listening attentively.

"I agree on one thing with Lenin; the war must end. I can't see what anyone is gaining by it."

Aron nodded in agreement. "Yes, but everything he's doing is evil. He's confiscating property without compensation, he's destroying the capitalists and the 'Kulaks' (small landowners). Do you realize that if we were under Russian rule, they would take away our land, the land that our family has worked so hard to keep? When this bloody was ever comes to an end, Poland must become an independent, democratic country, so we can live on our land and practice our beliefs. The Communists are evil. They don't worry about the means they use, as long as they reach their goal." Aron stopped.

Mendale said: "Right now, I'm most concerned about our own people under the Russians. The Bolsheviks claim that all Jews are capitalists, and should be eliminated. The White Russians claim that all of them are Bolsheviks, and they hound and kill them. The Ukrainians agree with them, and the Cossacks continue to murder indiscriminately, whenever they get a chance. I hate all these barbarians, and I'm sick of war and fighting. I just want to go home, and away from this miserable country."

Aron responded:

"I know, Mendale, it's been hard for you, but I have a feeling that all this will end soon, and you will come home to us. I must start heading home as soon as possible, and also keep my promise to Natasha and get her and the children out of the country."

The next afternoon, while playing chess in the garden and sipping cherry brandy, Aron received a note from two ladies sitting in a nearby gazebo. One was obviously older than the other. Her hair was swept back severely. The other, quite young, had long blond hair. Aron looked at the note and said to his brother:

"It's a note from the Countess Olga. I had absolutely no idea that she was here, nor that she was even alive. She's a close friend of Natasha's. I must go to her. I'll be right back." Aron walked across the garden, and approached the two ladies.

"My dear Countess, what a wonderful surprise for me. Thank God that you are safe." Aron bent over and kissed her hand. She was wearing a black dress, well fitted, which revealed her lovely figure, but her black hair was streaked with silver now.

"This is my daughter, Masha," she said. Then, turning to the young girl she said: "And this is Mr. Heller, an old friend from Moscow, dear," she added.

Aron noticed that the cigarette she was holding in her hand was without the accustomed silver holder. She had no jewelry on. He remembered her with her diamond tiara, resplendent at parties in Moscow. He shook Masha's hand, and thought how much like her father she was:

"How is your father, Countess Masha?" he asked.

The young girl was silent.

"Evgeny is no more," Countess Olga spoke for her. "The Bolsheviks murdered him. Now there are just two of us left, and we are under the protection of Hetman Skoropadski." Countess Olga sounded like she was resigned to her fate. Her once vivacious manner had vanished. Her lustrous dark eyes were sad. Aron tried to find the words to express his sorrow at what had happened to the count. She, however, didn't seem to be listening, as though she were trying to forget the bitter past. Then she motioned for Aron to sit down.

"I have my brother with me," Aron said. "He's in the Austrian Army and stationed nearby. I came to visit him here. May I call him over?"

"By all means, Mr. Heller, but for God's sake, don't call me countess. There are spies everywhere."

"I promise to be more careful, Madam Olga," Aron said obediently. He called Mendale over and introduced his as a specialist in the Austrian Army, and the ladies invited the two to sit down.

The two young people said very little to each other. While Aron and Olga talked about events that had changed their lives, the youngsters just looked at one another. The countess talked about her plans to go to France, where her uncle used to go on vacation before the war. He never returned, and continued to live in his villa near Cannes. He had promised to send a messenger who would get her and her daughter out of the country. Until that happened, the two women were safest here. Olga invited the brothers to have tea with her and Masha in her apartment the following day.

At the appointed time next afternoon, Aron and Mendale walked into a well-furnished suite in the same hotel where they were staying. Masha let them in, and Mendale was surprised to see how tall she was. She wore a white dress and seemed much happier than the day before.

A round table stood near the verandah, holding small sandwiches and cakes, and an elegant samovar. But what surprised the Hellers was that there were soldiers outside guarding the door. Under the protection of Skoropadski indeed!

It was wonderful and homelike to be here, Mendale thought. Masha flirted with him openly, and laughed when he told her a joke. Olga too, was in better spirits today than yesterday and made everyone promise that no sad subjects would be discussed that afternoon. They enjoyed their tea and spoke hopefully of the future. "You must come back again soon," said the countess as they were taking their leave. "Perhaps Thursday?"

Aron bowed and agreed, and the Hellers returned to their room.

But by Thursday, they found themselves not daring to leave their room. At noon a great commotion shook the hotel. Hetman Skoropadski himself arrived unexpectedly, riding a splendid horse, dressed in his tsarist uniform, and surrounded by a retinue of officers. Behind him rode a detachment of Cossacks, who were also dressed for a parade.

Mendale and Aron stayed put and rang for the bellman, who took nearly an hour to arrive. He apologized and explained that Hetman Skoropadski had come to visit Madam Olga, disrupting all hotel routines. Her suite had been sealed off, and Cossack guards were all over the hotel, to make sure that nothing would go wrong. The Hellers tried to see the countess again, but the Cossacks were suspicious and barred their way.

Very early the following morning, the Hetman and his retinue galloped out of the hotel grounds, leaving a contingent of Cossacks behind.

Back at the barracks, Captain Huzicki received the salute of Sergeant Charanter. The latter had just returned from Mariopol on a purchasing trip, and was attempting to give the captain all the details of his successful trip.

Huzicki cut him off abruptly.

"Yes, yes. . . . but make the report in writing. I must have exact figures and dates."

"Anything you say, Captain Huzicki. Your wish is my command," Charanter answered as he came to attention again.

"Well, as long as we got that straight, we can continue. I want to know exactly what the Hellers are up to. This is information that you have to give me orally, and in every minute detail. It's a question of security." The captain sat back, and lit a cigarette from the silver case.

The sergeant began anew:

"The Hellers are living luxuriantly at the hotel. Aron seems to have a great deal of money and is spending it freely. Corporal Heller is sporting a new, made to order uniform, and seems to be engaged in business transactions with his brother, although I have no definite proof of that."

The captain interrupted him again.

"Without proof, we can do nothing here. Get me facts, not silly stories." The captain was losing his patience. "I gave you a specific assignment and expect you to carry it out to perfection."

Charanter now decided to switch his strategy.

"Captain Huzicki, I have other information, and proof, that I know you will find interesting." He stopped for a moment to get his boss interested.

"Well, what is it, Charanter? Speak up."

"Both brothers have been seen in the presence of Madam Olga and Miss Masha. I know for a fact that they have been to tea in Madam Olga's suite. Corporal Heller was seen flirting shamelessly with Miss Masha."

Huzicki became livid at he mention of Masha's name.

"I can't believe that Madam Olga would allow such a state of affairs." The captain was shouting, totally out of control. "Masha, that beautiful angel, was with him, a member of your tribe, Charanter? That's unthinkable. Her mother has never even allowed me near her. Of course, they're aristocrats, and I'm just a Polish peasant." He became somber now. "But I have been given strict orders to watch for their safety. We can't take chances with these Hellers."

Finally the captain is responding, thought Charanter.

"And there is more," the sergeant said with a smile. "Hetman Skoropadski himself paid a visit to Madam Olga yesterday afternoon. He spent all night in the hotel, and left early this morning."

Huzicki seemed to go into shock at this latest news. When he finally recovered, he said:

"Well, did you find out who he spent the night with, the mother or the daughter?"

Charanter was scared now. Huzicki might get into one of his bad fits again, and slap him.

"My captain, unfortunately I do not have that information. The hotel was swarming with Cossacks. It was sealed off. It couldn't possibly be that Miss Masha. . . ." He stopped, as he realized that he might get himself in trouble. "At any rate, I will personally investigate the entire incident, this afternoon."

"You make sure that you do that. I hope that the whore hasn't sold her daughter to the old son-of-a-bitch Skoropadski. Use any method necessary to find out from the help at the hotel what really happened there." He was still angry, but tried to control himself. He had to rescue Masha. He would go to the hotel and insist on seeing her, he thought.

"We have to deal with the Hellers." Huzicki shouted for his assistant.

"Take this down," he said. "And see to it that it's dispatched to Corporal Heller immediately.

'Your leave has been cancelled. Return to the barracks immediately for questioning!' "

Charanter smiled, but inside he felt frustrated and bitter. He was thinking about his own bad luck. This captain was making his life miserable. He belittled him and he was never satisfied with all his efforts. He always wanted more and more of everything. Why should the Hellers have it so easy, and get special treatment?

"Captain Huzicki," he finally said. "What about Aron? Isn't he going to be punished too?"

Huzicki understood Charanter very well, and smiled.

"Unfortunately, I can't follow up on your idea. He's a civilian and not under my jurisdiction. He has permission to stay in this area as long as he wishes."

When Mendale returned to the barracks, he was questioned at length by Huzicki, concerning Madam Olga, Masha, the Hetman, and his alleged business dealings. The captain, however, didn't get too far. Mendale simply didn't seem to have the information he was seeking. It was back to the barracks for him, and repairing and laying down telephone lines.

Aron came to see the captain and brought him a gift again. Huzicki questioned him too, and got no satisfaction. Aron told him that Madam Olga and her husband had been friends of his in Moscow. He did not reveal her title. The captain realized that he had other ways of finding out what he wanted to know and now had to get rid of Heller. Only Masha and the filthy lecher Skoropadski were on his mind.

Livid with anger, he called on his assistant again. Ranting and raving incoherently, he shouted that he had no one to depend on. He had to do all the dirty work of investigating by himself. Ignoring Aron completely, he was out of the door in a flash.

Aron managed to get hold of Mendale outside headquarters. With Huzicki in a rage, there was no point in his hanging around any more. "With God's help," he said, "we will see each other soon. I'm going to Proskurov now to help Natasha, and from there I hope to make my way home."

Now that they had found each other again, it was hard for Mendale to part from his brother. As they hugged he said, "Take care of yourself Aron, and tell mother not to worry. I'll be back as soon as this is over." He tried to assume a confident tone, but didn't really believe it.

Chapter 22
ENOUGH OF WAR

In September 1918, after numerous encounters with the Reds, the Ninth Army finally left the Ukraine. Now a full-fledged civil war was on the way. Skoropadski was fighting Petlura, the leader of another Ukrainian faction, in addition to fighting the Bolsheviks.

Mendale was delighted to escape from that miserable country. The soldiers were told that they would now be going back to Poland. The rejoicing was great among the troops. There had been rumors that peace was near. Peace but not victory.

When they arrived near Lemberg, they first realized how badly the war was going for the Central Powers. Mendale's regiment had been totally isolated in the Ukraine, and knew nothing about the German defeat on the Western Front. They now heard that in June, at the battle of Chateau-Thierry, a massive German offensive was stopped, largely by the Americans, under the command of General Pershing. The Ottoman Empire (Turkey), Austria's other ally, was falling apart. Only the Austrian Army was still thought to be strong, and was poised with all its forces against the Italians. Marshall Foch of France, had been named to head the Unified Allied Command. He now called on the Italians to join in the general offensive by the Allies to smash the Central Powers once and for all, and bring an end to the war.

Rumors were rife at the camp. The soldiers were convinced that they were going to be sent to the Italian Front. Every day, Mendale heard new stories concerning the fighting there. Someone said that the Allies were now intensifying their use of poison gas. Another stated that the Italians were dislodging large boulders in the mountains to crush thousands of Austrian soldiers in the mountain passes. That way, they were saving their ammunition for future battles. Fear spread in the camp. Just as the war seemed to be ending, the soldiers were saying they were going to be sent to the front to be slaughtered by the Italians. The greatest anxiety concerned the possibility of being maimed for life. Even the seasoned soldiers dreaded that more than death.

One day, as Mendale was passing by the field hospital, he met Kowalski, who had been in Russia with him. The boy had his right arm in a sling. When Mendale asked him what had happened to him, he said that he had been wounded accidentally in the arm. Now, he would not have to be going to fight with their regiment. Mendale understood that it was a self-inflicted wound.

"I wish something like that would happen to me. I don't want to go either," Mendale said to his friend.

Kowalski then whispered in his ear:

"You're a smart fellow, Heller, smarter than most of us. Don't end up dead in some God-damned ditch in Italy, or get gasses, so you become a vegetable, not a human being. Save yourself." Mendale realized that his friend was right, and said:

"But how do I go about it, Kowalski?"

"You'll have to figure that out by yourself, my friend. Just think about it, and you'll come up with the answer."

That night, Mendale didn't sleep. he was ready to do anything not to have to go. But maybe Kowalski was wrong, and they weren't going to the Italian Front. The only one who might give him the right information was Charanter.

Mendale saw him the following morning in the hall, and asked what news he had from the front. The sergeant was very secretive, but finally said:

"Meet me this evening in front of the mess hall, and I'll tell you. Be sure you're alone. I can't talk here in front of all these people."

When they met in the evening, Charanter told him that most of the rumors about the Italian Front were true. It was also true that their regiment was to be transferred there soon. It was only a question of a specific date. He added:

"This information, Heller, is for you alone. Huzicki would kill me if he knew that I told you about this. We don't want to cause panic."

"Don't worry. No one will know anything from me. But tell me, what are you going to do, Charanter?" Mendale asked him.

"Oh, I've already been granted an exemption. I have to stay here to obtain additional arms, and I won't be able to leave with the regiment for the front."

"Charanter, you've done some pretty rotten things to me in the past. I've never asked you for help, but this is an emergency. Help me to get a transfer, or permission to stay here," Mendale pleaded.

"No, I couldn't do that. Huzicki would be suspicious, and it would be risking my own life." The sergeant seemed to be lost in thought for a moment, but then he said: "But I do want to help you. I'm not your enemy, on the contrary, I want to save your life." Charanter took out a slip of paper and wrote something on it.

"I'm giving you the name and address of a doctor who might be able to fix you up." Mendale looked at the slip of paper.

"Well, what exactly can Dr. Czerniakow do for me, Charanter?"

"I can't tell you that, Heller. But if you want to save yourself, you better go and see him right away." Then Charanter added, "And remember, my name is not to be mentioned. I've said nothing and know nothing. Our conversation never took place." The sergeant then walked away, leaving Mendale to ponder this new turn of events.

The same day, Mendale asked for leave to go to town. Dr. Czerniakow, an old man in his seventies, was short and chubby, and he had a cheerful smile. Most of the patients in his waiting room were women. Mendale waited a long time to be admitted.

"Dr. Czerniakow, they're going to send me to the Italian Front next week. I don't want to go. I've been in the army for three miserable years, and I've had enough. They told me you could help me."

Dr. Czerniakow didn't seem surprised at all at the request. He asked Mendale many questions, then said: "What I'm going to do for you is a matter of strict confidence. Even your family is not to know about it. Should the authorities find out, I could lose not only my license but my life. This is a very serious matter. I'm a pacifist, and as such do not believe that war is the solution to any national or international problem.

When I saw that this war has destroyed an entire generation in Europe, and caused horrible deaths and maiming of millions, I decided to take immediate action. I'm an old man, and have seen a great deal in my long life. I'm willing to take a chance to save lives." He stopped and got a Bible from the shelf. "Swear that you will not disclose any information to the authorities," the doctor said.

Then Dr. Czerniakow explained about the procedure. He was going to give Mendale pills, which when inserted into the eyes, would produce swelling and severe inflammation for a few days. The pills had to be inserted every three days, or else, the inflammation would wear off. The doctor assured Mendale that no permanent harm would result to the eyes if he used the pills only three weeks. After discontinuing them, it would take approximately two months for normal vision to return.

"Do you consent to this treatment, Mr. Heller?" the doctor asked. And when the answer was affirmative, he gave him a small envelope with small white pills. He inserted two of them into Mendale's eyes, and told him to return to the barracks immediately. The effect would be felt, he said, within minutes.

By the time Mendale returned to the barracks, his eyes were so swollen that he had trouble finding his bunk. His neighbor noticed the state he was in, and called the medics. They took him to the hospital and he was immediately examined by a doctor. An eye specialist was soon called in, but neither of them could determine what was wrong. They decided to put him under observation, and checked on him frequently. After three days, Mendale inserted two more pills, and his eyes got worse. That day, he heard from an orderly that his regiment had left for the Italian Front. It was October 15. Three days later, he slipped in two more pills. This time, his eyes were swollen shut. The doctors, fearing an epidemic, decided to place him in the isolation ward. He managed to get rid of the pills in the outhouse before they took him away.

After a week in isolation, Mendale was "miraculously" cured, though his vision was slightly impaired. The nurses took special good care of him, and he was dismissed from the hospital and declared fit for combat. Mendale felt disappointed and frustrated. He would still be sent to the Italian front.

On October 24, very early in the morning, Mendale and the rest of the members of his unit started their trip toward the Front. Their commander had assured them that the Austrians would be victorious. Everyone knew that the Italians weren't good soldiers, he added. They were good musicians and good lovers, great artists, great cooks, but soldiers? Bah! But Mendale didn't believe it. He had a feeling that the Austrian Army was doomed. They would arrive at the front on November 3, 1918, since they had a number of stops to make for more soldiers, ammunition, and food.

Chapter 23
THE WAR ENDS

The train arrived in the village of Horovaty near Fiume, the chief Hungarian port of the Adriatic Sea, then moved on. They stopped at some minor station for about an hour, then proceeded for about fifteen minutes more. The engine then turned off the main tracks and stopped in a sparsely wooded area. Here they were ordered off the train and made camp.

The next morning, the field kitchens were set up, and the men had a good meal. After that there seemed to be nothing to do, so the men scattered over the area and rested under the trees. They had expected a battle. Night came again. They heard no shooting and saw no approaching enemy. They had a good breakfast again the following morning, but began to feel uneasy about the continuing absence of the officers. Finally, a tall muscular corporal led a group of his buddies toward the train where the officers' quarters were and knocked on the door.

No answer. Really anxious now, they forced the door open. The car was empty except for a young lieutenant sprawled on the floor.

The corporal then tried to rouse the lieutenant, but he didn't stir. He reeked of liquor, so they poured a bucket of water over him, and that made him move a bit, though groggily. They dragged him over to a seat and sat him up.

"Hey, lieutenant, what happened to the other officers?" Corporal Nowakowski demanded.

"Town," he muttered. "Further orders. . ."

Nowakowski exchanged glances with the others, some of whom had begun to snicker. He reached into the lieutenant's pocket and took out his identification papers.

"Well, what do you know, fellows. He's got a 'von' in front of his name. He's a shitty aristocrat."

Someone suggested, only half as a joke, "Why don't we do to him what the Bolsheviks did to the tsar in Ekaterinburg?"

Nowakowski smiled.

"We're not barbarians like the Bolsheviks. We'll give him a chance. First we must get more information from his excellency." He kicked the lieutenant in the leg and began slapping his face.

"Come on, Lieutenant Aristocrat, tell us what really happened to your buddies."

The young man seemed to come halfway to life. "All right. . . all right," he groaned. "The war is over, that's all. . . ."

The war is over? They stared at one another, frozen between hope and doubt, afraid to believe and rejoice, for fear it was only one more false rumor.

Then with one accord they fell on the hungover lieutenant and forced the story out of him.

The night before, a courier had arrived from the high command with important information. He said that on October 24, the very day that the train left Lemburg, there was a climactic battle near the town of Vittario Veneto on the Piave River. Seventy-three Austro-Hungarian divisions fought against fifty-one Italian divisions, three British units, two French, one Czechoslovak, and one American. Although the Austro-Hungarian forces were greater in number, they were badly defeated by the Italians under General Armando Diaz.

"Our army is destroyed, annihilated, kaput," the lieutenant added. "Kaiser Karl is begging for an armistice on any terms. The war is over." The lieutenant seemed to collapse again. The effort of telling the story was too much for him.

"He's just telling a bunch of lies so we won't kill him," shouted one of the soldiers.

"We'll have to fight on, while these sons-of-bitches, these cowardly officers, run away. The commander will probably send us other pigs to order us into battle." The corporal now grabbed the lieutenant. The crowd was shouting! "String him up, hang him." They dragged him to a tree. He started to throw up. They got even angrier at him, and finally succeeded with the rope.

Mendale heard a commotion, from a distance, and ran over to see what was going on.

"Hey fellows, don't do that. Let him go. Can't you see that he's just a boy? He can't even hold his liquor." He got right into the circle next to Nowakowski.

"But he's a son-of-a-bitch Austrian aristocrat. They got us into this rotten war, now they'll pay for it." One of the men said.

Nowakowski looked threateningly at Mendale.

"Hey, Heller, what's it to you? Don't mix in to protect this pig. You suffered from the likes of him too."

"You're right, Nowakowski, but I'm not trying to protect him. I'm just thinking about what might happen next. What if the war isn't really over. They could shoot all of us for mutiny."

Nowakoski motioned for everyone to stop what they were doing. A hush came over the lynching crowd.

"You may be right, Heller." He finally said. "We never thought about that."

Mendale realized that the corporal was weakening, and said:

"Besides, he's probably the only one among the officers that's innocent and that seems to be the reason that they left him behind."

Nowakowski now let go of the lieutenant.

"Hey fellows, take this aristocrat pig to the car where we found him. If he recovers, we'll see what to do with him next." Two soldiers stepped forward and dragged the boy away.

Nowakowski felt frustrated. He had to do something to provide some other entertainment for his friends. They were still standing around waiting for something to happen. He said:

"Men, maybe it's true that the war is over, but maybe this stinking officer is lying to us. I'd fight those rotten cowards the Italians, and even the French, but not the Americans. Is there anyone here that hates the Americans?"

"No, never," the crowd shouted.

A tall muscular soldier stepped up to the corporal. He towered over him. The corporal, who was quite tall, looked small in comparison with this man.

"I have an uncle in Chicago," he said. "Maybe his son is in the army too. I refuse to kill my own cousin, who has the same Polish blood like I do."

"Hey, 'Chicago,' you're a man after my own heart." Nowakowski said. "Stay right here next to me." Then he turned to the crowd. "The war is over for us, brothers. We don't care a shit if Austria gets peace or not. We're finished with fighting. Tell me, aren't we through with this rotten war, boys?"

"Yes, we're through with it. Peace, peace now. . ." the crowd chanted.

Mendale, standing between the two tall men, began to worry as to what was coming next. He had stopped them from killing the lieutenant, but he might not be able to stop the next bloody act they may come up with. He then turned to Nowakowski and said: "I've got a very good idea, and I'd like to tell everybody."

"Go ahead Heller," the corporal said. "Quiet down, brothers, and listen to what my friend, Heller, has to say."

Mendale began. "Since everyone has decided not to fight anymore, I say let's go to the quartermaster, right now, and see what we can get from him. We don't want to go home without the proper provisions, and clothing. Why should all that stuff be left behind? Are you with me boys?"

"Hey, that's great. You lead us, Heller, and we'll follow," one fellow shouted, and the others agreed.

Then Mendale turned to Nowakowski. "What do you say my friend?"

"Great idea. Let's go." The corporal said.

With Mendale, Nowakowski, and Chicago in the lead, they headed for the quartermaster's car. Charanter wasn't there. Mendale knew that he must have been hiding. There was another sergeant in charge.

Mendale shouted. "In the name of all the fighting men here, I request that you issue coats, and boots for all of us. It's gotten very cold, and we're not properly dressed for this weather. We also want all the tobacco you've got."

The sergeant protested. "Sergeant Charanter isn't here. I don't have the authority to issue anything without his permission. . . ." He stopped, as he felt a rifle at his back. One of the soldiers, prodded him, pushed him aside and held him prisoner.

"Calm down, sergeant, the war is over and we're the authority now." Chicago said good naturedly.

Mendale appointed the other two leaders and a few of the soldiers that he trusted, to distribute the coats and boots. Everything was being done in an orderly manner. Mendale stood at the head of the line and gave each soldier some tobacco, and paper to roll the cigarettes in. Everyone seemed satisfied. Some said: "Thanks Corporal Heller. This is a great idea." A quiet, shy looking boy said to him, as he was handing him the tobacco. "Our "Lord, Jesus taught us 'Blessed are the peacemakers, for they shall inherit the kingdom of God.' You've turned us away from an evil act today. May Jesus bless you for this."

The distribution continued, and there was still a long line of soldiers who hadn't gotten their share. A fellow by the name of Gothilf was next in line. He shouted: "Hey Heller, who made you the boss here? Wait till the authorities find out. You'll be the one to hang."

Mendale tried to stay calm, as he doled out Gothilf's share of the tobacco. "Didn't you notice, Gothilf, that the soldiers were getting wild? They almost killed the lieutenant. I pacified them, so they won't try to kill anybody else. They were in such a bad mood, that they could have easily turned against you and me. Don't forget that we are members of a hated tribe."

"Don't give me your stupid explanations. You think you're so big." Gothilf shouted. "Just give me my tobacco, you crazy son-of-a-bitch, and shut your mouth."

"You're not getting any tobacco, Gothilf, until you learn to control your temper, and speak like a human being," Mendale said calmly.

"I'm going to kill you," Gothilf said, as he went for Mendale's throat. But Nowakowski felled him with a blow to the head. Gothilf lay there in a heap, his new boots and coat scattered about him.

"Get this stupid fool out of the way, Chicago." Mendale commanded, "and don't forget to dress him in his new coat and boots. We don't want the darling to freeze." The distribution continued.

"Hey, Chicago," someone on the line yelled. "Heller, and Nowakowski are now the generals, and you're the chief of staff." Everybody laughed.

Mendale asked Nowakowski to alert the cooks that they were to serve the best food they had available, including all the meat. The field kitchen was soon dispensing lunch and the soldiers got on line again to get their food, and then sat under the trees to eat and rest. After eating his meal and skipping the meat, which he had not eaten since the first time he had gone into battle, Mendale sent off by himself to rest.

The corporal, Chicago, and a group of their buddies decided to play cards. While they were playing, and talking about the events of the day, someone mentioned the fact that Charanter had made himself scarce during the day. "I wonder where that bastard is hiding?" he said.

"I saw him just a while ago, getting his lunch." Another fellow said.

"It looks like he didn't run away with his friends, the officer pigs" Nowakowski commented. "Something has just occurred to me, boys." He added. "Charanter must have a lot of cash on hand. As the quartermaster, he always has to buy stuff, so Huzicki must have given him a lot of money. Does this give you any ideas, boys?"

"The only way to get money out of Charanter, is by finishing him off. He'll never give up the money while he's alive." A stout, short fellow said.

"That's a great idea, buddy." Nowakowski interjected. "Nobody will miss that worm. Everybody hates his guts."

"But how are we going to divide the money, once we get it?" Chicago asked.

"We need Heller to help us with that. He's the brains of this outfit." Nowakowski said. "All right, Chicago, go and get Heller, and bring him here fast. I'm not planning to hang around here much longer. I'm going home in the morning."

When Chicago brought Mendale the news of the group's decision, Mendale knew that he had to think fast. While walking towards the group playing cards under the tree, he sat down next to Nowakowski, who started explaining the plan again. Mendale pretended to be listening attentively. When Nowakowski finished, he said:

"The basic plan is excellent. Nobody here likes Charanter, and I probably like him less than any of you. He did me a very bad turn in Russia, when we were with Hetman Skoropadski. He got me into a lot of trouble. I never thought I would lay eyes on him again, but here he is, the rat."

"Well, all right, Heller, let's get to the point." The corporal said.

"As to the plan, I'm trying to think about it logically, and I come back to the same question I asked this morning: What if the war isn't really over? But what if it is, and the officers come back with more men? We're still part of the Austrian army, according to them. We could justify taking coats and boots, because it's cold, but I doubt if we can convince them that we had to kill Charanter because we needed his money. We'd be shot without a trial."

Nowakowski got angry. "We didn't ask you here, Heller, to put the fear of God in us. We asked you to help us work out the problem of distributing the money."

"I know, my friend," Mendale answered calmly. "The first thing I did say was that it was an excellent plan. What I'm proposing now is that we wait until tomorrow. Let's sleep on it. We'll meet in the morning. If by then the officers haven't come back, we will work out your plan of action."

Nowakowski still wasn't pleased. He shook his head in disagreement, but Chicago said:

"Fellows, what Heller says sounds good. Our main purpose is to survive and get home to our families. We don't want to take chances this late in the game. Let's wait till tomorrow."

The others agreed but Nowakowski was still hostile.

"Hey, Heller, are you sure that you aren't trying to protect that son-of-a-bitch?"

"Look Nowakowski, I'm just making a suggestion. All of you have to make a final decision." Mendale said. "You're the leader here. Why don't you do it the American way. Take a vote. The question at hand is: Do we do it right now, or wait until tomorrow?"

"Yes Nowakowski, let's vote." Chicago said.

"Well, I guess we could do that. I've always believed that people have a right to decide." The corporal said. "Friends, raise your hand if you're for taking action today."

Only about ten of the men raised his hand.

"Is anybody else with me, guys?" he asked looking disappointed. No one else responded.

"Well, all right, who's for postponing it until tomorrow?"

Everybody else's hand went up. The corporal then stood up. They could tell that he was angry, and were wondering what he was going to say.

"Well Heller, I guess you win, fair and square." He shook Mendale's hand, and the men applauded.

"How about some smokes boys?" Mendale passed around his tobacco pouch. He took out a bottle of vodka from his knapsack and said: "Look what I found in the quartermaster's car. It's not much but let's toast our success. 'Na zdrowie'." He took a swig out of the bottle and passed it to Nowakowski.

The corporal then passed the bottle to the others. It didn't last long. Mendale took him aside so they could talk privately.

"My friend," Mendale said, as the two of them stood by the tree smoking. "I'm very proud to have participated in this vote. That's how democracy works. Maybe we can have this kind of government when peace comes to our wartorn country."

"So you're one of us. " He hugged Mendale. "You'll help us to fight to free Poland. I knew right off that you were different, not like the other. . . ." He stopped himself just in time. He felt very warm toward this Jew, and he wasn't going to insult him. He decided to change the subject. "Would you explain what happens to guys like me in this voting business when they disagree with the others?"

"Nothing happens. They feel frustrated, like you do right now, but they look for another chance to have their way. If they can convince enough people, then maybe they can win the next time," Mendale said.

"I like that idea," Nowakowski said. "If the Americans have this 'democracy', it must be a good thing, especially if they give a person a second chance." The corporal was totally pacified, and was smiling and joking now.

That night, Mendale couldn't fall asleep. He thought about Charanter. He disliked the man thoroughly, but he didn't want him to be murdered. The plot to kill him was totally bizarre. When he had told his friends to wait until tomorrow, he was just playing for time. He had to find a way to warn Charanter tonight, so he could escape.

When he was sure that everyone around him was asleep, Mendale tiptoed out of the car. Charanter was fast asleep, when Mendale shook him and whispered into his ear.

"Charanter, they're planning to kill you and take your money."

The sergeant woke up with a start and sat up looking as though he was in a state of shock. He finally said: "Who is it, Heller? Who is trying to kill me?" He was getting hysterical, and was now shaking.

"Calm down Charanter. I can't tell you who they are, because they trust me. I tried to talk them out of doing it, and only managed to convince them to wait until tomorrow. Save yourself, Charanter. Leave right now. You can escape under cover of darkness."

The sergeant got up and started to put some things into his knapsack.

"All right, all right. I'll go." He seemed totally incoherent. "Thanks Heller, for trying to help me. I can't believe this." He was shaking all over.

"Charanter, I'm going back now to my car. I don't want them to get suspicious." The sergeant grabbed Mendale's hand, and said:

"You're the only friend that I have in this rotten world. I hope that one day I can repay you."

"You already have, when you gave me the name of Dr. Czerniakow." Mendale said. "Go in peace." Mendale was practically out the door, when he felt Charanter pull him back.

"Heller, I just thought of something. Come," he whispered. "You're such a smart fellow, but you didn't think about your own safety when you came to warn me. What do you think those soldiers will do to you, when they find out that I'm gone? They'll surely kill you for spoiling their plan."

Mendale suddenly realized that he was trapped. Charanter had stopped trembling and seemed to be in control of himself.

"Go back and pretend to go to sleep, Heller. In exactly an hour from now, meet me right here. We'll just go home together by train."

"But I haven't got enough money for a ticket." Mendale felt cornered.

"Don't worry about that. I have enough for both of us." The sergeant said. "In an hour from now meet me near the big tree, just past the train. We'll walk to the station. From there we'll catch a train home." Charanter was smiling now. He was himself again, wheeling and dealing. "Well Heller, do we have a deal?"

"All right." Mendale said reluctantly. "I guess I'll see you later." He hated to do this to his friends. He really liked them a lot. But they could very well turn against him and kill him instead.

Mendale met Charanter at the agreed time. At first they ran, but slowed down when they realized that no one was following them. Mendale noticed that Charanter was limping.

"What's the matter with your foot?" he asked him.

"These old boots are full of holes, and are hurting my toes."

Mendale stopped, took a pair of boots out of his knapsack, and said:

"You can have these. I had them made in Russia, and I have the other extra pair that I got in the distribution today."

"You really are a friend, Heller. You care what happens to me. I'm truly sorry for what I did to you in Russia. It was Huzicki's fault. He's a devil of a man, and has a most vicious temper. He made me spy on you and your brother. I had to do it. Those were his orders." Charanter looked pleadingly at Mendale. "Say that you forgive me, so my conscience won't kill me. "

"Well, that's in the past. Let's forget about it. Now we have to concentrate on getting home safely." Mendale said.

They finally arrived at the station at dawn. The station master told them that the next train going north would be arriving at eight in the morning. Charanter bought two tickets and gave one to Mendale. He was looking to get something to eat, but couldn't find any vendors that early in the morning. Charanter suddenly said that he knew of a fine restaurant in town, where he could get a good meal. He'd be gone only half an hour. Mendale didn't know what the sergeant was up to now, nor did he care.

An hour passed and then another half hour, and there was no sign of Charanter. Mendale was thinking that his buddy must be up to some of his old tricks again. Mendale didn't have enough money to buy another ticket in Vienna, where they were supposed to change trains. He was lost in his thoughts, when a Hungarian soldier approached him. From the way he spoke Mendale surmised that he was Jewish.

"How about selling me the boots you have there?" the man said. Mendale had taken out his extra boots from his knapsack and was rearranging his things.

"Sorry, friend," Mendale answered him in Yiddish. "They're not for sale. I'm taking them home for my brother."

"Look, I've got the money. Just name your price." He took out a wad of paper money.

"I told you that they're not for sale." Mendale said angrily. And when the man continued to bother him, he told him to get lost.

"You'll be sorry for this," the man shouted, as he walked away. "I'll get those boots one way or another."

Within minutes he was back with an officer and two military policemen. They took the boots and the extra coat away from Mendale. He tried to explain, but they didn't listen. They let him keep the dress uniform that he had brought from Russia. He felt grateful that they didn't attempt to take his rifle or ask for his discharge papers.

The officer finally said:

"We'll let you go now. You're lucky that the war is over. In wartime, stealing is punishable by death, as you well know."

He sat down on the bench again feeling tired, cold, and despondent. Suddenly, he saw Charanter walking toward him. He wad carrying all kinds of packages, and humming a tune. Mendale was disgusted with his "friend". When he told him what had happened to his coat and shoes, Charanter said: "I'm sorry that it happened, but they weren't really yours anyway. Forget about it." Mendale didn't answer. This trip was turning out to be most unpleasant, and the worst part of it was that he would have to travel to Vienna with this fellow.

The train finally arrived in the capital and Mendale bought a loaf of bread, and feasted on it. He was really hungry. He tried not to talk to Charanter, who soon fell asleep, and was snoring loudly. Mendale watched the scenery from the window, thinking about the Hungarian girl he had known, when he came here three years before. It seemed so long ago, in the days of his innocence, before the carnage, and the cruelty of the war. He felt so tired of it all. The only ray of hope was that he was going home.

Charanter kept his word and bought him a ticket. The sergeant now told him that he planned to spend a few days in the capital, and then was going to return to Stryj, his home town. Mendale was glad to be rid of him, finally.

As Mendale approached the train that would take him to Kalusz, he saw that military police were checking everyone's identification, before allowing them to board. Most people, who were civilians, passed quickly through the check point, but the police stopped and searched Mendale. They then took away his rifle and his ammunition.

"The war is over, corporal. You won't need these any more." One of them said in a friendly manner. "Have a good journey home to your country."

On the train, a second miracle, he found a seat and put his almost empty pack under it. As he was falling asleep, he thanked the Creator for all His blessings. He was going home.

He must have been sleeping for hours, when he felt someone tugging on his arm. He looked up, and there was Stash.

"I'm dreaming!" Mendale said.

"No, you're not. I'm really here."

The two young men hugged and pounded each other on the back.

"I've been watching you sleep for a couple of hours, and didn't want to wake you," Stash said, sitting down next to him. He began to tell Mendale about his experiences. He had been in a fierce battle on the Italian front.

"I'm just lucky to be alive, brother. Once the slaughter started, thousands of Poles, Ukrainians, and Czechs gave up and surrendered. The Hungarians just took off. They said they didn't need the Austrians any more—they had their own country now."

Unbidden, Mendale seemed to hear the voice of young Moishe: "Once pressure is put on the empire, it could fly apart"

"I hid in the woods for days." Stash continued. "Then I met some other deserters, and we started going north. I sold my gun and ammunition, so I could buy a train ticket home."

Mendale resounded with his own adventures. They lasted across the Hungarian plain and through the Carpathians. And then at last, as they were leaving the station, two Ukrainian guards stopped them and asked for identification. They allowed Stash to pass immediately, but stopped Mendale. They searched his pack and found the uniform tunic, which they promptly confiscated. "You won't need that coat either, Jew. It's quite warm in November."

Mendale peeled it off and handed it over.

"You can go now, corporal, but remember, don't join the Poles. We'll be fighting them this winter, and you know what we do to Jews when they double-cross us?" He gestured with his hand across his throat.

Mendale said nothing. So this was his welcoming home committee.

Stash was waiting for him outside the gate. "I saw what those two beasts were doing." he said. "Here, take my extra shirt—it's something at least."

Mendale thanked him, and indeed the wool shirt did make a difference in the raw November day. They went to buy something to eat, but found the shelves almost empty—some kerosene bottles, candles, matches, and other small items, that was all. An old Hasidic man, sitting behind the counter, looked scared at the sight of them until Mendale addressed him in Yiddish.

"Sholom Aleichem, sir. Is there anything we can buy here to eat?"

"Aleichem sholom," answered the man, lifting his hands in reply. "I thought that you were a Ukrainian. No, there is nothing else here, except what you see. They emptied this place without paying a grosz."

"Are these local people?"

"They're mostly from the villages around here, but they have leaders who train them. They're murderers."

"We're just back from the Italian Front, sir, and on our way home. What is the situation like on the roads?"

"Things are very bad, young man, the woods are full of Ukrainian terrorists. They kill, pillage, and steal, and attack our people for no reason at all. This is being done under the name of patriotism. They say that they're fighting the Poles, but we are the ones to suffer." The old man looked very ancient at that moment, weighed down by his people's woes. Mendale pitied the old man and wished he could do something to halt such injustice. He said:

"From what you tell me, sir, we're embarking on a dangerous journey. Will you give us your blessing?"

"You will be safe, my son. The Creator will protect you from harm" He looked at Mendale with dark burning eyes, then closed his eyes, lifted up his arm, and spoke in a beautiful resonant voice:

"O Father in heaven, your people Israel have suffered enough. The nations have fought a bloody war. They took our sons and murdered them on the battlefields of Europe. The nations caused millions to be killed. While they were slaughtering each other, they were murdering our civilian people, and now that the war is over, they are turning their wrath against us again. O Creator of the world, save this young son of Israel and carry him safely to the people who love him."

The old man lowered his hands and sat there for a moment in deep meditation. Mendale didn't move, and neither did Stash. It was as if the old man had cast a spell on them.

Suddenly, the old man opened his eyes and seemed to come to life again. He bent down and took out half a loaf of brown bread from under the counter. He cut it in half and handed a piece to each of the boys. Then he gave them some water from a bottle on the counter.

"Go in peace, my son," he said to Mendale. "May the Holy One bless you and keep you safe." He then turned to Stash and addressed him in flawless Ukrainian:

"Don't let the terrorists harm your friend. Protect him. God bless you both."

"I promise you that I will protect him, holy man," Stash said.

They were a little dazed as they came out into the sun and started walking briskly toward Zbora. Neither of them spoke for a long time.

Chapter 24
THE RETURN

The two soldiers stopped by a small stream, drank some water, and then filled their canteens. Mendale glanced uneasily around. "Let's get out of here. I just saw someone watching us from the trees over there."

"I don't see anything, Heller," Stash whispered.

"He's hiding again."

They collected their things and were on their way. So far they'd been lucky. None of the guerrillas had stopped them. At times, they heard noises and knew that they were being observed, but nothing happened. These woods were near their home, and they were attuned to every natural sound.

Suddenly, as they rounded a bed in a the road, a fellow dressed in a tattered uniform stopped them. He had a rifle and a pistol that hung menacingly from his belt.

"I've been watching you for a while, and just wanted to get a closer look."

Stash said "We're going back to our village. We've been fighting for the Austrians. You know, brother, this wasn't our fight, but we were drafted and had to go."

"Well, I just wanted to make sure, so I can report to my commander." He seemed to linger and want something.

"Do you want to see our identification papers?" Mendale asked.

"No, brother, I couldn't read them anyway, but if you have some tobacco, I'd appreciate it." Mendale didn't have any left, but Stash took out his tobacco pouch and gave it to the man.

"Thank you, brother." He shook hands with both the soldiers. As he disappeared among the trees, he shouted: "Long live the Ukrainian Republic."

"Whew! That was a close call."

Stash crossed himself and whispered: "Thank you, Jesus. Mother of God, protect us from evil."

Now, as they were nearing Zbora, both of them prayed silently. They were tired soldiers of a defeated army, hoping for some rest, but there seemed to be no end to their troubles. Mendale recalled the order and comparative fairness imposed by Austrians. Now, with the Austrians gone, the countryside seemed in total chaos.

As they passed familiar landmarks, Mendale was stuck by how small things were in comparison with what he remembered. It all looked peaceful here. Unwillingly he found himself remembering the battles and the slaughter, the stench of dead bodies that he had to step on to get his work done. He saw again the remains of his friends, mutilated beyond recognition, and parts of their bodies strewn about them. He remembered the boy who went crazy in the trenches. How had he come through it all—alive and with all his limbs intact?

He was almost home now. Yes. There was the house in the distance. Here was a post that marked the beginning of his family's land. That tree—he used to rest under it. He looked about him curiously. The land had been harvested this year. Did that mean that Aron was back? He took a bit of earth into his hand and felt its cool moisture. Was this what men were fighting and dying for—a bit of territory, a piece of earth, as place to call their own?

Stash shivered. "Let's go, Heller. It's getting dark."

They continued on. On the other side of the road they saw some burnt=out houses and neglected fields. They rounded a bend in the road, and there was his house, very white in the starlight.

"You'll stay with us tonight, Stash. I don't want to see you travelling late at night." Stash agreed.

They approached the house. The front door was boarded up, but Mendale saw a light in the back. As they passed a window with its shutters closed, Mendale knocked and said in Ukrainian:

"Open the door. I'm back."

In his excitement, he forgot to knock on the back door and tried to open it.

Aron inside the house, heard someone shouting in Ukrainian and grabbed up his two revolvers. When he saw the door handle turn, he assumed it was terrorists, trying to break in. He cocked one gun and then the other, then unlocked the door and stood back.

Mendale had heard the two clicks, and stepped back from the door, pushing Stash behind him. "Aron, it's me," he shouted in Yiddish.

Aron's hand was just starting to squeeze the trigger. He stopped it just in time, and flung open the door.

"Thank God, Mendale, I almost killed you!" He picked up his brother like a child and started to kiss him. Soon Golda was hugging him, and then the rest of the family came running. The war years had changed Golda. Her hair, showing under the kerchief, was gray, and her face displayed new lines.

A strange red-headed young man sat at the table, studying Scripture. His sister Laichia introduced him.

"Avrumchi Silber and I are engaged to be married, Mendale," she said proudly.

"Mendale, don't be angry. For the dowry, we used the money you saved up before the war." Golda added.

"Angry? I'm delighted! I can't think of a better use for it."

Suddenly, Mendale remembered Stash. He whistled to him, and his friend came in shyly. Everybody made him feel welcome. Golda brought out a bottle of vodka, and Aron served all of them. Even the children got some in tiny glasses. They toasted "L'Chaim," and recited the prayer of thanksgiving for their safe return. Then Laichia set the table, and fed the two hungry soldiers.

Stash couldn't take his eyes off Laichia, and finally said to her: "You have beautiful hair, Miss Heller. It's like a flame." The girl looked embarrassed, and ran into the kitchen. Stash laughed and said to Mendale, "I like your sister a lot, but I know she's off limits to me, so don't look so worried."

After they finished eating, Ester put the children to bed, and the adults sat and talked for many hours. Mendale and Stash recounted their experiences, while Aron told a few interesting stories about his adventures in Russia. Stash kept looking at Laichia, and she finally excused herself and went to her room.

Moishe asked them a lot of questions. He was too young to be called up and had spent the war years at home. He had grown tall, and very thin. He looked like a scholar and was planning to be one. He told Mendale that he wanted to study law. He thought he might go to America, where there were more opportunities for Jewish people to practice in that field. Now, that the war was over, he would write to their brother, Meyer, and ask him for help and advice.

Aron felt that it wasn't necessary for Moishe to go so far away. Poland was now an independent country. Marshal Pilsudski had promised equality to all minorities in the country. Everyone would be able to live freely and study at the universities, in the newly reborn Polish Republic.

"The only major problem we have is the Ukrainians in Galicia, who do not want to accept Polish rule. There are terrorist bands all around us, in the woods and in other hiding places. But I believe that they really don't have the full support of their people. This problem will, I'm sure, be resolved soon."

"But meanwhile," Moishe said, "we live in a state of siege, always on the watch. Aron, you think so much of Pilsudski, but what about his General Haller and his followers. The Hallerczyks are with Pilsudski too, but one of their favorite sports is killing innocent Jews."

Stash spoke up: "There's too much hatred in this country. There's too much hatred all over Europe. I learned that during the war. I'm half Ukrainian and half Polish. The bigots on both sides have hated me since I was a little kid. While I was in the trenches, I made up my mind that if I lived through this slaughter, I would immigrate to America. I agree with you, Moishe. That's the only place to go. That's where they give a man an equal chance."

Golda asked the men to forget politics for now. She served them hot herbal tea and cookies, and Ester prepared a cot for Stash in the kitchen. Then everyone retired.

When Mendale was about to go to bed, Golda held him back. "Stay, my son. We have a lot to talk about. As soon as things quiet down, I want to go and visit Shainchi and her family in Germany. I might even go to see Max in America. I miss my other children too. It's time for me to step down and make place for you, the new generation."

"Mother, you know that I would never try to contradict you." Mendale said, his eyes almost closed. "But right now I'm too tired to think straight. Let's go to sleep.

Mendale slept fourteen hours straight. When he woke up, Stash had left, and he noticed that Josef too was missing—gone to live with his children, Golda said.

She served Mendale a huge breakfast and brought him a paper to read. The headlines said that Kaiser Karl had resigned. There was a picture of him and Empress Zita boarding the train which would take them into exile. He looked dignified, but very sad. The paper also printed his abdication speech of November 11, 1918, Mendale began to read:

"Since my accession, I have incessantly tried to rescue my people from this unfortunate war. I have not delayed the reestablishment of constitutional rights, nor have I impeded the people's striving toward national development.

The people have, through their deputies, taken charge of the Government. I now relinquish every participation in the administration of the State. . .

May the Austrian people realize a harmonious transition in their new political adjustments. The happiness of my people was my aim from the beginning. My fondest wishes are, that an internal peace will heal the wounds of this terrible war."

Mendale was glad that the Austrian people were behaving in a civilized manner toward their former emperor, and that the Kaiser didn't have to share the fate of the Tsar.

After 700 years, the Habsburg Dynasty has ended its rule in Austria. Along the route that was taking their emperor into exile, the people waved goodbye. Some were crying; others stood at attention. It was the end of an era.

Chapter 25
POLAND REGAINS ITS INDEPENDENCE

January 1919 was a cold and dismal monthly for many reasons. The hopes for peace and a return to normalcy, were battered by momentous events. It was only about six weeks since Mendale had returned from the war, and yet each day brought more distressing news to the Hellers.

Marshal Jozef Pilsudski, the great leader, and member of the P.P.S., The Polish Socialist Party, had been released by the Germans from the Megdenburg prison. He had received a tumultuous welcome in Warsaw from both the Polish and Jewish population. However, now his leadership was being challenged by another contender, Roman Dmowski, the head of the National Democratic Party. Dmowski's political platform centered on the idea that Poland was to be run only for and by ethnic Poles. He was not only virulently anti-Semitic, but openly against the Ukrainian minority as well. He lumped both of these groups together, as enemies of the new State. He had a considerable following among Poland's emerging elites, who wanted a "pure" Polish nation devoid of all "foreign" influences, and ideologies. A nation that would live by the traditional "Polish morality" of their powerful ancestors. His ideas were diametrically opposed to Marshal Pilsudski's concepts. The acclaimed leader of Poland believed that the newly independent country should be modeled on the American concept of democracy. This would mean a multi-ethnic republic, in which all the minorities would have equal rights, and would be able to practice their various religions.

The country was about to explode into a civil war because of the discord between these two opposing factions. The differences between these two opposing factions. The differences were exacerbated by the tendency of Dmowski's followers to use violence as a political tool. Only the good services of Ignacy Jan Paderewski, prevented a major catastrophe. This great patriot, pianist, and friend of Woodrow Wilson, finally agreed to head an interim government. Since both leaders trusted him, it was the only way the country could be rescued from disaster.

In January 1919, the first Sejm (Parliament) of independent Poland was convened and Marshal Pilsudski was confirmed as head of state. The Sejm proceeded with the task of drafting a full constitution.

And then, disaster. The liberation of Poland was followed by a series of violent pogroms against the Jewish population. It was perpetrated by Poles in the newly liberated cities of Warsaw, Krakow, Kielce, and many smaller towns.

In Zbora, as in all of Eastern Galicia, things were still in a state of turmoil. The Ukrainian terrorists continued to carry out raids against the civilian population, murdering Jewish people in particular.

The Ukrainian pogrom in Lemberg now was the closest one to the Heller home. European and American public opinion was aroused and a commission arrived in Poland from Britain to ascertain the facts concerning the atrocities that were being committed against the Jewish minority. The commission found that pogroms, murders and atrocities were perpetrated against Jews in 100 towns and villages between November 11, 1918 Armistice Day, and January of 1919.

The Jewish people realized, with finality, that they could not depend on their compatriots, the Poles, to stop the slaughter of the innocent. They looked to America and her allies, now hammering out a peace treaty and redefining the borders of Europe, to impose justice and order in their country.

Paderewski, beloved by all faction, and the foreign minister of Poland, represented his country at the Paris Peace Treaty on that fateful day of January 16, 1919.

When the Versailles Peace Treaty was signed in June, the Allies insisted that Poland, among other countries, sign an additional Minorities Treaty, guaranteeing equal rights to national and religious minorities.

When the news of this momentous event was telegraphed to Poland, there was general rejoicing among the Jewish population and Pilsudski's followers. Dmowski and his party, however, saw in this treaty an unwarranted interference in Polish autonomy. His hatred of Jews and Ukrainians became, if anything, more ferocious then ever.

Meanwhile, in Zbora, the Hellers tried to carry on some semblance of normalcy during the day. The animals had to be fed, and after four years of neglect, the house and other buildings had to be repaired.

At night, they took turns keeping watch. All the adults, in fact, stayed up later than they used to studying the Scriptures, conversing, playing cards or chess.

After a while, Yiddish papers were being printed again in Lvov. The Hellers were now able to get news, although often belated.

They were playing chess one evening, and the subject of Palestine, which would probably be made a British mandate, came up. Mendale saw this as a hopeful sign for the reestablishment of the Land of Israel, and suggested that the whole family consider emigration. But Aron, a Polish patriot, said, "No, no we must change our way of thinking and consider Poland our permanent home, now. We must help make her a true democracy. We are Polish by nationality. Our people have lived in this land for over a thousand years. Why, our great-grandfather fought in the Insurrection of 1863 against the Russians. This is our country, and we must strive to improve it."

Golda glanced up from her knitting. "Reb Chaim Soiffer," she said nodding. "He was a religious scribe, and a saintly man—and yet a devoted Polish patriot, too."

The children, bored and only half listening, now sensed a story. Chana, Aron's daughter said, "Grandma, tell us about Reb Chaim, please, Grandma."

It didn't take much coaxing. "Reb Chaim was a great scholar and disciple of Reb Mendale from Kotzk," Golda began. "

"From an early age he was revered for him goodness and wisdom. He wrote only one Torah scroll in all his life. As you know, the scroll is written entirely by hand and no mistake can be made on it. Reb Chaim, however, did something unusual. Each time that he came to the name of the Holy One, before he wrote it, he would go to the ritual bath to cleanse himself. In this fashion it took him many years to finish the scroll. But that's a separate story.

When the Insurrection of 1863 started, Reb Chaim offered his house as a meeting place for the Polish conspirators against the tsar. The great Reb Mendale Kotzker, of blessed memory, also lent his support to the insurrection. Among the patriots there were quite a few of our Jewish fighters.

Our patriotic tradition had started long before that. One of our own heroes was Berek Joselewicz, who fought with General Kosciuszko against the Russians, for Polish independence. But that was long before our story.

Let's get back to Reb Chaim, and the year 1863. The insurrection was in full swing, and its motto was "For our freedom and yours". The Russian, put all their forces into play. They weren't going to allow a victory for the oppressed. After a heroic struggle, the revolutionaries lost, and there were numerous reprisals,—shootings and hangings of the patriots. Reb Chaim the scholar was never suspected by the Russians, so he was able to help many of his friends flee to safety in Austria."

"One night"—Golda's story continued—"a high ranking officer of the uprising came to Reb Chaim's house for help. Reb Chaim hid him in a large unused oven. The officer stayed there for weeks. Each day his protector fed him and took care of his needs. In the morning, when Reb Chaim went to the synagogue to pray, he would get all the news he could of the Russians' activities and paid special attention to the decrees that were posted daily and other repressive measures. One day, he read a proclamation that an amnesty was to take effect that very day and that there was to be no further persecution of the patriots. Cautiously, Reb Chaim checked with one of the Polish leaders to confirm whether this wasn't a trick. He was told that it was safe for the officer to come out. Reb Chaim then borrowed a civilian suit from one of the neighbors, just to be on the safe side, and returned home with the good news.

"Sir, you are free," he called out as he opened the large doors of the oven. "Come out, sir. The Russians have declared an amnesty."

The officer crawled out of the oven. He had difficulty standing up erect, but finally managed to pull himself to his full height. In a militaristic fashion he shouted:

"Jew, take off your hat, when you are speaking to a Polish officer!"

Golda finished her story, and the room was quiet for a minute. They had all heard it before, but each time, the ending taught them a lesson.

Mendale looked up from the chessboard. "Yes, no matter what we do for Poland—even if we give our lives fighting for this country—we'll never be equal citizens. I want—I want—I want to go someplace where I can rest my nerves, and when things settle down here, make my plans for going to the land of Israel."

Everyone glanced up in surprise for Mendale had never said anything about leaving. But Golda was pleased. "I think Hamburg may be just the place," she said. "You have a sister there to take care of you, and in Germany there is always good order."

Mendale was relieved. It was always easier to do things if Golda was on your side. "I can't leave yet," he said, not with all these terrorists around here. But when things settle down. . ."

Chapter 26
GERMANY, A DEFEATED NATION (1919–1921)

Winter, 1919. It was over two years since Symcha had arrived in Altona. Things had changed drastically during that time. From a victorious and prosperous nation, Germany had turned into a defeated and starving one.

The Germans had refused to surrender to the Allies, like the Austrians had done on November 3, 1918. They were finally forced to do so on November 11. Then a period of strife began between the political parties within the country. The Spartacist League, led by Rosa Luxemburg and Karl Liebknect, fought the conservative Social Democrats. They hoped to establish a communist regime and changed their name to the Communist Party of Germany. Soon many working people rallied to their cause. They fought bloody battles against their opponents in the streets of the major cities of Germany. They had opposed the war from the very beginning, and now they claimed that all their predictions had proven to be right.

There was political strife between conservatives and Leftists, plus economic dislocation brought about by Allied blockade of German ports. This resulted in hunger and privation for the population.

The scientist, Albert Einstein, who together with Marie Curie, had been a peace activist before the war, but was not a member of any political party, now appealed to the Allied Powers to help the German people, and to feed those who were starving.

The blockade was finally lifted when Germany handed over her naval ships to the Allies and the Kaiser abdicated. But civil strife continued unabated.

One morning Symcha and two friends were on the way to school on the trolley. Suddenly someone shouted to the conductor to stop. The trolley came to a halt, and two young men, wearing red armbands, got on and shoved their way through the crowded car. They approached a dignified man in an officer's uniform, wearing a row of medals. The two young men made him stand up and, while shouting obscenities, tore his medals off his jacket. Then they hauled him off, and the trolley started up again. All along the route to school, the boys could see signs reading "Arbeiter und Soldaten Rat" (Workers and Soldiers Council), with young men congregating under them, shouting slogans. The terrified trolley riders whispered among themselves: "Revolution. . . insurrection. . ."

As Symcha and his friends got off at their school stop, they saw people gathering in the square. A loudspeaker announced that the city was now totally controlled by workers and soldiers, who were going to destroy the war mongers and imperialists who brought Germany so much sorrow. Only after getting rid of those enemies of the people, the orator shouted, would they be able to create a "just society."

As the lesson started, Symcha couldn't help worrying about what he had just seen. What did it mean? Then the custodian came in and whispered something in the teacher's ear. Their teacher turned very pale, but he faced the students, and they could see that he was trying to remain calm. "Boys," he said, "school is dismissed for the day. Hurry home, and don't linger in the streets. The revolution has begun."

A few days later Nehemiah, his uncle, was arrested, accused of being a capitalist. Shainchi was able to obtain his release, but since all private business was forbidden, he thought he had lost his means of livelihood. But within a few days, the leaders of the insurrection, Rosa Luxemburg and Karl Liebknecht were arrested.

In March of 1919, Mendale and Moishe arrived in Hamburg, after a long journey from Poland. Shainchi was waiting for them at the station. She had grown somewhat stouter and looked very German in her city-woman clothes. By then Nehemiah had recovered his losses and was able to open a store in Altona. He had also rented a more spacious apartment.

Mendale was happy to see Symcha, who had grown considerably since he had last seen him. Shainchi now had a little baby girl, Lily. Her three boys were thrilled to have their uncles visiting them. Mendale could hold them spellbound as he told them about his adventures in the war.

Meanwhile, he was looking around for a job or business he could get into, and Nehemiah introduced him to a friend in the fur business. Herman needed an assistant to work with him in the north, where he bought furs from the trappers and wholesalers to resell to furriers in Hamburg. It seemed interesting to Mendale, and he accepted the job.

After a few months of traveling through Schlewig-Holstein, with Herman, Mendale became quite proficient in this business. He learned to recognize the differences in quality of fox, stone marn, muskrat, and seal. Soon he decided to go into business for himself, and he started taking Moishe along, so his brother could share in the eventual profits. But Moishe had no head for business and often lost money in attempts to diversify.

Moishe felt frustrated. He really wanted a career in law, which he thought would enable him to help the Jewish people, the way the American labor lawyer and Zionist Louis Marshall had done. He would have liked to study in Germany but he didn't have the money to attend a German university. Mendale counseled him to continue working in the fur trade, and when he became financially secure, he could continue his studies.

Mendale's business began to prosper, and he was soon able to rent an elegant apartment and furnished it handsomely. He bought Shainchi a gold watch and often took her out to a café in the evenings, for a treat. Mendale was stylish and handsome, and with his excellent German, he was accepted everywhere.

Nehemiah and Shainchi had brought his cousin Pepi to help Shainchi with her growing family. Mendale was attracted to her from the moment they met. Soon he was taking her to the movies, to the theater, and to parties. They took long walks in the park, and one day, rowing on the lake, he kissed her and held her close.

But she moved away from him. "I don't want to get too serious with you, Mendale," she said shyly, "because I'm going to America soon."

Mendale understood. She wanted him to make a commitment. Kissing her was one thing, but he wasn't ready for marriage.

"Pepi, don't go away. Let's get to know each other better. America is far away."

"My cousin wrote me that she would be sending me a Schiffskarte [a ticket for passage] as soon as she has the money"

So this talk of America was serious then. She really meant to go.

"Don't look like that!" she cried. "I don't want to be a nanny forever. It's time for me to have my own family."

Neither of them said another word till he took her back home. After that, when Mendale visited his sister, Pepi would avoid him. The more she tried to ignore him, the more he was drawn to her. He knew that she would stay if he asked her to marry him, but he couldn't bring himself to do it. He tried to forget her. His immediate plan was to return to Poland and then prepare to go to the land of Israel.

The political situation in Germany changed again when the Social Democrats, the Catholic Center, and the Democrats formed a coalition. From this union, there emerged the new and democratic Weimar Republic, which promised to bring a better life to the people,* However this didn't cure the economic ills of Germany. Many people were going hungry. In the countryside to the north, where Mendale spent a great deal of his time, things seemed to improve, but in the rest of Germany distressing poverty was everywhere.

People were talking about the breaking up of the big Junker estates, and giving land to the people. Some feared the Communists. It was said that if they were left to do what they wanted, they would destroy the country, like they had done in Russia. Most were glad that the Kaiser was no longer in power, but were also very doubtful about a democratic system. They said that they weren't used to democracy and didn't understand how it worked. It was felt by all strata of society that the Versailles Treaty had sentenced the German people to a long period of slavery. Poland had gotten mineral rich Upper Silesia, and West Prussia. Alsace and Lorraine went to France. German territories west of the Rhine were occupied by Allied troops. "Where was self-determination," the Germans were asking. "Where were Wilson's 14 points? Was Germany the only country that these humanitarian laws didn't apply to? Was she the only one guilty in the war?" The answers to those questions never came. The Versailles Treaty was finally ratified by the government, but the bulk of the German people never accepted it, or agreed to it.

The desire of the government to fulfill the terms of the Treaty resulted in the polarization of the right and the left. On March 13, 1920, a military clique occupied Berlin and made a right wing politician,

---

* On July 31, 1919, a new democratic constitution was adopted at Weimar.

Wolfgang Kapp, chancellor. The Weimar government fled Berlin, but a general strike of tremendous proportions broke out, all over Germany, and soon Kapp and his group were turned out. Shortly after, a left-wing unit in the Ruhr attempted to start a social revolution, which the army put down. From that point on, the political situation seemed to stabilize, but hard times still hung over Germany like a miasma.

For some time now, Mendale had a new assistant in his work, Oscar, one of Nehemiah's nephews. He had left his wife Lutka behind in Poland, and now wanted to bring her to Altona. Lutka traveled as far as the new German border, but was refused entry. She wired to her husband for help.

At a family meeting, it was decided that Mendale would be the best person to bring her across the border in safety. His appearance and speech were both impressive, and he had military medals to display—now again an asset in Germany.

He traveled first class and wore his best clothes. When he reached the border town where Lutka had been stopped, both German and Polish officials treated him with great respect. A good omen. Poland was now at war with the Soviet Union, and there was an outpouring of patriotism among the people.

Lutka was staying in a small hotel near the station. "You're Mendale?" she said. "My, I've heard so much about you. Do you really think you can help me?" Mendale showed her the papers he had brought from Germany with official permission to join her husband in Altona. "As soon as I've rested and have some lunch," he told her, "I'll start making my rounds to the proper authorities."

The following day, Mendale was back in Altona with Lutka. The young couple smothered him with gratitude for his help, and since Lutka was expecting their first child and apartments were hard to find, Mendale suggested that they stay with him. He had begun to think seriously about leaving Germany for good, and if so, they could have the apartment to themselves.

Mendale had heard from Shainchi that Pepi was about to sail for America. He hadn't seen her in quite a while, and now the spring weather reminded him of the days when he and she had been so close. He decided to see her alone again. He still wasn't ready to propose, but—well, he wanted to see and talk to her.

They met in a café that afternoon. She looked prettier than ever in a new dress. It was short in the latest fashion and revealed her beautiful legs. Her straw hat with spring flowers on it was tilted to one side. For a fleeting moment he felt sorry that he hadn't asked her to marry him. He hated to see her leave. Suddenly he found himself blurting out his own half-formed plans:

"I wrote a letter to Chicago a few days ago, to my brother Meyer—he calls himself Max now. I asked him if he thought it was a good idea for me to visit him in America."

"Moishe would come with me," he went on. "He would study law and I really don't know what I'd do there. What do you think?"

Pepi's face lighted up, but she didn't say a word.

"I think it's wonderful, Mendale! People get rich there sometimes. I'm sure you'd become very rich."

Mendale sipped his coffee and lighted a cigarette.

"I don't know about that," he said. "I'd certainly like to see the United States, but I don't think I'd want to stay for good. Eventually I'm going to the Land of Israel."

Pepi's pretty face sagged. Obviously, Palestine had not occurred to her, and this made her seem remote to Mendale.

"I feel that the time hasn't come for that move, yet," he went on, "but I don't want to stay in Germany. There's so much hunger and political strife, and the leftists and rightists are constantly battling with each other."

"Are you afraid that there'll be a revolution then, like in Russia?" Pepi asked in a small voice.

"Who knows? There's upheaval on all sides. Look at Poland. Pilsudski has just attacked the Ukraine, supported by bloodthirsty Petlura, whose idea of fun is murdering Jews. I'm just fed up with things. I'd like to leave this depraved continent of Europe."

"So come to America with me," Pepi said cocking her head and smiling. "Let's not talk about all these sad things anymore! The music is playing 'Wiener Blut', and I must dance this last dance with the handsomest man I know."

Mendale swept her up in his arms and they felt carefree again, as they used to when they first met.

The following week Pepi sailed for New York on the Hamburg-America Line. He stood waving to her as the ship sailed slowly down the Elbe toward Auxhaven, the North Sea, and the Atlantic. He felt abandoned. Since the war began, happiness had seemed to elude him. He had had brief glimpses of it, and then it vanished.

In August, Pilsudski won a great victory against the Bolsheviks, and things quieted down at Zbora. Mendale received a letter from Max, telling him not to come to America. Things were very difficult in Chicago. He himself was working full-time and studying at the university, and he didn't think Mendale could prosper in the United States as he had in Germany. Besides, he argued, Mendale was better off going home to Zbora, where his business acumen was needed.

Mendale couldn't quite agree with this analysis, and he saw very little hope for his own future on the continent. But he lingered on in Germany, staying away from Altona for long stretches of time. Then he received a letter from his mother. Golda wanted him to come home. She needed his help.

Symcha was finishing the school year with great success, one of the best students in his class. But he was sad when he thought about his Uncle Mendale leaving Altona. Mendale was his favorite uncle and a link with home. He was tired *Realschule*, and he wanted to go home to the fields around the house, his parents, and his brothers and sister, and the new baby that was on the way. He hadn't seen his father, Aron, since the beginning of the war, and he missed him.

His teacher pulled down the wall map with a rattle, jerking Symcha from his daydream. Geography was his favorite subject, particularly the study of distant lands, but today, his teacher, wanted to discuss German geography—the new geography in a Germany stripped of much of its territory.

"As he pointed to these areas on the map, the elderly teacher began to cry."Do you see what has become of our Fatherland?" he said, tears glistening on his cheeks. With a gesture, he indicated the former borders. "All this was Germany, and now look!" Suddenly, Symcha burst out laughing. He tried to stop but couldn't. The teacher stopped crying and shouted, "Heller, what do you find so funny?"

Symcha stood up. "What difference does all this stuff about Germany make to us? We're Jews, and if I'm going to cry, I'll cry for the thousands of our people who have been murdered in this war."

"Heller, what are you saying?"

Symcha raised his voice in defiance. "And something else; Poland has suffered enough. It's time for justice in this world!"

Pale with rage, the teacher pointed to the door. "You will leave this classroom immediately and report to the director, Dr. Carlbach. You insolent nonentity, get out of my sight!"

Uncle Nehemiah was called to school and defended Symcha's right to speak his mind. He told the director that if Smycha were expelled, he would withdraw his own three boys. The director merely suspended Symcha for two days and advised him to save politics for outside the classroom. But when the school year ended, Symcha had made up his mind to return home. He too had been disappointed in Germany.

Chapter 27
A BRIDE FOR MENDALE

In February 1921, Mendale Heller returned to Zbora. He had arrived in Germany with one small suitcase, but was leaving it with an extensive wardrobe, plus gifts for his mother, brother, and the rest of the family. His blond hair was fashionably cut, and he was proudly sporting a small mustache. He had a gold pocket watch that he had bought from an impoverished Russian nobleman, but he kept it hidden, in order not to be too conspicuous.

The conductor who came to check his ticket treated him with utmost courtesy. Seeing the medals that Mendale wore, he confided that he too had been on the Russian front, and they compared experiences. At the Polish border, he had to submit to a check of passports and credentials, but all went well.

When Mendale left his compartment to get some fresh air, he noticed that there was a commotion inside a third class car. Two men, dressed in traditional Jewish clothes, were being pushed and beaten up by soldiers. From their insignia, Mendale identified them as Second Polish Brigade—Hallerczyks.

Mendale opened the car door and slipped inside. Three ruffians were battering a young Jew and a bearded elder. Mendale thought fast. He couldn't fight three men by himself, and besides, other people in the compartment were amused by the scene—no help there. It had to be diplomacy or nothing.

He grabbed the Hallerczyk, who was banging the young man's head against the wall, by the back of the neck, and in the most commanding way he could muster, he shouted: "Shame, shame. Is this the way we Poles celebrate our independence—by hurting defenseless people?"

The ruffian released his victim and began to squirm in Mendale's grasp. "Let go of me, whoever you are."

Mendale turned him around. "You're lucky that I'm in a good mood today, or you'd be a dead man." He shoved him roughly against the other two soldiers who by then had released the old man. "Get out of my sight, you sons of bitches. It's people like you that give our country a bad name"

The people in the car seemed amused at that remark, and Mendale felt that he had gained their sympathy. The other two soldiers sidled out of the car, but their leader turned back to Mendale.

"Who made you the protector of the dirty Jews? A plague on you, dog's blood."

Mendale wanted to appear cool and logical, but he was losing his temper. Fortunately, just then, the conductor appeared and wanted to know what was going on, and in the rush of explanation, Mendale regained his self-possession.

The young man with the battered head tried to thank Mendale in Polish. "You saved our lives."

"It's nothing, nothing. Come, let's wash up."

In the privacy of the washroom, Mendale addressed the men in Yiddish. "Now you can recite the prayer of Thanksgiving on being saved from danger."

Both men looked surprised. They had assumed that Mendale was a righteous gentile.

"I'm Menachem Mendel ben Symcha Shlomo. Shalom aleichem." He extended his hand to the old man.

"Aleichem shalom," the old man answered, and they introduced themselves and told him a little of their history.

Eli, the younger man, had missed being drafted in the war because of his youth but his parents and younger brother had been killed by the Cossacks in the first Russian offensive. Eli hid in the woods and saved himself by begging. After the Russians were defeated, the boy met Reb Duvid when he wandered into a house of prayer.

"We do not believe in brute force," Reb Duvid explained. "We believe in peace and love, and the triumph of good over evil. The barbarism of these times makes us aware that the Messiah is about to appear to redeem the world, and bring Israel back to our own land."

"Reb Duvid," Mendale said dubiously, "with all due respect to your belief, I don't think we can survive to see the Messiah if we don't defend ourselves."

"No, my son," Reb Duvid said. "Using force is not the way. We believe in passive resistance. We resist evil without using physical force. This is a higher way."

"Then, Reb Duvid, you had better be ready to die at any moment, if you run into any more Hallerczyks."

Aron and Golda were waiting for Mendale at the station in Kalusz. They had been driven there in a new sleigh behind two sleek new horses. Obviously the farm was prospering. The war years had taken their toll of Golda, but she still walked erect, and her small body didn't have an extra pound on it. Aron did look older but more serene and sedate.

The countryside was white and still, and the sky a clear blue. Smoke hovered over the thatched roofs of the villagers. How different this was from Altona and the other German places. It all seemed so small—the villages, the houses, everything. It was not at all the way he remembered it.

He suddenly remembered his father's words of long ago:

"We are in exile only temporarily. One day we will return to our own country, the Land of Israel, and no one will be able to mistreat us there." Maybe it was time for him to go to his real home. He couldn't shake off the experience on the train with the Hallerczyks, and told his mother and Aron about it.

Aron tried to still his fears.

"It's a temporary phenomenon, Mendale. When things settle down, people will prosper, and the disorder will cease. We have to be patient and give the republic a chance." Mendale wished that he were as confident as Aron was.

Next evening there was a party, with all the people from the neighboring villages coming to welcome him. Natan Glass, a man who rented a piece of land from Golda, seemed particularly cheerful. He approached Mendale.

"How come that a handsome and accomplished young man like you isn't married? The girls here would be thrilled if you chose one of them."

"I haven't found the one I'm looking for," Mendale answered, and tried to slip away from him, but Natan persisted.

"Do you know something? I have thought of a girl who would be perfect for you. She's beautiful, intelligent, and modest, and she comes from a most distinguished family. Her father is an outstanding scholar and cabalist. She is an only child and the apple of her parents' eye. Her name is Idisel Rosenmann."

"Mr. Glass, I'm not interested in an arranged marriage," Mendale said as politely as he could, but Nathan was not discouraged.

"If you happen to be in Stryj, you might just want to look her up," he said, and turning, he called over his stepson. "Leib, tell Mendale about Idisel Rosenmann."

Leib confirmed everything that Natan had said, and added ruefully, "I wish she would consider me. But I don't have a chance with her."

"I'm not interested in marriage at this point," Mendale said, a trifle testily, "and when the time comes, I'll choose my own bride."

At the end of March, Avrumchi, Mendale's brother-in-law, needed to buy leather for his business, so he asked Mendale to come with him to Stryj. After they had completed their transactions, they went to have lunch at a restaurant near the train station, and there they ran into Icha Charanter, the farmer sergeant, whom Mendale hadn't seen since the war.

Charanter seemed pleased to see Mendale. He began telling some comical stories from the war years and had them both in stitches. Then he became very serious:"Mendale saved my life at the end of the war," he said. "I will never forget what he did for me." He started telling one of the stories, but suddenly changed the subject, and told about his girl friends in town. The young men listened, but didn't really believe all he said.

"Well, what about you, Mendale?" Itcha asked.

"I heard that the girls in Germany are terrific. You must have had a lot of fun there."

"I can't complain, Charanter, but I don't really like German women. They're too hardened and mechanical. I prefer our own girls."

"Well, if that's the case, let me find you the prettiest virgin in Stryj. But if you go for her, I will have to be paid well for my matchmaking."

"Don't bother. You'd just be wasting your time." Then Mendale added, "What's going on here? Everybody I talk to is trying to marry me off."

As if on cue, Avrumchi now joined the conversation. Laichia had asked him to find a wife for Mendale, without letting her brother know what he was up to. And he'd been waiting for an opening. "From what I've heard," he said to Icha, "there's a very special girl in Stryj. Quite a few people are trying to interest Mendale in her, but he refuses to listen."

Mendale stared at his brother-in-law suspiciously. "What is this—a conspiracy?"

Charanter said, "Well, who is this girl?"

"Her name is Idisel Rosenmann."

"Idisel Rosenmann! Why, the owner of this very restaurant knows this Idisel—she's a close friend of his daughter Blima."

Mendale stared at him. "What a coincidence," he said ironically.

"Now don't be difficult, Heller. This is beautiful girl with lots of suitors. Let me call Reb Yosef over, and we can find out more about her."

Charanter got up and went to speak to the owner. Soon he brought him over to the table. The older man was friendly and confirmed all that Icha had said. "My daughter, Blima, is married now and lives in Vienna," he told them, "so I don't see Idisel as often as I used to. But this girl is a gem. She is a beauty, both in body and in spirit." He stopped, resumed awkwardly, "But excuse me, pan Heller, her father Reb Shaul, would not even consider a prospective son-in-law who is not learned in the Torah. I see by your clothes that you are a modern man. Forgive me, but you'd only be refused."

Mendale smiled. Now that he'd been refused, he was beginning to get interested.

"Well, now, this is becoming a challenge." Then he added, "as a small boy, I studied with Rabbi Rosenfeld, who lived with us on our estate for many years. His great erudition is well known, and he inspired me and my brothers with a desire to continue with our studies always."

He rattled off some of the subjects he had studied under that earnest young scholar, and Reb Yosef listened carefully.

"There is another obstacle, Pan Heller," he finally said. "I'm not sure that Reb Shaul would consent to his daughter marrying a man from the country. As you probably know, many city people look down on folks from the villages. Well, even the Rosenmanns might have that prejudice." Reb Yosef stopped when he saw the expression on Mendale's face. Then he continued in a more cheerful vein: "But what am I talking about? You haven't even seen the girl, nor has she seen you. You might not like each other at all, so all these factors will have no meaning."

Mendale didn't say a word. He had decided that he was going to meet Idisel, come hell or high water. So when Reb Yosef suggested, "I could send a message to Reb Shaul that you would like to meet Idisel after prayers tonight," he readily agreed.

Reb Yosef went back to the counter and wrote a note, which he sent off by one of his waiters. He then returned to the table with a bottle of slivovitz and four small glasses.

"L'Chaim," he said joyfully. "To the success of your mission, Pan Heller." They all emptied their glasses in one shot. They were still chatting when the waiter returned with the message. The Rosenmanns would be pleased to receive Mendale that evening.

It was four o'clock. They planned to take a walk, make some purchases of gifts, then clean up at their hotel before prayers, but suddenly Itcha grabbed Mendale's arm. "There she goes. That's Idisel."

The young girl disappeared into a doorway before Mendale could really see her. All he noticed was her lovely figure, but her face had been hidden by her shawl. His enthusiasm diminished. This wonder woman turned out, after all, to be fairly ordinary. He really didn't feel like going to the Rosenmanns at six.

At the cafe, a group of Charanter's friends arrived. One of them, a member of Betar, was leaving for the Land of Israel. He was charming, as well as eloquent, and tried to convince the others to go with him. He talked about Jabotinsky, and referred to him as his teacher. Jabotinsky had been released from Acre Prison in Palestine, and he needed young men to protect the Jewish settlements, and communities in the Land of Israel, from Arab attacks. Again Mendale was caught up in his dream of Zion.

Back at his hotel room, Mendale made himself presentable, then followed Icha through the streets of Stryj, en route to their appointment.They passed the Rosenmann's store. It was a small grocery, the windows tastefully decorated with products from Hungary displaying bags of spices and dried fruit. As they entered the hall of the house, they could smell freshly baked cake and bread.

Suya, Idisel's mother, greeted them. She was tall and majestic and wore a wig, her own golden blond curls showing at the hairline, and looked elegant in a graceful purple dress.

Charanter took his leave, explaining that he had only come to show his friend the way. Suya showed Mendale into the living room.

Reb Shaul stood up to welcome his guest. He was a man of short stature, shorter than his wife. A number of books were spread out on the table, where he had apparently been studying.

"Blessed is he who has come to us," he said. They shook hands, and Reb Shaul motioned for Mendale to sit down, and the younger man had a chance to observe him. He had a brown beard and dreamy hazel eyes, and he seemed kind and good-humored.

"My daughter will be here shortly. Meanwhile, I'd like you to tell me about yourself." he said.

Mendale began describing his background, his upbringing, and the war years. He hadn't really intended to talk that much, but somehow found himself speaking at length about many things. He was being encouraged to do this by his attentive listener.

Now Reb Shaul asked him about his studies of the Torah, and Mendale quoted many passages from the Scriptures, naming chapter and verse. When the older man realized the extent of Mendale's knowledge, he asked him a number of questions about Rashi's contribution toward understanding of the law. When he was satisfied with the answers, he turned to a discussion of "the Ari." Reb Shaul spoke of him as "My guide and teacher," although Mendale knew that the Cabalist,* Rabbi Isaac Luria, known as the Ari, had lived in the sixteenth century, in Safed, in the Land of Israel.

"My boy," the older man continued, "when I decided to study Cabala as a very young man, I had to obtain my father's permission, of course. But I was also examined by a committee of very learned rabbis. They asked me many questions and probed into every crevice of my being, to determine if I was worthy, and if I possessed the emotional stability required. They wanted to be sure that I would not break down under the weight of this new experience. A prospective student had to be psychologically strong, for he was about to embark on a voyage into the

---

* Believer in ancient Jewish mysticism. The Ari was a central figure in the evolving ideas of a new way of looking at the Cabala.

depth of hitherto undiscovered mysteries. Then the rabbis tested me about my belief in the Creator. The study of the Cabala, as you probably know, has turned some men into atheists, because they began to believe only in the symbols, and their own power, rather than in the totality of the mystical concepts, whose ultimate aim is communion with the Almighty, and loss of the "self." The rabbis spoke to me, each in his turn, about meditation, and asked me if I had experienced it. I told them that I had already had some knowledge of that subject and that I had been practicing some of the meditation exercises. That seemed to please them, but one of the elders suggested that I had a great deal to learn in that realm. Finally he expounded on the self-concealing and self-revealing aspects of the Creator.

"The rabbis finally adjourned, and I had to wait for their verdict. My fate hung in the balance, but I didn't despair. My father was with me. He always imbued me with courage. After about half an hour, I was called back. They asked my father to come as well. The same rabbi who had found me lacking in meditation, spoke for the entire committee. He stated that they had found me to be strong in my faith in the Almighty, and that I had passed all the other tests they had placed before me. I was elated to enter the world of Cabala. I approached it with purity of heart, with awe, and with great reverence." Reb Shaul pronounced the last words with awe.

Now the door opened and the girl came in.

Her father's voice fell silent, and as the two men rose, Mendale was conscious only of two violet blue eyes. He was transfixed, only dully aware of her father's introduction. "My daughter, Idisel. . ."

He must have stammered something, but he could not remember what it was. He could not seem to get enough of looking at her. She was a striking beauty of medium height and curvaceous figure. Her hair was curly and golden brown and her skin was flawless, touched with a natural rosy glow. She smiled as they shook hands then sat down demurely at the table opposite him.

Somebody—perhaps the girl herself—asked him about himself, so he began a rambling and mechanical narrative of his many adventures. It was only when he strayed into the suffering of the Jews that he had seen, as each side in the battles took out its defeats and frustrations on them, that he came momentarily alive.

Idisel seemed to hang on every word, but she made no comment. After a moment of silence, her mother took up their war story:

"When the Russians came to Stryj, they took all our men away. They said that they were taking them to work. They came into our house, pointed a gun at Shaul's back, and ordered him to come with them. I looked out of the window, and saw a long column of our men led by Cossacks on horseback. The two Cossacks who'd come in didn't touch men and they didn't go into the kitchen, the Blessed One be praised.

"We had hidden Idisel in the small cellar near the oven when we heard the Cossack coming. When I saw that everybody had gone, I then went over to the cellar door and let Idisel out. She had heard every word of what the Cossacks had said. 'Mother,' she said to me. 'We must follow them and see what these beasts are going to do to father. Maybe I can get him released.' I protested. The thought of losing them both was too much for me to bear. 'Mother, don't cry.' she said. 'I have a plan.'

"She quickly smeared soot from the wood stove all over her face, put on some old clothing, and tied on an old flowered kerchief that almost entire covered her face. She took off her shoes and stockings and bent over. She really looked like an old Ukrainian peasant. She ran out and after about half an hour, caught up with the column.

"She found her father, and walked alongside him until they came to a wooded area, where the Cossacks began dividing them into groups for cutting wood. Reb Shaul urged her to leave quickly before his turn came for selection. He said that they had not been beaten on the way nor had anyone been killed. Well, at least we knew where he was. So she whispered good-bye and left him.

"We tried to get a group of old men together," her mother continued, "to go to the Russian authorities and bargain for their release, but everyone was afraid. Within a few days the Russians realized that all the stores were closed, everyone was hiding behind bolted doors, and no business was being done, so they released the men. We, the whole family, decided to leave our homes and flee west. These people are barbarians, and we weren't going to take any chances with our lives under such a cruel rule. We made our way to Czechoslovakia, dressed as peasants, and we did not return until the war was over."

"You showed great courage, Pani Rosenmann. You and your daughter are true heroines."

"On the contrary," Idisel said spiritedly, "I was terribly afraid, I wouldn't have gone if it hadn't been so important."

"Panna Ido," Mendale said, addressing Idisel for the first time, using her Polish name, "courage is not being without fear. Courage is doing what must be done *despite* fear."

There was a moment of silence, then Suya said briskly, "That's enough now about war and sadness. Let's get something to eat."

They were seated at the table, laughing and chatting gaily, when Avrumchi arrived. It was time for them to return to the hotel.

Mendale shrugged himself into his coat, which Idisel held, and whispered hastily into her ear: "Will you have me as your husband, Idisel?"

She seemed speechless for a minute. Usually there were long preliminary discussions before this kind of a declaration. But suddenly she started laughing, and when she finally stopped, she whispered back into his ear: "Yes, yes, with all my heart."

In the few hours he was with her, this girl had totally bewitched him. He was like a man under a spell. He couldn't quite believe that this exquisite young woman had consented to be his wife. He had such fears that her father might yet oppose the marriage, that he couldn't wait for the long formal preliminaries.

"Reb Shaul," he said straight out, "when can we write the engagement contract? Your daughter pleases me very much. I want to marry her."

Consent was given. Reb Shaul and Suya seemed overjoyed. They drank "L'Chaim," and the young couple was left to discuss their plans.

When Mendale returned to Zbora the following day and told Golda about Idisel, his mother was overjoyed. They all drank a toast to the bride and groom at dinner time. The following day Golda sent for the dressmaker to sew a new silk dress for her for the engagement, which was to take place in two weeks.

On the appointed day, Mendale, looking extremely elegant, and Golda in her new outfit, were driven to the station by Aron. En route, one of the horses hurt his leg against a rock, and this slowed them down, so that when they arrived at the station, the train to Stryj had just pulled out. Mendale was upset at first, but then said to his mother:

"Perhaps this delay is a sign that I acted too hastily. I really don't know Idisel very well. Maybe we need some time to get to know each other better, before we announce our engagement."

Golda looked at in disbelief. "Did you or didn't you make an appointment with the Rosenmanns for the engagement today?" she demanded angrily.

"I did, Mother, but this may be an opportunity to postpone everything for a while." Mendale suddenly felt trapped by this commitment, and yet he didn't want to lose Idisel entirely. He added, "I need more time, Mother. Try to understand my feelings."

"I understand nothing of what is happening here," she snapped.

"I'm simply saying that I will not be going to Stryj today."

"I consider your behavior entire irresponsible!" she stormed at him. "You made a promise to be in Stryj for the engagement today. If you don't appear, you will embarrass the Rosenmanns and especially Idisel, whom you told me you were in love with. They must have invited guests and prepared food for the occasion. They may never forgive you, and you'll lose her."

"Sorry, Mother, I'm not going. Maybe tomorrow I'll feel differently, but right now the answer is negative."

Golda realized that her son wasn't going to change his mind. "Well, I'll go to the Rosenmanns and try to give some excuse for your failing to keep your promise. Shall I tell them that you have changed your mind about the girl?"

"No, Mother, I haven't. I just want to think about it," Mendale said. "I'll stay in Kalusz at the Hotel Excelsior overnight, and wait for you to return."

Golda got on the next train and arrived at the Rosenmanns late in the afternoon. She was very pleased with Idisel and impressed with her parents. Mendale would be marrying up in Jewish society and getting a beautiful bride in the bargain. Golda excused Mendale's absence as something that couldn't be helped: They had missed the train; he was tired and disappointed, and didn't feel well. The war had made him somewhat moody and superstitious. He believed that it was fated that he shouldn't go to Stryj today. Then she made a suggestion:

"Why don't you come with me to Kalusz tomorrow morning? We could have the engagement where Mendale is staying."

The Rosenmanns had been deeply humiliated, and Reb Shaul wasn't sure that it was a good idea, but he and Suya finally consented to go. It took them a long time to persuade Idisel, however; she was hurt and upset, but in the end she said that she would go because she had made a promise.

Golda slept over at the Rosenmanns that night, and next morning they took the train to Kalusz. They arrived in the early afternoon. Mendale had just come down to have his lunch, when he was called to the lobby. The minute he saw Idisel again, looking so downcast, he was bitterly sorry that he had made her suffer.

"Forgive me," he said, kissing her hand. He took her aside and sat down on the couch with her. "I have become very a moody person since the war. Perhaps it's good that you found this out before it's too late. Do you still want to go through with the engagement?"

She looked at him sadly: "I've committed myself to you. I don't break my promises easily." Her eyes filled with tears, but she managed a smile and added: "You are my *zivik,** so let's make the best of it."

They now went hand in hand to where their parents were waiting. Mendale apologized to Reb Shaul and Suya, and asked everyone to come to his room to write the engagement contract.

They went upstairs. Golda was anxious to get things going without any further delay, but she wanted everything spelled out.

"There is one matter that we haven't discussed yet at all," she said to Reb Shaul. "I'm talking about the dowry."

Reb Shaul looked down, as though pained by the statement.

"Unfortunately, I'm not a rich man," he said. "I'm a storekeeper of modest means. But I do possess one great treasure, my only child, Idisel. She will bring joy and tranquility into your house. She is pure, gentle, and lovely, as you can see." He now turned to Mendale: "You will get my most prized possession when you marry her, and I will have a son at last."

---

* According to legend, when a child is born, the angels call out the name of its betrothed and true love.

Mendale had heard in Stryj that Reb Shaul was poor. Although he owned a store, he could never refuse people when they asked for credit. Many took advantage of his kindness, and as a result, he was barely keeping his head above water.

"Reb Shaul," he said, "I'm sorry my mother brought up this subject." He shot an angry glance at Golda. "If I'd been interested in a dowry, I would have discussed it with you when I proposed to your daughter. I have enough money for all our future needs. Please don't worry about a dowry."

"My Idisel will have a complete trousseau," Suya put in loftily. "She will have linens, pillows, down quilts, clothing, and many valuable family heirlooms. She shall have some of the things from her grandmother Tova, who died in the Land of Israel." Then she added proudly, "And she will have a wedding befitting a daughter of Reb Shaul Hakohen Rosenmann. You can rest assured, Frau* Heller—there will be nothing lacking."

"Well," Mendale pressed. "Let's get started on the contract."

The young couple parted the next day. She was to come to visit him in Zbora the following week.

---

* Mrs. in Yiddish.

The engagement picture of Idisel Rosenmann and Mendale Heller, 1922.

Chapter 28
CITY, TOWN, OR COUNTRY

As Idisel's carriage drew near Zbora, the countryside was aglow with thousands of spring flowers: daisies, chamomile blossoms, and corn-flowers. Soon she saw a rider approaching them. It was Mendale on horseback, dressed in English fashion, in riding breeches, black boots and a bowler hat. He looked like the dashing hero of a romantic novel. Idisel ordered the driver to stop, Mendale dismounted, jumped into the carriage, and covered her face with kisses.

"Welcome, my beautiful girl," he said. "I dreamed about this moment for the entire week."

He only stopped kissing her when the driver looked around and cleared his throat. "All right," Mendale said. "Drive on." With the saddle horse hitched behind, they drove on to the house.

"Why are you so serious all of a sudden?" she heard Mendale asking, and awoke with a start, realizing that she had been brooding a lit-tle.

"I was thinking of long ago, but now my life will be altogether dif-ferent with you. No more sadness," she replied, and began to smile again. She was beginning to care deeply for the man sitting next to her. He was a ray of sunshine in her life. She began to laugh out of sheer joy.

By the time they rode into the courtyard of the farm, Idisel's clothing was quite dusty from the open carriage ride. After she met the entire family, she changed into a white batiste dress, and white stockings. She was a picture to behold, and Mendale couldn't take his eyes off her. There was a holiday spirit about the house. A table was set on the veranda with all the good products of the countryside: fresh fish from the lake, cold sorrel soup, parsleyed potatoes, huge bowls of wild strawberries, sour cream in an even larger bowl, brown bread, and fresh butter. After lunch everyone else rested, but Mendale took Idisel for a walk and showed her his favorite places in the woods behind their house.

Next day was Friday, and preparations had to be made for the Sabbath. Golda suggested that the young couple go out to the woods for a picnic, but Idisel wouldn't hear of it. She wanted to show Mendale that she could cook.

While Golda was braiding the Sabbath bread, Idisel prepared a Viennese cake, which she filled with strawberry preserves. She beat the meringue quickly and skillfully. She made sure that the oven was the right temperature, as the meringue had to be only very slightly browned. She asked permission to prepare the *kugel*, for which she made a very thin dough and filled it with fresh cherries.

Now everyone bathed, and the men and boys got ready to pray. Golda dressed in her new dress and wore a gold watch around her neck. She told Idisel that Mendale had brought it for her from Germany. Idisel also had a new dress. It was lavender colored and matched her eyes.

When the men returned from their prayers and everyone was gathered for the Sabbath meal, Mendale took a small box out of his pocket. He took Idisel's hand, opened the box, and she saw a diamond ring set in gold.

"This ring is for you, Idisel," he said, putting it on her finger. Idisel turned a lovely shade of rose pink. "Oh, Mendale. I've never had anything so beautiful!"

"Nothing can compare to your beauty, Idisel," he said. "You make this diamond look like glass."

Now everyone applauded and gathered around to examine the ring more closely. Afterward they said the appropriate prayers, and then sat down to eat. In between courses they gleefully sang Sabbath songs. Idisel felt very much a part of this boisterous happy family. As an only child, she was accustomed to quiet and decorum.

During Saturday lunch everyone praised Idisel's dishes. Mendale said that he had never eaten such a delicious cake before, and that pleased her most. After the meal, everyone napped, except Mendale and Idisel. They sneaked out and ran into the fields. They lay down to rest in the tall grass and began to make love, while butterflies flew lazily about them.

Reb Shaul stayed up late into the night studying. He was getting very tired, and the words on the page were beginning to blur. He closed his eyes and thought of Idisel. She was away in Zbora for almost a week now, and he missed her. He realized that he too was entering a new phase in his existence.

He was 52, but suddenly felt very old. He had hoped that Mendale wouldn't insist on taking Idisel to live in Zbora after the wedding. But the Torah clearly stated that a wife must follow her husband. But Suya. . . he would still have Suya. After all these years, he still loved Suya with the same fervent love of long ago. "I remember you at our aspausals," he whispered a quote from the Bible. And, indeed, he saw her again as she was when they first met.

She was tall, slim, and had a shock of reddish blond hair. She was devastatingly beautiful. Both sets of parents were already making arrangements for the wedding, when she walked in. It was obvious that the two families were well matched. His father was a wealthy man, who owned a wholesale hardware store in Skole, at the foothills of the Carpathian Mountains. He was also a leader of the community, and a great scholar. Suya was the daughter of well-to-do parents and scholars, who supported yeshivot* in the Holy Land, in Jerusalem and Safed.

The parents were now discussing the dowry, but the young people hadn't even said a word to each other. They sat at a separate table seemingly forgotten by their elders. Shaul couldn't keep still any more. He couldn't believe that a girl as beautiful as Suya would consent to be his wife. From his limited experience, he knew that very beautiful people seemed to be lacking in character. He decided to talk to her.

"I know that I'm not supposed to say this yet, because custom doesn't permit it," he said. But I find you very pretty, *Fraulein*** Suya," he whispered.

She smiled and said: "I hope that you will find my character and personality to your liking, as well." Her large blue eyes sparkled as she talked.

Shaul was totally enchanted by her.

"Still, I'm amazed that you would consider marriage to a quiet scholar like me. You must have many worldly and handsome suitors."

"I decided to become your wife before I even met you," she answered. "The matchmaker and others told me about your gentle spirit and your kindness. When I saw your picture, I knew that you were the

---

*   Universities for the study of theology.

** Miss in Yiddish.

right man for me. Our parents agree that we're a good match, and want us to be married. That is very important to me."

Now she stood up as though waiting for their parents to finish. She smiled at him encouragingly. He got up too, as though drawn by a magnet. He really wanted to hug her but that wasn't permitted. She too seemed to feel the same way. Her face became very flushed, and she whispered, looking at him lovingly:

"I will be very proud to be your wife, Shaul Hakohen Rosenmann. I hope that you will grow to love me."

When their parents interrupted to tell them that everything had been arranged, and only their consent was required, they both answered at the same time: "Yes, yes."

Shaul felt that he was the luckiest man on earth. Suya was enchanting and he was also getting a sizable dowry from her parents. What surprised him more was that he had fallen in love with her.

Through the many tribulations that were to follow their marriage, they drew even closer. First, the death of their two boys within one year, and then the war years, and the suffering and dislocation, made their love even stronger. Suya was his refuge. She understood him better than he understood himself. She was "a woman of valor," as it is said.

He seemed to be wide awake now, and went back to study the page he had read earlier without true comprehension. After some time, he fell asleep, his head leaning in the book.

He woke up in the middle of the night. But between waking and sleeping, it seemed to him that he was in Czordkow, at his Rebbe's court. He recalled Rabbi Israel saying to him:

"Shaul, when you are near me, my soul rejoices." He felt the same way about his Rebbe. He was a Tzadik, a holy man of great purity. Reb Shaul longed to be near him and to hear his words of wisdom. He would tell him about Idisel's engagement, and ask for his blessing. Reb Shaul now resolved to visit Rebbe Israel the following Sabbath.

The April sun was setting when Reb Shaul arrived at the Rebbe's court in Czordkow. He was a familiar figure to the Rebbe's entourage, just as his own father had been at the court of Rebbe Israel's father, Rebbe David Moses of blessed memory. The older Rebbe was considered to be one of the great men of his time in Poland.

As Reb Shaul walked up the marble stairs of the great house, he remembered with nostalgia, when he'd come to this court for the first time. . . when he became bar Mitzvah. The opulence and riches of the court were dazzling to the boy. When Shaul and his father entered the great hall, Rebbe David Moses was seated on a golden throne, like a king.

Shaul and his father were announced with great pomp by the chamberlain. Rebbe David Moses motioned for them to get close. He stood up to shake hands with Reb Yosef, Shaul's father. Then he shook hands with the boy, saying:

"Shaul ben Yosef Hakohen, you are about to become Bar Mitzvah. Soon you will have the responsibility of fulfilling all the commandments. I will have the honor to initiate you into a new period of your life." The Rebbe now sat down, and continued: "It has been told me that you are already an outstanding scholar, and that you know a great part of the Torah by heart. What's more, I hear that you have a deep understanding of its teaching, and can expound about it in a manner that amazes your teachers. I, too, would like to hear some words of your wisdom." He stopped and waited for Shaul to speak.

Shaul's voice trembled, but he had to answer as best as he could.

"My beloved Rebbe Davis Moses. You are one of the wisest, holiest, and compassionate men in the world. How can I, with my humble and limited knowledge, enlighten you?"

The Rebbe looked at him kindly. Then Shaul felt his warm embrace, as the holy man said:

"The answer you gave me tells me a great deal about you. There will be a time to discuss Torah later. Reb Yosef, you are justly proud of this young *talmid haham* (wise student)." Then, turning to Shaul, he said:

"Let me bless you, my son."

The gentle hands of the Rebbe and his prayer, filled Shaul with a spirit of peace, that he never experienced before. When his father and he left the throne area, Shaul was in a state of ecstasy.

When he recovered later, Shaul thanked his father for bringing him to the Rebbe. He had always heard about the wonders of the Rebbe's court, and now he had an opportunity to see it.

Reb Yosef was one of Rebbe David Moses' staunchest supporters and followers. He contributed a great deal of money for the upkeep of the court, as his own father, Reb Gedalia Regirer (the leader), of blessed memory, had done before him. The Rebbe had many wealthy followers, who contributed generously to his budget. But unlike the others, Reb Yosef was not only rich, but a learned scholar. When he visited Czordkow, he always sat on the Rebbe's right. This was the greatest honor of him.

Reb Shaul remembered that before he was accepted for the study of Cabala, it was Rebbe Davis Moses who encouraged him to be tested. He saw the old Rebbe for the last time after his engagement to Suya. By then Rebbe Davis Moses looked very ancient, but was still full possession of his faculties. He told Reb Shaul how proud he was of him and his accomplishments. He had followed Shaul's progress very closely. Shaul had for many years kept up a correspondence with Israel, the Rebbe's son. It was through him that the old Rebbe knew so much about Shaul. After Rebbe Davis Moses' death, Israel became the Rebbe of Czordkow. Shaul and he now drew even closer. Whenever Shaul came to the court at Czordkow, he was received by the Rebbe with great honor. Since the war, Shaul could no longer send contributions to his Rebbe, but he was still as welcome as before.

Today Rebbe Israel greeted Shaul in the great hall again, but it no longer was splendid as in Shaul's youth. It was time for the evening prayer, and the two friends walked to the court's house of prayer, the Claus. Afterwards they had a light supper together in the Rebbe's study. The next day would be a very busy one for Rebbe Israel, as many of his Hasidim would be coming to share the Sabbath with him, and Shaul and he would have little opportunity to talk.

Their conversation now turned to the engagement of Idisel and Mendale. Reb Shaul told his friend about his future son-in-law. He ended by saying:

"Although Menachem Mendel was raised on a farm, he is very learned in the Torah, and has a worldly education as well. He fought in the war, but his experiences have not made him cruel. On the contrary, he seems to be more compassionate because of what he lived through. They make a beautiful pair, like two angels."

"May the Creator bring them great joy together, and many grandchildren for you, my friend." Rebbe Israel said.

"My Idisel asked me to talk to you about a certain matter that seems very important to her," Reb Shaul said. "But right now it seems so trivial." He stopped and hesitated for a moment.

"If it's important to her, how could it possibly be trivial, Shaul? What is it? Tell me." the Rebbe said.

"Well, Idisel doesn't want to cut her hair off and put on a wig, as is customary. When she asked me permission I couldn't bring myself to let her have her way, and break with tradition. What do you advise, Rebbe Israel?"

The Rebbe began to laugh, and said:

"You know Shaul, that I believe in being modern if it doesn't conflict with the teachings of the Torah. I was laughing just now, because my own daughter has made the same request. I must admit that I was somewhat shocked at first, but I tried to approach the subject logically. I brought up my daughter to think for herself. She is educated and knows what's going on in the world. You have brought up Idisel the same way. Both these girls are very intelligent. We must consider the views and aspirations of the new generation, especially after all our suffering in the war. After considering carefully my daughter's decision, I gave her permission to keep her own hair. You should do the same, Shaul."

Shaul smiled. "I certainly will Rebbe Israel. Idisel will be overjoyed with your verdict."

Now the Rebbe had something unpleasant to tell his friend. He was planning to move his court to Vienna. The war years had caused so much change in the lives of his followers. Many of them could no longer contribute, and others had moved away from Poland to the capital of Austria. They were concerned about his safety, if there should be another Ukrainian uprising. The cost of keeping up his court had reached enormous proportions, and he had to rely mainly on his Viennese followers for most of his income. Rebbe Israel became very sad.

"I don't like to leave Czordkow. It's always been my home. Who will help the poor followers with a few zlotys,* or a bit of advice? What am I to do, my dear friend?"

---

* Polish currency.

Shaul was saddened by this news. He would miss his Rebbe and friend. Nothing would be the same any more. He was searching for words of comfort, and he finally said:

"Rebbe Israel, Vienna is a beautiful city, and there are many devout people there. They need your holy presence there to guide them, because there is a great deal of perversity and evil in the city as well. Your Hasidim will make you feel at home in no time. They will be proud to have you among them. As for me, I promise that I will come to see you even in Vienna, my dear friend."

The Rebbe thanked Shaul for his comforting words, and added:

"It was ordained by the Almighty that his people Israel should be wanderers, until he redeems us, and brings us back to our land. It is my fate too, for I am his humble servant and a member of his chosen people.

"My disciple, Dr. Chaim, tells me that he and other professional men are creating a special fund, so I can come back to Poland from time to time. You know that most of my Hasidim here are poor, and can't afford to come to Vienna, but our charity for them will continue, with the Creator's help. They are, however, loyal and steadfast in spirit, and need less guidance than the Viennese Jews.

"I'm grateful to the Almighty for all his blessings. I thank Him tonight, especially for your friendship, Shaul, my brother."

It was Saturday, and time for the second meal of the Sabbath. Rebbe Israel was seated at the head of a large table, which was covered with a white damask cloth. His followers sat around him. Reb Shaul, sitting on his right, noticed that the Rebbe didn't speak much, but he joined, wholeheartedly, in the singing in praise of the Holy Sabbath. He and Rebbe Israel harmonized, as they had always done before, through some of the joyful passages. Reb Shaul had a deep melodic voice, and the Rebbe was a tenor. They tried to be happy, for it is written that on the Sabbath one mustn't dwell on sadness, but rather must rejoice.

It was sweet to be at the Rebbe's table. All the cares of the weekday world were forgotten, as the Hasidim united in spiritual uplifting togetherness. Rebbe Israel shared his food with them, eating only a morsel of each dish that was served for him. The Hasidim then passed the plate around, eating of the food that they had shared with this holy man, and feeling blessed.

After the closing prayer, the dancing began, as all joined arms and sang "V'taher Libenu."

"Let our hearts serve You with purity." They kept chanting the same few words again and again, until they were in a trance. Rebbe Israel and Reb Shaul were thrust in the middle of the circle and, holding each other's arms, they danced and sang, entranced as well.

After rejoicing, everyone went to rest and nap, in order to be ready for the events of the evening.

Reb Shaul planned to take leave that evening, after the Melaveh Malkah, the Farewell to the departing Sabbath Queen. Rebbe Israel finished the prayer over the wine. This separated the Holy Sabbath from the rest of the week. He put out the flame on the two braided candles with great ceremony. He was then handed the spice box. He held it lovingly for a moment, inhaling its fragrance. He seemed transported to another world. These spices represent the spiritual beauty of the soul, the Sabbath soul, to which he was saying farewell. He then passed around the spice box, a small silver tower, to his Hasidim. He now began to sing the closing song, "Hamavdil ben Kodesh," and the Hasidim joined in with a great chorus.

Rebbe Israel blessed all the congregation. When he had finished, he laid his hands on Reb Shaul's head, and said:

"A special blessing for you Reb Shaul ben Yosef Hakohen. My love for you may be compared to David's love for Jonathan. May we always keep that love in our hearts." He stopped for a moment as though controlling his emotions, and then continued. "May the Creator, the source of all our blessing, watch over you and your family. May He bestow His loving kindness on your dear wife, Suya, and on your daughter Idisel, and her groom Menachem Mendel. May they find peace and harmony under the bridal canopy."

Rebbe Israel embraced Reb Shaul warmly. They both felt that they were seeing each other for the last time, but neither dared to phrase that fear in words. Reb Shaul didn't cry easily, but seeing the Rebbe so moved, he had to fight back his own tears.

Happy as the young couple were at being together, it soon became evident that Idisel was not pleased about the prospect of living in Zbora. The war years had left the Rosenmanns rattled and anxious. Her father's danger, the many months they had spent as refugees, the constant fear for one another's safety—all those experiences had proved how very important her parents were to her.

Golda tried to persuade Idisel that country living was really wonderful, especially for raising a family, and Idisel tried to be tactful about her feelings. She was accustomed to city life, she pointed out, and her parents had no other children. She liked the country—to visit, perhaps even for an entire summer—but for living—well, she was a city girl. Her future mother-in-law was not at all pleased, but her future husband was on her side.

Mendale agreed that village life was no longer for him. His success as a businessman in Germany had proved very challenging, and he made up his mind that, after the wedding, he would go into business in Stryj. But how to break the news to Golda?

Fortunately, she herself gave him the opening. It was the beginning of July, and Mendale had just returned from a visit to Idisel, when Golda called him and Aron in to discuss financial matters. She said that the income from their properties was twice as much as it had been the year before, and that they were doing very well, better than she had ever expected.

"So," she said, "this is a good time for me to retire."

"Retire?" they echoed in astonishment.

"Yes, I'm an old woman now—no, no, don't protest— and I feel tired most of the time. I want to turn the farm over to you two and be a lady of leisure."

Mendale felt that this was the proper time to break the news of his decision to his mother. He added that he no longer liked the village atmosphere. The Lemkes and Ukrainians had become even more hostile. They were totally frustrated by Pilsudski's victory, and knew that their dream of independence was shattered. Mendale wanted to live in the more peaceful atmosphere of the city. He concluded finally by saying:

"Many of our people are leaving this area. I believe that it is in our interest to put the property up for sale."

It cut Golda like a knife. She couldn't say a word. Aron, obviously upset, spoke for her:

"Just as we have built this place up, with our hard work and sacrifice, you want us to give it up?"

"Aron, you know very well what a precarious area this is," Mendale answered him. "Do you want to bring up your children in a part of Poland where there's always political trouble? Or are you going to try for some stability for your family? You should not be blinded by economic factors alone."

Aron listened and then said: "Let's think about what you've just proposed. Frankly, I'm too shocked at the moment to make any logical decision. I think Mother feels the same way too. When we've had a chance to sleep on it, We can come to a more wise conclusion." Then he added: "If you've definitely decided to leave for good, it will be difficult to keep this place. We've increased our holding, with the hope that you'd stay. We've also rented out some of our less desirable land. All this needs administration, and tending to. I don't think we can continue without your help, Mendale, so you think over your idea of leaving, as well."

Golda listened and said absolutely nothing. She couldn't bear the thought of giving up her home. What would she do now? She would be totally lost without her land. At 50, she would have to start anew. A soft breeze coming through the window interrupted her thoughts. It was the smell of new cut hay. Would she ever be able to live in the city? Was her life ending? She decided not to dwell on morbid thoughts, and said: "Sons, let's not talk about this any more tonight. Let's go out and get some fresh air."

The stars filled the sky. It seemed that if you reached out your hand, you could touch them. They sat on the verandah, and contemplated the beauty of the clear night. Mendale remembered again the things his father had said about how temporary their stay was in exile. Idisel and he would live near her parents, until they made enough money to go to the Land of Israel, all four of them. Idisel shared his dream. She even spoke modern Hebrew. His Hebrew was of the Torah, but she had promised to teach him the new words and the Sephardic pronunciation. They had a clear plan at last, a true direction.

The next morning, at breakfast, Golda was pale and looked tired, but she had made her decision. "People," she addressed the whole family, "we have decided to sell the farm."

Aron had pondered the question through most of the night and had been won over by Mendale's argument. His change of mind had been the deciding factor for Golda.

Three brothers came to look at the Hellers' property. They were Lemkes, but not like the ones who lived in the village. They arrived in a carriage and were dressed in American ready-made clothes. They brought a smart-looking city lawyer with them.

After they looked over the land, the buildings, and the inventory, Golda invited them to the main house for refreshments. Dun, who seemed to be the oldest among the brothers, was their spokesman. The lawyer only listened, and from time to time whispered something into a Lemke's ear.

Dun told the Hellers that he and his brothers came from the mountains, about eighty kilometers away, but that he had just recently returned from America. "We worked in Detroit for eleven years and saved our money so we could come back to our own country and buy ourselves a real farm."

"I have a son in America, too," Golda said. "In Chicago. Is that anywhere near this—this whatever-you-said?"

"About four hundred fifty kilometers—that's nothing in America. Everything's miles from everything else."

"Tell me, Pan Dun, what's it like over there now?"

"America is a land of hard work, Pani Heller. A man works as hard as a horse does here. On the other hand, a horse is treated like a human being. We're not afraid of work, my brothers and I. We were young and strong, and we persevered. Now we've come back home, and can afford to buy an estate like you have here."

Golda offered them tea and small plates of strawberry jam. While they were drinking and conversing, the lawyer looked at his watch.

"Gentlemen," he said, "I believe that we came here on business. Shall we get on with it?

"Pan Lawyer," said Dun heavily, "for eleven years in America, it was hurry-hurry-hurry. When we came home, we vowed not to be in a hurry. I'm paying you for your time, so don't complain."

The brothers asked Golda many things about the farm, about the crops, about the financial details. Golda brought out the accounting ledgers, and the lawyer helped explain them to Dun, who couldn't read.

Finally Dun stood up. He was a tall and powerful man with a pleasant smile. He addressed Golda:

"Pani Heller, I like your place very much. It would be just the right size for my entire family, and we could live here in peace and comfort." He looked at his brothers, and they nodded in agreement. "I want you now, to give me a figure, the most reasonable price for a quick sale. I mean for everything, including all the buildings, the school and the church, as well. I also want all the furnishings. Everything as is."

And when Golda hesitated, overwhelmed, he added: "I'll pay you in American gold dollars." He pulled one out of his pocket and showed it to her. "The United States of America," it read. "Twenty Dollars."

Twenty Dollars! In Polish zlotys that was worth— oh, one couldn't tell, because the zloty changed value every day. But American currency was rock solid, the most stable in the world.

"Excuse me, Pan Dun," Golda said in a flurry. "We must talk this over."

The Hellers retired to an inner room, but they hardly needed to consult with each other. This was the best deal they could possibly get. They returned soon, and Golda told Dun the price they had decided on—slightly jacked up because they expected Dun to bargain.

Without blinking an eye, Dun said, "It's a deal, my lady." Then he motioned to the lawyer. "Pan Lawyer, draw up the contract and the bill of sale." As the lawyer was writing, Dun motioned to the brother sitting next to him, who was holding a small sack in his lap. The brother handed Dun the sack, who emptied in onto the verandah table.

The Hellers goggled, wide-eyed, at the cascade of golden coins that tumbled out of the sack. Dun began counting out the price of the farm. When he reached the agreed-upon amount, he poured the coins into Golda's lap and returned the rest to the sack.

When the lawyer finished writing the documents and all the signatures were in place, Dun asked Aron to read the papers aloud. Somewhat embarrasses, he said, "I never went to school, but my memory is very good, so if I can hear it read, I'll remember what it says."

When Aron finished reading and Dun was satisfied that everything was in order, they shook hands all around, and Aron brought the vodka, with the big glasses that the Lemkes liked to drink in. He filled them up to the brim for the brothers and used smaller glasses for himself, his mother, and Mendale.

"To your health, my dear lady, to your health, gentlemen," Dun stood up and toasted them festively.

Golda's eyes glowed."*Na zdrowie* [to your health], gentlemen, and may you prosper in peace on this beloved land, which has been so good to us." Her voice faltered a triple on the last words, for in one month, the Hellers would have to leave.

The large rooms of the dining room looked out onto the property; the houses, the fields, the land. Aron stood at one window, and Golda at the other. They were both crying. In between their heaving sobs, they managed to communicate. It was so painful. How could they have done it? How could they have given up their land, even for all that gold money? Aron walked over to his mother. They were both still crying quietly. He hugged her and said: "Mother, if it makes you so unhappy, perhaps we can still do something about it."

"What can we do now?" she asked sadly. "It's too late, my son."

"It may not be too late. We could go after them, give them back their money, and stay," Aron said firmly.

"No, Aron," she wiped her tears, her voice was a bit shaky. "We've made a commitment. . . a promise to Dun. It's too late. . . but my heart is breaking."

It was August 8, 1921. Mendale stood before the mirror, dressing for his wedding. His blond hair glistened as the light struck it. He put on his starched shirt, gates-ajar collar, striped pants, cutaway coat and tie, and surveyed himself. It was the first time he had worn this outfit, which the tailor had delivered that very morning. He added the finishing touches— diamond cufflinks and stick pin—-and smiled sheepishly at his image. Pretty grand, pretty grand.

He looked out of the window. A slow drizzle had been falling since early morning. He remembered the saying that if it rained on the day of the wedding, the bride loved sweets. Mendale smiled. Idisel loved chocolates. He had brought her bonbons last week, and it had disappeared in no time.

He went over to the closet to close it, and took a fresh look at the coat with the white fox collar, and the skirts and blouses he had bought Idisel in Lvov. On the shelf lay a silver mesh bag that would set off the new outfits. Soon Idisel would be here with him to put them on, bring them to life.

Their new apartment had only three rooms, but they were large and had high ceilings, of excellent prewar construction. The furniture had been delivered just a few days before, all of mahogany, fine quality. Their marriage would have a good start.

Mendale felt strange and full of both misgivings and expectations. He was twenty-four years old, almost a quarter of a century. The war and all the experiences in Germany were behind him, and he had left Zbora for good as well. Tomorrow he would begin a new life and would have to share it with another human being. It was a frightening thing to let another person into one's life, to be responsible for Idisel as well as himself. . . .

At that moment, the Heller family arrived to pick him up—cheerful, happy, full of noise. Only Aron was serious. He took Mendale into another room, and his face made plain to the younger man that he could expect a high-minded lecture.

Sure enough. "Since our father, of blessed memory, is not with us," Aron began, "I have the responsibility to take his place and to lead you to the bridal canopy. The Torah states clearly that the purpose of marriage is companionship and procreation. We all believe that you have found in Idisel a true gem of great beauty and depth. Your main responsibility will now be to her and your new family. It is written in Genesis: 'Therefore shall a man leave his father and his mother, and shall cleave unto his wife, and they shall be one flesh.' As an old married man, I can tell you—"

Mendale cut him short: "Aron, please—you know me better than that." He clapped his brother on the back. "I shall continue to value your advice through life, my dear brother."

The brothers embraced, and then the entire party left for the House of Prayer.

The rain had stopped by the time the wedding procession left the Rosenmanns' house. It was led by the musicians, playing the wedding march, and then *badchan* (poet entertainer). The bride came next, pale with excitement but exquisitely lovely in her gown and train. She was accompanied by her mother and soon-to-be mother-in-law, and followed by Reb Shaul and his male relatives and friends.

At a command from the *badchan*, the musicians began to play the marriage march. They all danced as they went along, turning to the bride from time to time. The master of ceremonies danced and sang also. And so the procession wound its way through town, followed by everyone who cared to join. They finally arrived at the front of the House of Prayer.

The groom and his party were waiting near the red velvet bridal canopy. Reb Shaul stepped out from the procession and took his place next to Mendale. Then he and Aron led the groom under the *huppah*. Now the musicians began to play again, and the bride, her face covered by a veil, was led under the *huppah* by her mother and her mother-in-law. Holding lighted candles, they walked Idisel around the groom seven times. Then they placed her on Mendale's right, and the rabbi began the ceremony.

When the rabbi had finished reading the *ketubah* (marriage contract), Mendale placed the ring on Idisel's right forefinger and recited the marriage vows. They drank from the consecrated wine, and finally the groom placed the glass on the floor and stamped on it. Everyone shouted, "*Mazel tov!*" and showered them with candy.

The musicians struck up the traditional song, "*Mazel tov* to the Bride and Groom," and led the crowd to the hall nearby, where the wedding feast was to take place.

Chapter 29
A FAMILY MAN

The old midwife, Miriam, entered the apartment and took off her shawl, revealing a white apron. The starched white cap on her black wig looked immaculate. She removed her gloves and began taking bandages and bottles out of her large bag.

Idisel's father, Reb Shaul, was standing in the corner of the dining room, his back was to Miriam, but she knew he was in deep meditation and shouldn't be disturbed. Even as she gave directions to the maid in a whisper, she heard Reb Shaul start to recite softly: "Even as the sparrow has found a house, and the swallow a nest for herself, where she may bear her young, beside your alter, O Lord of Hosts, my King." Miriam recognized it as a psalm (84th), but didn't really understand the Hebrew words. It sounded lovely to her ear anyway. Reb Shaul was praying to the Almighty to help Idisel and make her delivery easy and to bring her a healthy baby.

Miriam tiptoed toward the door of the bedroom, but stopped when she saw Mendale standing sadly near the door.

"Good evening, Reb Mendale," she said with a curtsy. "Please don't be nervous, sir. Everything will be all right soon." I delivered your Idisel, you know. She was the most beautiful baby I have ever seen. She had the physical beauty of her mother and the heavenly beauty of her father. . . ." Abruptly, she added, "I'd better get in there and examine her."

She then disappeared in the bedroom, followed by the maid and leaving the door slightly ajar. Mendale tried to peek in, but the midwife shooed him away, and he could only pace the floor to relieve his tension.

After what seemed an eternity, Miriam came out. She called to Reb Shaul to come over, too, and said, "The pains are coming very close now, and the baby's head is in place. It looks like a very normal birth. Idisel has been a good girl so far, but don't be surprised if she cries out when the baby is being born."

Again the door closed, and the two men were left alone. Mendale continued pacing, and Reb Shaul went back to his corner. Then suddenly they heard a cry, and both men ran to the door. A painfully long moment of silence, then Suya shouted, "it's a girl. Mazel tov!," and she let the men come in.

Mendale was doing quite well. The apartment in Stryj was beautiful. Idisel had all the clothes and jewelry she wanted. Mendale had also stocked Reb Shaul's store with plentiful inventory of good quality. At this point he could afford to help his in-laws a bit.

His daily routine consisted of trading in grain, visiting his stockbroker, and in the afternoons meeting with his friends in their favorite café. In the evening he loved to play with his little daughter, Chipale, who was a bright and pretty little girl, with his blond hair and lovely blue eyes.

But he found himself thinking more about the future, now that he was a family man. He was looking for a business to invest in with some of the money left from his German fur trade. One day, a real estate man, he knew, approached him about a partnership that was for sale in Kije, a small town in Kielce Province in former Russian Poland, and quite a distance from Stryj.

The property consisted of a gypsum factory and a flour mill. Mendale who went to see the place, was particularly impressed by the gypsum factory. He saw the immense piles of stone being milled into powder, which when processed would be used in building. There was a great deal of construction going on now in eastern Europe, to replace the structures destroyed in the war, so gypsum was in demand. The flour mill was successful too. It was in a very fertile part of Poland, and all the farmers roundabouts brought their grain to be milled there. Mendale checked the accounts and found that both businesses were very profitable. The partnership was for sale, because the owner a recent widow, was unable to run the business by herself.

When Mendale returned to Stryj, he and his mother and Aron decided to buy the partnership. It would mean moving to Kije, which was than a small village. Idisel was again faced with the same problem she had faced as a bride. But she understood that Mendale's talents and aspirations had to be considered, so she agreed to move. Suya comforted her: "The Torah teaches us that a woman must follow her husband. You must go where Mendale chooses to go."

They moved to Kije shortly after. It was a small village and quite different from the villages they were accustomed to. Here the farmers were all Polish. The house that went with the business consisted of three apartments. The Kestenbergs, their new partners, lived in one, Aron and his family moved into the second apartment, and Mendale and Idisel lived in the third. After a few months, Aron decided that the local schools weren't advanced enough for his children and he moved his family to Kielce, a city about thirty kilometers north of Kije.

Mendale was left to run the business as he saw fit. But it was quiet and lonely for the young couple after Aron and his family left. Mendale had spent many hours with Aron and Symcha, discussing business and playing chess, and the women had socialized, talked, and embroidered. Idisel missed that, but she missed her home in Stryj more, not only her parents but also her circle of friends. At least she again had time to read a great deal. She loved novels, and recalled the old days when she and her girlfriends formed a literary club. Some of their favorite writers were Schiller, Goethe, Tolstoy and Dostoyevsky.

One day, a delivery of gypsum was sent by Mendale to Kielce, to be shipped to a customer in Warsaw the following day. A week passed, and Mendale received inquiries from the firm in Warsaw. The gypsum hadn't arrived. Mendale and Aron went to the Kielce expeditor to trace the shipment. The man, whose name was Bernstein, made a search of the premises, but couldn't find the gypsums. He was very apologetic. "I'm sorry gentlemen," he said, "but I believe that the gypsum has been stolen."

Aron flew off the handle. "Is this the way you take care of our property, Bernstein," he shouted. Mendale stepped between them just as it looked as if it would come to blows. "Brother," he said, "I'm sure that these people must be insured against such eventualities." He then turned to Bernstein and said, "Please make out the claim, and let me know when the company can make good on it."

The young man was grateful to Mendale for stopping the fight, and he assured the Hellers that they would get their money back just as soon as he received it, and so they did.

Bernstein and Mendale became friends from that day on.

Aron had purchased an apartment on the main square in Kielce, from a man by the name of Szlomowicz. It was an elegant place, and he had paid the man in American dollars. After they had moved in, he was informed that the apartment had been sold illegally, since it had been consigned to the chief of police, a man named Iwanow.

After a few days, the chief visited Aron personally. Aron was just wondering how much trouble he was really in when the chief said matter-of-factly, "Pan Heller, I came to see for myself what kind of a person it was who could snatch this place from under my nose."

"Chief Iwanow," Aron threw up his hands in a gesture of helplessness. " I purchased this place from Szlomowicz in good faith. I had no idea that I was involved in a shady deal." He showed the chief the certificate of purchase and the receipt for the payment in full. "What am I supposed to do?"

The chief looked through the documents and said. "Hmm." Then he glanced up. "I came here, Pan Heller, for the purpose of informing you that you are to move out immediately. However, from what I can determine, you are an innocent party to this deal. I will see to it that Szlomowicz returns your money, and that he is adequately punished."

Aron thanked the chief for being so understanding. The official then added, "My family will not be arriving from Warsaw for two months, so you can stay in the apartment until then. That will give you time to find another place to live."

The chief left Aron in a very cordial mood and continued to be his friend for many years thereafter.

Aron soon found a new apartment, but it came as part of a complicated business deal: The owner, Meyer Kaufman, wanted to sell half of a brewery and soft-drink bottling plant, and the apartment was part of the package. The business seemed to be doing very well, so Aron bought it and soon was absorbed in his new enterprise. He had begun to lose interest in the gypsum plant anyway, once he'd moved to Kielce, and when Mendale too found a new business to invest in, they agreed to sell the partnership in Kije. That took several months, during which Mendale also conducted negotiations with his new partner, one Henryk Weiss, a highly respected trader in wheat.

Mendale's new enterprise involved exporting Polish grain. One great advantage to it was that he could locate to Kielce and need not be isolated any longer in a small village. Idisel was delighted with the idea. The partnership papers were drawn up, and Idisel moved in with Aron and Ester while they hunted for their own apartment.

Then calamity struck. On the day he was to take over his new partnership, Mendale went down to the firm's offices, which were located in the main square of the city, and found the door closed. No one answered his knock, and he could see no light under the door. That was odd. Where was Pan Weiss? Or, if he was ill, was his secretary or assistant?

In growing anxiety, Mendale hurried to the offices of the lawyer who had drawn up the partnership agreement and witnessed the transfer of the money. The lawyer was as puzzled as Mendale, but as he made several phone calls, his face grew longer and longer with each informant he spoke to. Then he hung up and faced his client.

"I'm sorry, Pan Heller. The man seems to have absconded."

Sick with disbelief, Mendale stared at the lawyer. "That's impossible! The man came highly recommended—you know that. There must be some mistake."

"I agree that it's hard to credit, but there is no other explanation."

"But—but I can't run the business without him! His knowledge and contacts were what made it a success."

"I'm truly sorry, Pan Heller."

"You can't be sure. Suppose he's just sick?"

"I've called his apartment, Pan Heller," the lawyer said compassionately, "and was told he moved out last week, leaving no forwarding address."

Mendale, staring into an abyss of ruin, faced the truth. He had been swindled. Every penny he owned had gone into the partnership. He had nothing left, nothing. He was nearly thirty years old, with a wife and child to support, and as penniless as a boy just starting out.

The lawyer was saying something about the police and putting a tracer on the absconding Weiss, but Mendale hardly heard him. "Thank you," he said faintly and left the office.

He wandered the streets for a while, then found a park and sat down on a bench, shivering. Gradually he pulled himself together. The first thing he had to do—perhaps the hardest thing in his life—was go home and tell Idisel. Yes, and Aron and Ester too.

He made his way home on foot, trying to marshal his nerve. Reaching the apartment house, he climbed the stairs, and entered. Idisel was in the entryway and turned to greet him with a radiant smile. It vanished instantly.

"Mendale, what's the matter? Are you ill?"

He stammered it all out—the discovery, the lawyer's phone calls, the police, the fact that it was hopeless. He was braced for recriminations. He deserved them. He wanted them. Instead, Idisel said, "Oh, Mendale, it's all my fault."

"*Your's?*"

"I should have been happy in Kije, instead I complained."

He wanted to shake her for being so silly, and he wanted to wrap his arms around her for being the most wonderful wife in the world, and he ended up weeping on her shoulder with shame.

Gradually, in the next weeks, they changed they way of living to suit their new circumstances. Mendale found that he wasn't quite broke—a minor investment in Stryj paid him a small dividend—and with that, he began trading in grain. He soon established a reputation in Kielce for honesty and punctuality in deliveries. It was hard to start again on such a small scale, but at least he was managing. Idisel and Chipale weren't starving.

Golda had been staying at Laichia's house in Rozwadow, out of touch, and she hadn't heard about the absconding partner and Mendale's devastating loss. When she arrived at Aron's for a visit and found out, she was very distressed. "Mendale, I have to speak to you alone," she said briskly, and ushered him into another room.

He half expected a lecture, but she surprised him: "I must say that I admire you for bouncing back so quickly, Mendale. You are also a very lucky man, in your choice of a wife."

"I know that, Mother."

"Well, now that that's settled, let's get down to business. I'd like to remind you that you have never received a single zloty from me from the sale of Zbora, nor did you ever ask for any money. Aron has already gotten his share. Now it's your turn. How much do you need to set yourself up in a business?"

"What?"

"How much do you—"

"You're going to *give* me money, set me up in business?"

"Yes."

He couldn't answer for a minute. Then, with an effort, he said, "I will accept a loan, only a loan."

When Mendale told her how much he needed, Golda said, "All right, my stubborn boy. I'm going to give you the money in American currency, just the way I received it at the sale of Zbora." She pulled out her purse and showed him the beautiful double eagles it contained.

"Call it a loan, if that what pleases you. As far as I'm concerned, it's yours to keep."

Mendale hugged his mother. "May I become as good a businessman as my generous little mother."

Chapter 30
STOCZEK, THE NEW HOME

The bus from Warsaw passed towns and villages and finally neared its destination. They drove through the woods. The bus driver explained to Mendale that the historic fight against the Russians took place here, and was known as the "Battle of Stoczek." Mendale remarked that he had heard the song with that title. A young woman sitting next to him then started singing it. It told about the Polish hero, Dwernicki, who fought the Muscovites, and led his loyal troops in a victory against the oppressor. Soon she was joined by other patriotic travelers who evoked the scene of long ago; with cannons booming, and the Polish boys bravely fighting the enemy.

They passed a lake and a water mill, the green countryside radiant in the setting sun. They drove past the church with its high steeple. There were beggars sitting by the main gate, waiting for alms from the worshippers. And now the bus entered the town square, where it stopped. Mendale asked the bus driver how to get to Nosal's inn.

"Nosal's place is over there." He pointed to the other side of the square, adding, "But that's a Jewish inn, sir. Are you sure it's the place you're looking for?"

"Yes, I'm sure. I want to be among my own people."

The driver had been very pleasant to Mendale throughout the journey, and now he knew why: he thought Mendale was a Catholic. They never allowed you to forget that you weren't their equal. "Good night, driver," he said politely and climbed down.

The cobbled square looked ancient, surrounded by small, neat houses. On the far corner, he recognized a synagogue, a wooden structure, large in comparison with other buildings. Jews of all ages were hurrying toward it for the evening prayer, their dark coats and round caps proclaiming their identity. Mendale, carrying his small suitcase, followed them into the house of worship. The service was already in progress, and he joined the other men in their devotions.

The prayer over, the *Shames* (sexton) took him up to the rabbi, whom he greeted in Hebrew. Mendale explained that he had come to Stoczek to buy the flour mill on the other side of town. If he was successful in purchasing it, he would then bring his family and settle there. The rabbi was very pleased, but he warned Mendale about the mill owner, who was a hard man to deal with. "And no lover of Jews, either," he added, "although he does love money."

He introduced Mendale to the secular leader of the community, Reb Shea Halpern, a dignified graybeard of about fifty.

"Reb Shea is the brother of Senator Halpern, who represents us in the Sejm," said the rabbi, smiling. "We believe that Reb Shea even outdoes his brother in oratory."

Mendale liked the rabbi right away, but he was also impressed by Reb Shea. After they had chatted briefly, Halpern said, "Reb Mendale, I imagine you will be busy tomorrow with your business, but please come to my home in the evening when you're through." He handed Mendale his calling card, and added: "If there is anything I can help you with, I will be glad to do it."

They left the synagogue, and Reb Shea went on, while Mendale stopped at Nosal's. After a good dinner, he was shown to a small, clean room and was soon asleep.

He started out the following morning a bit later than usual and was astonished to find the square transformed. A sea of small, colorful stands had filled it during the night, displaying hats, kerchiefs, ribbons, beads, clothes of all kinds, shoes, fabrics, trinkets, candy, and drinks. It was Tuesday, market day, in Stoczek. Almost at the end of the square, Lukowska Street he saw a line of peasant wagons, filled with farm produce, waiting their turn to enter the square. They would sell their vegetables and eggs and chickens, and some of the vendors were already doing a brisk business.

Lukowska Street went downhill now, and soon Mendale was passing a big field and some small homes and orchards. Finally, on the very outskirts of town, he spotted the mill, a large brick building. He entered the gate, and the watchman showed him to the owner's officer.

The owner was a *Volksdeutsch* (an ethnic German born in Poland) by the name of Hans Werner. He was tall, and heavyset and had blue watery eyes. He looked as though he'd been drinking. He told Mendale that he was selling the mill because he was about to immigrate to Argentina. He wasn't comfortable in Poland any more since independence.

"My country was defeated in the war," he added very sadly. "I can't bear the shame of it any more. We used to be respected before. Now the whole world hates us."

Mendale noticed that Werner had trouble expressing himself in Polish, and Mendale said:

"Herr Werner, you can speak to me in German, if it's easier for you. I'm from Galicia."

The watery eyes lighted up. "Ah, thank you, Herr Heller. It is kind of you."

As I was saying, I'm planning to start a new life on a new continent. It will be in the Pampas of Argentina, where my brother owns a cattle ranch. There is a large German colony nearby. I will feel at home there."

After an extensive explanation about the mill and its business dealings, Werner showed Mendale the account books. Then he said:

"It's really a pleasure to deal with you, Herr Heller. In this godforsaken town, there's no one that I can speak to freely. My family have always felt isolated here. The people are very provincial and ignorant." Then remembering that he was trying to sell the mill, he added: "Of course, you will fit in better with this environment. There are a few Jews and Poles in town who are educated and sophisticated like you. You will adjust more easily."

"You're right," Mendale said ironically. "I lived in Germany for a year, and I was even able to get along well with Germans."

When Werner found out that Mendale had American money, he lowered the price. (Not for the first time, Mendale thanked the Lord for Dun and his brothers and their sack of double eagles.) "Herr Weintraub will be glad to hear that," he said, for at that moment his prospective partner was ushered into Herr Werner's office.

Reb Noah Weintraub was a miller, whom Mendale had met some weeks before in Warsaw. For many generations, his people had run a water mill in a small town nearby, but since the war, business hadn't been too good, so he had decided to sell out and buy the mill in Stoczek, which was more modern. In order to do that, he needed a partner, and Mendale had decided that this would be a good deal for him, as well. Reb Noah was an expert in the field of milling, while he himself had had considerable experience in the grain trade.

This time, however, Mendale wasn't going to take any chances on partners. He had sent inquiries to the rabbi of the town where Reb Noah lived and also contacted the Hasidic Kozienice rebbe, whose follower Weintraub was. He had received excellent references from both these sources. The Kozienice rebbe wrote him personally that Reb Noah was a big contributor to his court—a quiet man, married but without children, and honest and God fearing.

Reb Noah was dressed in the customary black garb of the Jews of central Poland. He greeted Werner in Polish and Mendale in Hebrew, and the three men then proceeded to look over the property, Reb Noah whispering into Mendale's ear when Werner exaggerated or misrepresented any of the equipment. As they went from floor to floor of the extensive building, Werner explained the workings of the different grinding stones. The place was very impressive, the only mill in the area that was driven by its own electric generator.

Tour completed, they went back to Werner's office, where they drew up the contract, and then walked to the city hall, to finish the transaction. When the deal was concluded, they all smiled and shook hands.Mendale had the feeling that he was going to be very happy in this quaint little shtetl, which had been liberated from the Russians only six years before.

That evening, Mendale walked to the Halpern house, not far from the inn. It turned out to be a large wooden, Victorian structure, decorated with numerous ornate carvings and balconies. A maid led him in to the sitting room, where Reb Shea was and his wife Bushia were seated. Introductions were made and a light supper served. Mendale met two of the Halpern children. Estusia was about fifteen, and a striking beauty, with very dark hair, light skin, and the bluest of eyes. The younger girl, Hudka, was very bashful, and seemed to be trying not to be noticed. Frau Bushia who was now serving tea, from a samovar, said to Mendale:

"We have a son too, Yakov Mayer, but he's not home very much since he joined the Betar. I'm not sure that he's old enough to get involved in politics. He's just a boy."

Reb Shea smiled congenially at his wife: "You know, Bushia, we must all become political. Without understanding the workings of this new government and our rights as a minority, we cannot survive in modern times."

"Yes, but I feel that Poland is our country, and we must help it to become more democratic. The Land of Israel is only a dream, yet our son is talking about going to live there, and to fight for the land. We've had enough of war. I don't want my boy to carry arms or even to talk about it. He's just a kid, and should find something better to do."

"Oh, let him play soldier, Bushia," Reb Shea said. "The leader of his party, Jabotinski, believes that all of us must prepare for a struggle yet to come. He preaches armed self-defense for all Jews. I can't dispute his right to his opinion. But as far as I'm concerned a great deal can be accomplished. by peaceful means. What do you think Reb Mendale?"

"I have some faith in the League of Nations, and its attempts to protect the rights of minorities in this country. But I also know human nature, and our history. Like your son I have a dream to live in the land of Israel, but I need money to that and must succeed in my new business. I plan to work hard right here and to win equal rights for our people who prefer to call Poland their home."

The discussion continued late into the night. Frau Bushia and the girls went to sleep, and Reb Shea and Mendale played chess, until Yakov Mayer came home. Mendale left the Halpern house with a very good feeling. It seemed to him that he had finally found a father and a mentor. He knew that Reb Shea felt the same way about him.

The following, day, Mendale located a place to live. Pani Glinka's house was not too far from the mill, and exquisitely neat cottage, painted white and surrounded by a lovely garden from which rose the scent of dill and other herbs. Pan Glinka showed him the two rooms that were available. The space was cramped but with summer coming, they would be outdoors most of the time. He rented it for six months and gave the Glinkas a deposit. He went home to Kielce feeling satisfied with his new arrangement.

Two weeks later, Mendale returned to Stoczek with Idisel and Chipale. They quickly settled into their new quarters, Mendale began working at the mill, and Idisel made plans for the new house they were about to build. She liked the simple people in this town, and was learning to cope with shtetl life.

Mayer Celnik was glad that he could be home at this particular time. He was on the roof of the Heller's new house putting on the shingles. Mendale had employed him for the entire season. He'd also be working to repair the roof of the mill, and the other house on the premises.

Celnik felt lucky. Generally he had to travel to his job, to the next town or further. New houses in Stoczek were few, and far between. But now that he got this job, he would be close to his wife, Paya, when she gave birth. She was due any day now. Mayer was hoping for a boy. Four daughters were a burden to a poor man. He's have to work very hard to provide a dowry for them. He was ready to work hard and long hours, but there was little work in this area for his specialty. When he did a job, people would always say, that he had "golden hands." They were very satisfied. He prayed to the Almighty to bring him work always, so he could support his family.

He thought of Paya again, and prayed right there on the roof, that the Creator would take pity on him, and give him a son. A boy would be different. He would be at his side, and some day he would teach him his trade, or maybe he would choose a more lucrative profession. Besides, he would have someone to say the mourners prayer after he and Paya died. Yes, a boy would indeed be a blessing for a poor man.

The sun was beating down strongly now, and he was getting tired. From the roof, he could see someone coming out of the house now. It was Royza, his oldest girl, and probably the most beautiful girl in town. Now she was running toward him and shouting, "Tateh,* two boys, twins."

Celnik scrambled down from the roof, like a cat. He hugged his daughter, and they both ran home. His eyes filled with tears, as he whispered a prayer of thanksgiving.

Mayer Celnik and his family lived in a building called "The Bar-

---

* Father in Yiddish

racks." It was across the main road from the mill, and had been built by the Russians to house soldiers. With the retreat and defeat of the Russian armies, the building was abandoned, and the Jewish poor were allowed to move in. Each of the families occupied one room, with an earthen floor.

As he approached his home Mayer could hear a great deal of talking. The window was open, and he stuck in his head to see what was going on. Paya was resting after her ordeal, and looked exhausted, but there was a strange smile on her face. The girls were cleaning up the room, and fussing over the babies. The midwife had already left, not even waiting to collect her fee. She knew that Mayer would bring it to her when he got paid.

Now he got to look at his two boys. They were each so different. One was dark and round with a head of jet black hair, and the other very white, and thin, with fuzzy red hair. The dark one was quiet, and red-head was crying. Mayer bent over and kissed Paya's face. Mayer had to get ready to go to synagogue. He would have to arrange for the Mohel, and make all other preparations. He picked up each of his boys, in turn, and marveled at the tiny little creatures. He uttered a prayer: "Father in heaven, help me, so that they will never go hungry."

Now he stopped by the office at the mill, and told Reb Mendale about his good luck. Mendale wished him "Mazal Tov", and shook his hand. He asked Heller for an advance on his pay, and Mendale immediately complied.

"May our Father in heaven bless you with many sons, Reb Mendale," he said as he was leaving.

"May the Creator bring you and your family good health, and security, Reb Mayer."

When the boys were a few weeks old, Paya would come across the road with Yohevet, their youngest girl, at lunch time. They would sit under the shade tree in the yard of the house. The boys were nursing, each at one breast.

"Things are looking up, Paya," Mayer said to her one day. "We have the boys, and I have a steady job close to home." She smiled, and he continued. "It still isn't enough for us to live on, and dress the children properly. Reb Mendale asked me today if I knew of a laundress, and I promised him that I would ask around. Mayer stopped. He couldn't ask Paya outright to go to work. He really would have preferred if she could just stay home, and take care of the twins, but what was he to do. He let her decide.

And Paya responded immediately: "Mayer, I could do the wash for them. With the money I'll make, we'll be able to feed all our little birds, and I may even be able to save a little. Maybe Idisel will let me bring our Sura to help out. That would be easier for me."

The future seemed a bit brighter now, especially on this beautiful summer day.

It took almost a year for the Hellers to build their new house, but once the new furniture from Warsaw was in place and all the curtains hung, they surveyed it with great satisfaction. Their own home, solid secure and all theirs,

Life in Stoczek was good.

The Hellers had made a small circle of friends and many acquaintances. The Halperns were closest to them. Although they lived on the opposite ends of the shtetl, Mendale saw them almost every day.

Reb Shea encouraged him to get involved in the political life of the town, and when Mendale ran in the election for city councilman, he won. He also joined the executive committee of the Jewish Community Organization, which had responsibility for the welfare of the poor and needy.

In both these capacities, he became aware of the extent of poverty among the Jewish population in town. Unlike the Poles, they didn't own land—a legacy of Russian rule—but lived from small trade, crafts, or cottage industries. Times were bad for trade and so many lived on the edge of indigence earning barely enough to feed themselves. Mendale began to visit them in their homes, and found them to be, for most part, hard working, honest, and diligent but nonetheless often in need of the basic necessities. Their diet consisted mainly of bread, potatoes, and onions, and he noticed that many small children had rickets, a calcium and vitamin D deficiency.

Mendale began to organize the executive committee for action. First, they established a special fund for nutrition, with each of the ten committeemen contributing a substantial basic sum of money. Then they assessed the capacity of the more wealthy citizens of Stoczek, and asked them to pay a regular monthly amount. Mendale, who went in person to solicit the aid of these people, found most of them to be generous and caring. He was also able to get the help of the doctor in town, as a free medical consultant for the needy. He had begun to care a great deal for this little shtetl he had chosen as his home. He felt wanted and appreciated by all.

His philanthropic efforts had made Mendale think about what would bring true prosperity to his shtetl. Modernizing and industrialization were the answer. The rich as well as the poor used kerosene lamps to illuminate their homes. Only the mill, which operated its own generator, was electrified. Mendale resolved that all of Stoczek should have electricity, even if he had to do it single-handed.

He and Reb Noah worked out a plan of action. The first step was to get the government permission for the construction of a privately owned electrical installation. At the next city council meeting, he put the plan before the mayor and the council. There was a hush in the room, while the group recovered from the surprise.

"These are big plans for a little town like Stoczek," said the mayor, Pan Wielgosek, slowly. " It would be a great boost for out local business, of course. But how much will it cost?" Mendale indicated that he and Pan Weintraub would finance the deal. He explained how the plan would work, and as he spoke, he could see opposition melting away.

Pan Wielgosek was positively excited by the time he finished. "I will not only approve, Pan Heller, "I will personally see to it that all the applications and permits are taken care of."

There was a great deal of applause, and congratulations all around. Mendale breathed a sigh of relief. First step accomplished.

Now frequent trips to Warsaw began for the ordering and purchase of machinery. Symcha, who had joined his uncle and aunt in Stoczek, acted as adviser in this area. He suggested the use of coke, a byproduct of coal, for firing the generators. This was being widely used in Germany as a cheap efficient fuel, and in became a great success in Stoczek. It was also cheap, and could be purchased in great quantities. Mendale and Symcha had rejected the other possibility, the use of oil. They had inquired at Idisel's relatives in Drohobych, which was the center of the Polish petroleum industry. They owned a number of oil wells there. The price they quoted, even with a special discount, proved to be prohibitive.

Once they knew how much machinery was to be housed, they could start building the plant. It took over a year to complete and consumed a great deal of their efforts. The cables and poles had to be installed and wires run into the homes of subscribers. The township itself purchased electricity from Heller and Weintraub; soon the streets would have electric light at night. Stores, the church and the synagogue all subscribed.

The great day came when service was to be inaugurated. The festivities took place in the town square, and everyone in Stoczek was invited. The mayor, Pan Wielgosek, spoke first, of course, followed by Pan Shea Halpern. "And now the men to whom this progressive advance is owing," he concluded, "Pan Emanuel Heller."

When Mendale stepped up on the podium, to the uninhibited cheers of the crowd, Idisel and Chipale next to him, he felt that it was the proudest moment in his life.

"Friends and fellow citizens of free Poland," he began. "We are about to light our town—to light and energize our town—from a new source. This new electric plant of ours has created jobs for many of you already. In the future it will spin off many more jobs and make possible machines to take over much drudgery. Within a few years, I can envision, every one of you having at least one electric light in your home. We will make electricity so cheap that it will be within everyone's reach." The crowd applauded.

It was getting dark. Mendale looked at his watch to make sure of the time and had trouble reading the dial. Never mind. The moment had come. He seized the handle of the switch the engineer had set up. "And now," he shouted, "as it is said in Genesis: 'Let there be light!' " He pulled down the switch. The lights around the square blazed on. The large lamps in front of the courthouse glowed brilliantly, and one by one windows of houses turned golden.

"Oh-h-h," said the crowd and then burst into cheers.

Mendale, carrying Chipale and hand in hand with Idisel, walked home, surrounded by friends. People on Lukowska Street stopped them every few feet with congratulations. Many—including some who had scoffed at the idea of electrification—announced their conversion: "How soon can we be wired in?" they clamored.

At home, there was food and drinks for everyone, and the festivities continued until early in the morning.

Soon, Idisel found that she was pregnant again. She and Mendale hoped for a son this time. He bought her a very special gift: a crystal set with earphones. The three of them would sit around it and listen to music and cultural broadcasts. It was one of the few radios in town.

Idisel particularly liked the music of Strauss and Lehar. She would sing along in German in her lilting voice. Of the classical composers she preferred Chopin and especially as played by Artur Rubinstein. The Polish folk opera *Halka* by Stanislaw Moniuskzko was her very favorite. It was broadcast live one evening from the Warsaw Opera House, with Jan Kiepura, a world-famous Polish tenor, and soprano Marta Eggert, his wife. Idisel was thrilled.

In May, the country was startled by the news that Pilsudski had seized power and named himself head of the government. The majority of Polish people rejoiced. They trusted strong men. With their beloved "granddad" at the helm, there was hope that Poland would be safe and orderly, and the task of reconstruction could begin. Mendale wasn't so sure. Pilsudski was firm for the rights of minorities, and he was said to favor the Jews, but Mendale mistrusted coups d'état ending in one-man rule. It was safer to work problems out one at a time, the disorderly democratic way.

Fall came that year with a great deal of rain. It was muddy and dreary. Mendale, who was now a member of the active reserve of the Polish army, received notice to report for reserve duty in the Lvov area. It was strange to be back in uniform again, and it brought back some memories he would rather not have entertained.

Moreover, he found his weeks in the army most uncomfortable and depressing. He was no longer used to the rigors of the barracks. Most of the soldiers were difficult to handle and obeyed orders reluctantly—particularly the Ukrainians, who comprised the majority here in Galicia. They hated Poland and were resentful of having to train in the Polish army.

When his stint was over, Mendale went to visit his in-laws in nearby Stryj before returning home. At dinner time, the conversation turned to the political situation in Poland.

"Well, father-in-law, what is your opinion of Pilsudski's takeover?" Mendale asked.

"Let's pray that the hand of the Creator will guide this great leader," Reb Shaul answered dreamily. "But the children of Israel cannot pin their hopes on earthly leaders. We must continue to pray for the redemption, for the coming of the Messiah, when true peace and justice will reign over the entire world."

"Amen," Mendale said. "But I'm still confused. I'm not sure I ought to care what happens to Poland. At every turn I'm reminded that I'm not one of 'them.'"

"You're not one of 'them,' my son. You are of the seed of Jacob."

Yes, but that simply left him torn between two realities: one was the Land of Israel, and the other his home is Stoczek, where he had achieved personal fulfillment and peace. "I'm about to be a father again, Reb Shaul, and I want my children to be brought up in an atmosphere of freedom in the land of Israel, not in exile."

Reb Shaul thought for a moment, then said—decisively for him: "If you decide to go to our land, Mendale, Suya and I will go with you. But I believe that it's not time yet. The last messenger who came from Jerusalem told me that there is great hunger and unemployment in the Land of Israel now. You must wait until times improve."

That made sense to Mendale. At least it postponed the decision once again.

Next morning Mendale took leave of his in-laws. On the train to Warsaw, he had a minor adventure. He fell into conversation with the pretty young woman sitting opposite him. She made some comment on his uniform and he was just explaining the circumstances when a large middle-aged man barged into their compartment, interrupting their talk.

The new arrival stretched out his hand and shook Mendale's: "I'm honored to share this compartment with a member of our own Polish Army. I myself was in Pilsudski's First Brigade." He pointed to the scar on his face. "This is my souvenir from the Russians, the rotten Bolsheviks."

Mendale and the girl exchanged amused glances. The man took a flask from his pocket, called the porter for some glasses, and poured a drink for himself and for Mendale.

"It's early for me," he protested mildly.

"Come brother, you must drink to our Fatherland." He pressed the glass into Mendale's hand and said to the young lady, "Forgive me, miss. Would you like to join us too?"

"No, thank you," she said politely.

"Then, *na zdrowie*! To independent Poland!"

Now he stepped down beside Mendale and began telling a story of a battle with the Bolsheviks, and some vulgar jokes which he whispered into his ear. After some twenty minutes, Mendale had had enough and, getting up, excused himself. He went to the washroom and when he returned to the compartment, the man was no longer there.

The young woman glanced up and grinned at his relieved expression, but a moment later, her own expression changed. "My watch," she said, touching her lapel. "It was right here."

Mendale reached for his own pocket watch, and realized that it was gone, too. They looked at each other, wide-eyed.

"Our self-styled patriot!" she said angrily. "He tried to kiss my hand when he left."

Mendale checked his pocket for his wallet. At least that was still there. He then said to the young lady, "You had better check your money."

She looked and found that her purse hadn't been touched.

"Well," Mendale said, "we should be grateful that the thief was selective. I'd better call the conductor."

The conductor explained that the man in question had gotten off in Radom, but he would report the theft to the police at the next station.

The girl pulled out a lunch box and said, "Would you care to join me? There's enough here for the both of us."

Mendale thanked her but refused. He was about to add some polite excuse when something made him blurt out the truth: "My name is Emanuel Heller, at your service, and my religion restricts what I may eat."

Her eyes popped, but she gave him a nice smile. "Well, Emanuel Heller," she said gaily, "many of your coreligionists eat everything we do, so don't blame me if I accidentally offer you ham. But if you won't partake, at least converse with me while I do."

So as the train rattled on, they talked quite freely at length. Mendale found himself saying things he though never to say to a gentile. "We Jews love Poland, madam. We fought and spilled our blood for her, and yet the majority of Christians do not accept us as free and equal citizens. The new Constitution guarantees our rights, but things work differently in practice. People hate us and seek to do us harm."

"Oh, I admit there are many ignorant people in this country," she said. "But you have to give them the chance to become civilized. Eventually they will see this hatred as a detriment to the development of our country. We who believe in democracy will have to teach them. You, Pan Heller, must do your part to help teach them."

"You're very convincing," he said. "I will try to help in any way I can."

Dusk fell. The steel blue January sky changed to orange, and suddenly it was dark. It was snowing lightly when they arrived at the station in Warsaw. Mendale took her hand to say good bye.

"I'm so glad that we had an opportunity to meet and talk," he said. "It gives me great hope for the future to know that there are people like you in this country." He handed her his card. "If you should ever need my help or want to see me, I'm very easy to get in touch with. Our little town is very close to Warsaw." He bent over and kissed her hand.

When Mendale arrived home, Idisel was heavy with child. The doctor said that the infant would come in about a week more. Pani Halpern, who had stopped in to see her, told Mendale that she should rest, not be disturbed by petty problems this last week, and he readily agreed to see that she was untroubled. "Good. Oh, and Mendale, my husband wants to see you as soon as possible."

"Very well, I'll go in the morning. Thank you for your concern, Pani Halpern. You are a good woman."

The message from Reb Shea didn't seem particularly important, so it was nearly noon by the time Mendale reached his friend's house the next day. "Sit down, Mendale," said the older man and showed him a letter. "This is from Reb Shaul Rosenmann."

Instantly Mendale took alarm. "What is it? What's the matter?"

"Your mother-in-law was sick. . . ."

"Yes, but she was feeling much better." Suya had had an operation on her leg, but it had come out well—she had told him she was quite free of pain and on the mend. "You mean, she's had a—a—"

"A relapse, yes."

His heart was pounding furiously. Her love, his quiet, saintly mother-in-law. "Well? How bad?"

Reb Shea licked his lips. "She is no longer in this world, my dear friend. She has gone to paradise." He handed over Reb Shaul's letter.

Mendale's eyes raced across his father-in-law's shaky writing. "The Almighty has seen fit to take my greatest treasure from me. His will be done. But under no circumstances are you to tell Idisel about it, until the child is born, and she recovers her strength. She is very delicate now, and we don't want to cause her grief."

Mendale had to stop because the words were swimming on the pages. Just a few days ago he had seen Suya, and she had looked so beautiful. How could all this have happened so quickly? He pulled out a handkerchief and blotted his eyes, then continued reading.

She had died of a heart attack in her sleep. She had gone to bed looking forward to a visit with her daughter. But—she didn't wake up in the morning.

Mendale did not return home until he had himself under control. When Idisel asked him idly what Reb Shea had wanted, he managed a tone of indifference: "Oh, politics, my love. Nothing urgent. Now you must take good care of yourself these last days. . . ."

Reb Shaul arrived a few days later on the bus from Warsaw. He had put his store up for sale, he confided privately to Mendale, and did not intend to return to Stryj. "Good, Reb Shaul. You're home is here now."

When Idisel asked her father why Suya didn't come, he told her that her leg had been bothering her, and it would have been difficult for her to get around. But she had wanted one of them to be there for the birth.

On February 9, during a snowstorm, a pretty blond baby girl was born in the Heller house. Idisel was in labor for a very short time and felt very little pain. At the naming party, they named her Sara, but pretended it was Hanna, so Idisel wouldn't be aware of what happened to her mother.* Back in Stryj, Idisel's cousin, imitating Suya's writing corresponded with Idisel, and pretended to be her mother. This subterfuge worked so well that Idisel was never aware of the truth until Reb Shaul thought it proper to tell her.

It was a pleasant April day and Idisel dressed the baby, preparatory to taking a walk with her father. They set out together, Surale in the pram, Chipale chattering alongside. they headed for a nearby pine woods, where they sat down in a clearing.

"I've wanted to speak to you for a long time about this, Idisel," Reb Shaul began.

"What is it, Father?"

"It's your mother. She was very sick, my child. . . ."

"You mean to say that's why she didn't come with you? How sick was she? She said nothing in her letters."

He tried to speak, but the words came out wrong: "They weren't her letters, Idisel."

Now really alarmed, Idisel jumped up. "Father, what *is* it? What are you trying to tell me?"

"Our beloved Suya is no more," he whispered.

She guessed the whole truth in a flash. "Four months ago? She's been—been gone for two months?"

"I though it best to postpone the bad news. We were worried about what the shock might do to you and your baby."

"Yes, but *two months*! She stared at nothing, trying to visualize her beloved mother lying cold in her grave all this time. She thought her alive in their little house in Stryj.

---

* In the Ashkenazi tradition babies are named only after deceased relatives. Suya is a diminutive of Sara, as is Surale.

"Forgive me," he begged. "I'm to blame. It was my idea to keep it from you." He moved closer to her, comforting her and stroking her hair. "Idisel, the Almighty took your mother but He gave us another beautiful soul, little Surale. We named her after your mother, but we didn't let you know."

Idisel kissed her father and hugged him. then she stood up and went over to the carriage and lifted up her little Sara, Surale. After a while she began nursing Surale. So this was the Creator's way of comforting her. The baby did look like Suya. Perhaps the child was a reincarnation of her beloved mother.

Reb Shaul walked away leaving Idisel alone. Now it was up to the baby to fill the void for her.

Chapter 31
LIFE GOES ON

The Hellers were going back to Zbora for a visit. Golda had retained a sizable piece of land at the time she had sold most of her property to Dun. She had wanted to have the security of being able to return if she ever changed her mind. She knew now that she would not go back to the land, and she had decided to sell it. By letter through his lawyer, Dun had agreed to buy.

Aron and Mendale had come with her and her grandson Symcha was driving the Packard. They went south at first, following the main highway through and then turned off onto the "Polish roads"—mere dirt paths, not meant for automobile travel. The weather was clear and bright, and the fields were ripe with wheat and rye, swaying in the summer breeze.

Aron thought nostalgically of the prewar years. The other farmers had considered him an authority on agriculture and cattle breeding, and they had often come to him for advice. He had studied many books on the subject, and had enjoyed being able to improve his crops.

"It's like old times, with all of us together like this," he said, sighing.

"It seems to me like yesterday," Golda agreed. "All of us were working here in the fields. And the Lemkes! Mendale, you were such a menace to them."

"Maybe we were all too hard on them, Mother," Mendale said.. "Remember when they wanted to use the clay from our clay pit, free of charge? They claimed that the Germans had promised them the use of it." That probably wasn't true, but, in retrospect, it seemed to him that they should have let them use the clay free anyway. They used it for their floors. They were very poor and that's how they kept their houses warm in the winter.

"They had no right to the clay," Golda said angrily. "But they took it anyway. They were a thieving lot, those Lemkes. But Dun is different. He's an honest and decent man, and I have a great deal of respect for him."

Their former land was very close, and soon their house came into view. Everyone became silent, remembering something different. Now they were approaching the gate, and Symcha turned the car into the courtyard.

Golda and her sons entered the house, fighting dismay. Everything was so different. A large cross hung over the door, and the furniture looked old and neglected.

But Dun and his wife greeted them warmly. He looked a great deal older and somewhat stooped. He was dressed in his traditional Lemke clothes, a white embroidered linen shirt over dark pants. His American suit hung inn the open closet for Sunday use. He invited them to sit down at the large rustic table, and called his daughter to bring some fresh water from the well. He plunked down a large bottle of vodka on the table, one hundred proof *Wyborowa*. They would have a drink when they concluded the sale.

After Dun's words of welcome, Golda said, "Well, now Pan Dun, are you happy as owner of a large farm?"

Dun considered the question for a moment, and then said: "Happy— that's funny, Pani Heller. Sometimes I'm sorry that I bought this land from you. We Lemkes are despised by the Ukrainians here, as you well know. Perhaps I should have gone a little further west of here, closer to my native village." He spread his hands. "But then maybe not. My two brothers went back to our village and married women with a lot of land, and I guess they're not that happy either. The land over there is rocky and mountainous and doesn't produce well. So, if you have one thing, you lack another."

They chatted idly for a while. Mendale wanted to ask Dun if he got along with his fellow Lemkes, but didn't know how to phrase it tactfully. Then after a bit, Dun volunteered the information: "There is a lot of envy here because we own all this land. Even my own people, the Lemkes in the village who should be my friends, try to rob us. We have to be constantly on guard."

"O, dear" said Golda with sympathy. "We had the same problem with them, and so did the German who owned it before us. But I thought that they'd be more neighborly to one of their own."

"They don't seem to realize," said Dun, "that I was only able to buy this property because I worked like a slave in America. And before." He began to speak bitterly of his early years. "At twenty-five I was a poor farmer with two small children to support. No matter how hard I worked my small piece of land, it didn't yield enough to feed us all. In the winter there was never enough to eat and in spring not enough money to buy seed. One day, a man came into our village and told us that he could get us jobs in America. We would make a lot of money, and be able to send it to our families here. We could even get rich. My wife and I decided, right then and there, that if he chose me, I would sign up for five years." He and his brothers were glad to have been picked.

"After we were all brought together, they took us on a train to Hamburg, where each man was given a number and put on a ship to America. In New York, they stamped us like cattle. A Polish man met us and took us by train to Detroit. That's where the work really started. We had to work continuous shifts, totaling fourteen hours, before we were allowed to go home to rest. Home was an apartment, where ten men lived in two rooms."

Most of the men drank, but Dun had more character. He sent money home every month, so his wife and children could live fairly well, and they both saved every spare penny. His brothers, too, were careful.

"We drank only once in a while," he explained, "on holidays or at weddings, because we wanted to go home rich men. None of our friends knew how much money we had saved. Some of them bought cars, rented nice apartments, or married American women. Their wives took their money each payday and gave them back only enough to buy cigarettes."

The brothers stuck to their dream and spent very little. By the time their five years were up, the war was on, and they signed on for five more years. Dun's wife managed to scrape by the war years on the money she had saved up. When the three finally came home, it was with a sack of gold coins.

"But sometimes," Dun added dreamily, "I think to myself, Why didn't I take that money and go to California? Or to Kansas. I could have brought my wife and children to America. For the money I saved, I could have bought myself a big wheat farm—you can't imagine how big, Pani Heller. As far as the eye can see, and all mine. Farmed by machine, too. We could have started a new life in a new country, and my son wouldn't have to serve now in the god-damned Polish army." Dun stopped, some-what embarrasses. "I'm sorry. I got carried away. I should appreciate what I have—a beautiful piece of land, cattle, and good sturdy buildings. I should be satisfied." He laughed good naturedly. "What about you, Pani Heller? How has life been treating you?"

Golda enumerated her blessings: "Two sons in America, Max (Meyer) a dentist, and just became a father for the first time; Morris (Moishe's new name) studying law at Columbia University; one daughter in Altona with seven children, and expecting an eighth; Aron here with six, living in Kielce; Laichia in Rozwadow, with four; and Mendale here from Stoczek, father of three little girls.

"You see, the Creator has blessed me with twenty-one healthy grandchildren, Pan Dun, and a twenty-second on the way. The money you will pay me today for my last piece of land will take me to Germany and then to America to visit those I have not yet seen."

"I hope the trip to America will not be disappointing to you, noble lady. You know that I wish you all the best," Dun said.

Now Dun paid out the money he had agreed on for the land, and Golda handed over the deed. They signed the papers and shook hands, then toasted each other's health with the vodka.

The Hellers drove off in silence, leaving the land behind.

America was not only a disappointment to Golda. It was a downright shock.

She had been impressed by her first glimpse of the port of New York. The Manhattan skyline overwhelmed her, and so did the Statue of Liberty, presiding tranquilly over the harbor. And when Meyer and Moishe— only she had to remind herself that they were Max and Morris now—met her on the great slab of a pier, she cried for joy.

She hardly recognized Max, he looked so American. She remembered that he was only nineteen when she last saw him, and now he was a mature man of thirty-five. He held her in his arms for a long time, and they both cried for all the years of separation.

"Enough of that," said Morris finally. "I want to say hello to Mother, too." As he embraced her, all three began to laugh through their tears.

"No more sadness. We're together again," Golda said, putting an arm around each of them. "I thank the Lord for allowing me to come to America to see my sons once more."

They whisked her into their new car and then drove through the magnificent city full of skyscrapers. When it got dark now, lights seemed to appear in the windows as if by magic, and signs in the streets in colored lights too. She had never seen anything as exciting.

Max explained that they were going to his house, which was "out in Queens," whatever that meant. It took a long time to get there through incredible swarms of cars and trolleys and overhead railroads. Max described his new office to her and Morris told her that he had finished his studies and would soon be taking his bar exam.

In time Golda learned that New York was a city of many nationalities and seemed to be quite peaceful in spite of it. "There are more Jews here than Ukrainians," Max said with a stifled laugh. There was so much freedom here—perhaps too much, though Golda. Max's Italian neighbors were particularly pleasant to her, and they seemed like her own people in their close family ties.

But Jewish life in America seemed all wrong. There were many synagogues in New York and even some religious Jews, but the vast majority of them did not follow the precepts of the Torah. For Golda, the worst shock was discovering that her own sons violated the holy Sabbath. For Max, Saturday was the busiest day in the week, and he explained to her that his livelihood depended on working on that day. In fact many Jews worked on Saturday and thought little of it. Max's wife Ruth was born in New York and she brought American ways into their home. It seemed very foreign to Golda.

When she voiced some of her feelings to her sons, they decided it would be better if she stayed with Morris, who lived in a section of Queens where there was more of a religious community. She soon knew all the shopkeepers and most of the people at the House of Prayer. She met other women who were much like her—spoke no English, sat in separate pews from the men, and prayed on the Sabbath and holidays. They wore wigs and were very observant.

Golda felt the weight of her years. At night, when she lay awake, she remembered the years of happiness and sorrow, so long ago. She recalled the saying that when people get old they think a great deal about the past, rather than the future. She would get up again and begin reading the *Tse'enah Ure'enah,** and find inspiration and solace in its pages. She would always keep it near her, wherever she went. After a few months she began thinking of returning home.

One day, she read an article in *The Forward*, the Yiddish labor paper, which appalled her. A Jewish butcher had been convicted of selling non-kosher meat, and passing it off for kosher. A shock wave ran through the entire Orthodox community in New York. In all her years, Golda had never heard of such a sinful act. She stopped eating meat entirely and remained a vegetarian until the day she left.

The month before she sailed, all America experienced a shocking upheaval. The stock market crashed. Many financiers threw themselves from the windows of their fashionable offices and homes, or took their lives in other ways. The financial world was in a shambles. Nobody knew what it meant, but it left one more bad taste in Golda's mouth.

As Max drove her to the Hamburg-America pier, she was happy to be going back to her home and her other children. America was not for her. She would never return. She told Max if he or Morris wanted to see her again, they would have to come to Poland.

Altona seemed more prosperous than ever. The people on the streets were now elegantly dressed, the cafés full of young people, the shops well-stocked with luxury items.

"Germany hasn't yet felt the impact of the Depression in America," Golda thought. She worried that the situation in America would now effect the economy in this seemingly prosperous country. But her son-in-law, Nehemiah told her that business was fine. The democratic Weimar government had things under control, he assured her. He explained that since 1924, Germany had received a total of seven billion dollars in loans, mostly from the United States, and that was certainly a cushion against any possible financial trouble. On the contrary, the money received had generated great prosperity for everyone, especially for the workers and

---

* The Pentateuch, or Five Books of Moses, translated into Yiddish for the use of women, by Jacob Ashkenazi (1559–1623), also known as the "Women's Bible."

the small shop keepers. The stock market crash in New York on October 4, 1929 would, in his opinion, not affect Germany.

"We have more serious worries here," Nehemiah added. "It's those Nazi terrorists. They're full of hatred against our people. They are becoming very strong, particularly in Bavaria. Their leader, Adolf Hitler, has written a book called *Mein Kampf* ("My Struggle"). In this book he vows to destroy the Jewish people once he becomes leader of Germany."

"Leader of a civilized country like this?" Golda scoffed, "Why, we used to have anti-Semites in Austria. Once they got in office—if they did—it all fizzled out. I don't see the solid, sensible Germans following a lunatic."

Shainchi now joined the conversation: "I read in the paper that many poor people and even criminals are joining his party. People with nothing to lose. He promises them that he'll take money away from us and give it to them."

"But, my dear girl," Nehemiah corrected her, "some of the wealthiest people in this country also support this criminal. They even got him out of jail, so he could carry on his vicious propaganda against us. They *want* him to topple the government."

"All right, the poorest *and* the richest. What bothers me is that he tells them both that *we* caused all their misfortunes—the Versailles Treaty and all the evil that befell them."

"That's true enough, Mother Heller, you should see their newspaper, *Völkischer Boebachter*. It's a piece of filthy anti-Semitic trash."

"Couldn't anything be done about him and these what-do-you-call-them, Nazis?" Golda asked.

"We can only hope," Nehemiah said, "that the Weimar Republic can survive their antidemocratic assaults," Nehemiah answered.

Back again in Stoczek, in the warmth and comfort of her bed, Golda now recalled her trip to America and Germany. Both of these countries were having troubles. One was collapsing financially, the other politically. She had an uneasy feeling that evil things were about to happen. She hoped that her children and grandchildren would not have to be in another war.

But she felt safe here in Stoczek. Maybe Poland would escape bad times. It had experienced too much suffering in the past. Now she prayed silently for peace in the world, and for a tranquil life for her children and all the Children of Israel.

Hitler was raging in Germany. On January 30, 1933, the former Austrian corporal and vagabond was sworn in by President Paul von Hindenberg as Chancellor of the Republic. It was the death toll for the democratic government, which had lasted for fourteen years.

This event ushered in a reign of terror against all anti-Nazis. The Reichstag fire was staged, followed by the suspension of all civil rights. Storm troopers roamed the streets, breaking into houses and arresting members of opposition parties. Some persons were tortured, beaten, and murdered. Newspapers were shut down and their editors imprisoned, trade union leaders arrested. At Dachau near Munich, a camp was built to hold dissidents—the first of an infamous many.

The worst was saved for Germany's Jews. Hitler, now absolute dictator of the country, declared that they were not Germans, and turned his thugs loose to beat, rob, and murder them. The more influential and wealthy among them suffered the worst treatment. Jews were excluded from public service, the universities, and the professions. On April 1, 1933, Hitler proclaimed a national boycott of Jewish shops.

All over the world, Nazi tactics were denounced as barbaric, but that only spurred Hitler on. At the urging of his new propaganda minister, Joseph Goebbles, thousands of students gathered, built tremendous bonfires, and burned books considered subversive by the Nazis. Secretly, in contravention to the Versailles Treaty, he began to rearm Germany.

In Poland, Hitler's assurances of peace didn't sit well with Marshal Pilsudski. He was one of the few European leaders who understood Hitler's aims. Pilsudski felt that the only way this madman could be stopped, was for France to join Poland in a preventive war against Germany. France declined to participate in such an effort. Pilsudski's hopes for destroying Hitler collapsed.

The dictator's speeches—raving, screaming, rabble-rousing—were broadcast by his propaganda machine from large stadiums, where crowds were shown chanting hypnotically "Sieg Heil!" (Victory Hail!) after every point. Newscasts in the movie theaters showed uniformed men and women saluting their leader. The performance over, the crowds pushed out into the streets seeking vengeance.

The Hellers were particularly concerned for the safety of Shainchi and her family—and indeed the entire Jewish community in Germany. There was little they could do to help them, but Mendale wrote, encouraging them to leave for Palestine.

Soon the Polish army was mobilized, and Mendale was again called up. When he said good-bye to Idisel and his three little girls, Surale clung to him. "Daddy, are you going to be fighting in a war?"

"No, my sweet," he said. "We're only practicing. I'll be home soon."

Surale missed him terribly. What if she never saw him again? There was an anxious pain in her heart.

On a gray, drizzly afternoon, a few days later, she heard a rumbling form the highway and ran to her parents' bedroom, which overlooked the main road to Warsaw. Columns of soldiers were marching by, dressed in drab green uniforms. Every unit carried banners at its head, including the red and white colors of Poland. It gave her a thrill to see them float by. Occasionally an officer rode past on a horse, and batteries of field artillery rumbled by from time to time.

Surale wondered where they were going and why. Fear struck again, lingering in the pit of her stomach. Was it another war like the one she'd heard so much about? Would her father be killed and buried in a grave no one knew?

Those graves in the woods, where the family would go walking on Saturday afternoons, had haunted her for a long time. Before you go to the lake, near the ruins of an old palace, you came across stones with inscriptions carved on them in a strange language.

"What does it say, Daddy?" she asked him.

He read them in German, which she understood, and then added, "They were killed during the war, long before you were born. That's the war I fought in."

"So, where did they come from, and why did they fight?"

"They were from Germany, and they fought for Germany. There's no one here who knows them"

Now they walked on, and joined the others. Soon she was distracted by the ducks and swans on the lake. Large, white water lilies floated on its surface. Everything was very still here, but in the distance you could hear the sound of a water mill, on the other side of the lake.

Now, looking out of the window at the soldier vanishing up the road, she couldn't shake off the connection between her father and forgotten graves.

A few weeks went by, and her father came back. There was no war. Everything was normal and ordinary. Mendale took her along on one of his trips to Warsaw, and when they returned to Stoczek that evening, they found that a circus had magically sprouted in the town square.

"Oh, Daddy, can we go? Can we?"

"I don't see why not."

This wonderful treat made up for the weeks of worry for the child. She decided during the performance, that when she grew up, she would join the circus. She would be a tightrope artist and wear a pink dress, and carry a parasol, just like the girl she was watching. Circus people were never sad and didn't worry about war.

Mendale was returning home from one of his trips to Ternopol, where he had recently purchased a linseed oil factory. When his train arrived in Siedlce, he saw a tremendous crowd of people waiting at the station— Hasidim dressed in their Sabbath clothing. He asked out the window what was happening and was told that Rebbe Israel of Czordkow was passing through Siedlce on the way to Lublin and was going to stop to visit his Hasidim. People had gathered here from all the surrounding towns to greet him and to receive his blessings.

Reb Shaul had often told his son-in-law of his love and admiration for this great teacher, so Mendale got off his train, curious to see him. He could take a later train.

Soon the rebbe's train appeared in the distance, and everyone surged forward to see it. It consisted of an engine pulling only one car, but the station master stepped forward, straightened up in a military fashion, and saluted. He was not a Jew. He must have assumed that it was some national dignitary, for who else would travel in this manner?

Now the train stopped, and the rebbe appeared at the window. The crowd rushed forward, but was kept back by police while a group of guards got off the train, led by the rebbe's secretary. The guards made a path through the crowd, pushing people back until the secretary was able to speak:

"Now people, don't shove. Quiet down. This must be an orderly proceeding. All those with urgent requests for the rebbe will be able to see him, but first you must line up and take your turn. Remember, the rebbe has very little time. There are other needy people waiting for us in other towns."

People started pushing from all directions now, and Mendale, propelled by them, found himself in a line. Rebbe Israel now came out to the back of the train, surrounded by a number of his young disciples. A hush came over the assembled multitude. As Rebbe Israel stretched out his hands to bless them, the crowd seemed to sway toward him. Then his resonant voice was raised in blessing. Women began to cry, and the whole crowd started singing:

"Let the Redemption come soon.
Let the Messiah come in our days."

"Loz shoin zain die geule
Mashiach zol shoin kimen." (Folk song)

Rebbe Israel sang with them as they repeated the two phrases again and again. Then, surrounded by his disciples, the rebbe disappeared into his car, and the secretary began to move down the line collecting notes handed to him by people on the line. When it was Mendale's turn, he gave the secretary a note stating that he was Reb Shaul son-in-law and would like to meet the rebbe.

When the secretary finished collecting, two young Hasidim got off the train and helped him sort out the requests, which selection process reduced the collection to a mere handful. They began reading off the names, and each lucky chosen one was escorted into the rebbe's car.

Suddenly, Mendale heard his own name: "Reb Menachem Mendel Heller, son-in-law of the renowned scholar, Reb Shaul HaKohen Rosenmann. Step forward."

The guards cleared the way, and soon a surprised Mendale found himself in the car, half-blinded after the bright sunshine outside.

"Reb Shaul HaKohen's son-in-law, let me see you up closer," said a commanding voice.

As his eyes adjusted, he made out the majestic-looking rebbe seated at a small table in the middle of the car. His face held the serenity of a saint.

"Is it really Reb Shaul's son-in-law?" the rebbe said in surprise. "Stand here, a little closer."

"What's the meaning of this modern clothing, Menachem Mendel? Does my beloved friend's son-in-law actually dress in the manner of the gentiles?"

"Forgive me, Rebbe, These are earning-a-living clothes. In my heart I'm a Jew and an observing one at that."

"I'm glad to hear those words, Reb Menachem Mendel," the rebbe said. "Now sit down and tell me how my friend is. I haven't seen him in many years, in fact not since I moved to Vienna. I know of his great loss. May our Heavenly Father comfort him in his grief, and give him long and peaceful years."

"As you know, Rebbe," Mendale said, "he lives with us, and we are honored to have him in our house. The rabbi in Stoczek keeps him busy, enriching the learning of his most outstanding Torah scholars. There is no one else in town that can compare to Reb Shaul in erudition."

"Ah, it pleases me that the young people of your town are benefiting from his knowledge and piety. But Reb Shaul always believed in work as well as study."

"He hasn't retired from work, Rebbe," Mendale explained, answering the implied question. "Reb Shaul works daily in our flour mill. He's in charge of weighing transactions, especially the grain that the farmers and bakers bring for grinding."

Mendale smiled, remembering his diligent father-in-law at work. Many grain merchants tried to cheat the illiterate peasants, but they knew that with Reb Shaul in charge, that would never happen, so even if they were not selling grain to Heller & Weintraub, they brought their scales to Reb Shaul for an honest measure.

"He's extraordinary in observing our laws concerning weights and measures," he added.

"I know the purity of his heart, my son," the rebbe said. "Tell him to come to Lublin to see me next week, or, better still, you take him there."

"I promise, Rebbe, God willing," Mendale said.

Rebbe Israel looked like he was concluding the interview, and Mendale stood up to go.

"Is there anything I can do for you, Menachem Mendel?" the rebbe asked.

"I'm content with the bounty that the Holy One has bestowed upon me," Mendale said. "I have prosperous businesses, a good wife, and three wonderful children."

"Tell me about the little doves," the rebbe commanded.

"I have three little girls, each one a blessing."

"And no son?" the rebbe asked.

"No, Rebbe, not yet."

"Then I shall pray that Idisel, the only child of my beloved friend, give birth to a son."

"Rebbe, it is my fervent prayer as well."

Mendale left the train with a light feeling. He didn't really believe that the "wonder rebbes" could perform miracles, as many Jews did. But this one seemed—spiritual, of another category.

Chapter 32
HAPPINESS AND DESPAIR

The following year, the Hellers became the proud parents of a beautiful curly-haired boy, whom they named Symcha—after Mendale's father. There was a great deal of rejoicing in the Heller house.

On the eighth day after his birth, the Covenant of Circumcision ceremony was to take place. A famous local cook was employed to prepare the feast, the house was readied for the occasion, and arrangements were made to welcome half the town of Stoczek.

By ten o'clock on the great day, the mohel and the rabbi arrived, followed by a crowd of men and women. The doctor placed himself near the mohel, so he could see that all hygienic measures were strictly observed and oversaw the mohel's preparations: the instruments, the medication, a glass tube, and cotton. He placed these items on a small table covered with a white cloth, washed his hands, and then recited a blessing.

Idisel appeared at the door of the bedroom, carrying the baby. She showed his lovely pink face to the crowd. They all began singing "*Baruch HaBa*" (Blessed is he who comes) as she handed the baby to the godmother, who gave it to the godfather. The mohel then took the infant and placed him on a pillow, and handed him to his Uncle Aron who was the *Sandak* (the holder).

Idisel remained standing at the door as the operation was taking place. She couldn't bring herself to watch what was happening to her baby. Suddenly she heard him cry out, and she winced, still not daring to look in his direction. Anyway, the men were all around him.

Golda whispers in her ear: "Dear girl, your son is being brought into the Covenant of Abraham. Be proud and content."

Soon the baby stopped crying and when some of the men moved away, she could see that he was sucking on something the mohel had put in his mouth—some wine on a piece of cotton. Now she heard Mendale's voice, reciting the benediction:

"Blessed art Thou. . . who hast hallowed us by Thy commandments, and hast commanded us to make our sons enter into the Covenant of Abraham our father."

Mendale was how holding the baby proudly. He was very quiet as the mohel recited the benediction praising God and added a prayer for the welfare of the boy. Finally he called out the name, Symcha. Mendale now came over to Idisel and gave her the baby. His ordeal over, he was already falling asleep.

Then the party began and lasted into the night.

The radio broadcast was interrupted by solemn music and patriotic Polish songs. The announcer then stated that Marshal Jozef Pilsudski had just died. It was May 12, 1935.

Mendale was shaken by the news. The old marshal had run Poland single-handedly for nearly ten years and had held the nation together. Even his pact with Hitler the year before, 1934, could be defended. Pilsudski would have preferred to fight Hitler, but without the help of France, that had not been possible. In view of the more serious threat to Poland's security from the communists on its eastern frontier, the pact with Hitler had been inevitable.

This event began to have tremendous repercussions on what happened in Poland. As Hitler's measures against the German Jews grew harsher by the day, Poland's right wing strove to emulate his behavior, and they put pressure on the government to enact similar laws. Only the marshal's sense of fairness and sturdy opposition to such measures had stopped them. Now Pilsudski was dead, and the future for Poland looked bleak, and even bleaker for Poland's Jews.

The following day at dinner Mendale formally addressed the family:

"I have a feeling that great changes are about to take place in this country. The anti-Semites may take over the government and try to destroy us. They may not go as far as the Nazis have done, but they already have a blueprint for action.

"I promise you, my children, that we will no longer submit to the cruelty of these evil people. Within a short time, we will be going to the Land of Israel."

Later that week, a traveling group of musicians came to town and many adults and children surrounded them in the square, where they played and sang a number of popular songs. For the finale, however, they sang a song that no one had ever hear before:

"To the Land of Israel, fellow Jews,
There we must go right now,
For that is our own beloved land.

"Since the world has been in existence,
Jews have never suffered so much,
For everywhere, all over the world,
There are now anti-Semites.

"They hate us and degrade us.
Why do we persist in living in fear?
Let's pack our bags and get going,
To the Land of Israel."

The singer, a young man in tattered clothing and a sad face, asked everyone to join in the refrain, and the crown responded loudly:

"To the Land of Israel, fellow Jews,
There we must go right now,
*For that is our own beloved land."**

Some heckler in the back shouted, "That's right, Jews, go to Palestine. We're sick of you."

Then some others joined in, chanting angrily: "Jews go to Palestine, Jews go to Palestine."

Pilsudski's death was followed by many changes, most of them oppressive to the minorities. Compulsory religious instruction was introduced in the public schools for the first time. The Catholic children in Stoczek were to be taught by a Jesuit priest and the Jewish children by an accredited Jewish teacher who had had religious training.

Soon Pan Meht was hired by the educational system. He was a graduate of a Hebrew teachers' academy, as well as a certified secular teacher. He spoke fluent Hebrew, was modern and at the same time observant.

It occurred to Mendale that here was the ideal person to do private

---

* "Kan Eretz Israel"—composer unknown

tutoring as well as teach the Heller children modern Hebrew, a language they would need when they got to Palestine. Meht agreed, but since he was un-married, he asked that, instead of payment, he be allowed to have dinner each day with the family. The agreement was made and the lessons started.

A new world opened for the three little girls. They read stories about the land and the people, about ancient Jerusalem, the city that King David built. Meht taught them poetry of Chaim Nachman Bialik, who wrote about the contemporary Land of Israel.

The stories in their readers told about the new city of Tel Aviv, and showed pictures of children playing on the beach and others swimming in the sea. It was a land of sunshine and oranges, a magical land they were soon to be part of. Meht had also taught them the songs of the *halutzim*, young pioneers on the *kibbutz*, the collective farm, and the songs children sang in school. Soon they were speaking the language with ease and look-ing forward to their travels.

Pan Meht was quite different when he taught religion at public school. He was stricter and tried not to show favoritism to the Heller children. They had to learn the sad facts of their long history, which was difficult and painful. They also studied parts of the Bible and read about the great heroes and marvelous events of ancient days. Many of these stories were quite familiar to them because Grandma Golda read them every Sabbath to the children from the "Woman's Bible."

There was also a private school for boys in Stoczek called Talmud Torah, with instruction centered on the study of the Torah, plus Jewish values, laws, and ethics. A new requirement had been introduced by the Ministry of Education that all religious schools were also required to hire accredited teachers to teach the Polish language and history. At Talmud Torah, the new teacher's name was Bela, and she came from Siedlce. Meht and she fell in love.

They came to tell Mendale about their plans to get married and that they had applied to go to Palestine. They had already started saving money for the journey. Both of them had jobs as teachers waiting for then in the Land of Israel and had official requests for their services.

Mendale wished them well and offered to help them in any way he could. He was glad that at least some people were having an opportunity to get out of Poland.

It was a Sabbath, and a beautiful summer's day, but in Mendale's heart there was only a desperate anxiety. Symchale, his son, was ill. The boy had filled the life of his proud father. Mendale had taken time from important business matters to push the infant's pram through the park. He had played with him and bathed him. He had felt guilty that he had not devoted so much time to his girls when they were small.

Soon after his first birthday, Symchale had started walking and was able to say many words. He delighted them all with his sweet disposition and his intelligence. But then, just when everything was going so well, the boy fell sick.

The doctor, who'd been at the Hellers' since early that Sabbath morning, emerged from the sickroom.

"Pan Heller," he said in response to Mendale's frantic questions, "your son has an advanced case of pneumonia. His temperature has increased very rapidly, and as you can see, his breathing is becoming more difficult."

Idisel came into the room, and it was obvious she had heard all the doctor said. She was pale but resolute. "What must be done, Doctor?" she said in a voice that was nearly steady.

"To prevent any further deterioration," he said to both parents, "I would recommend that we take him to Warsaw to the hospital. There he will get the best care possible."

"If that's what we must do," Mendale said, "I'm ready to go right now. Idisel, what do you think?" She readily agreed.

"Then I will call the hospital, and make all the arrangements," the doctor said. "Meanwhile, keep putting cold compresses on his head, and sponge him to reduce the fever."

"I'm going with you, Doctor. I'd like to get a specialist to come here, no matter what the cost, so he can treat him before the ambulance arrives."

Both men now left the room, and Idisel was alone with her baby, and hung over the crib. Little Symchale made fretful, sick kinds of noises, quite unlike his usual healthy wail, and his color was bad. It terrified her. Surely the Creator did not mean to take away their baby. They had only had him for such a short time. . . .

She wished her father were here. He was always able to calm her fears. But Reb Shaul had gone to visit his sister Malka in Skole and would not be home for some weeks. She must be strong on her own. She must be strong for Mendale all through this ordeal.

In the afternoon the specialist arrived. He consulted briefly with the doctor, and examined the baby. Then he turned to Mendale and Idisel.

"I concur with your doctor. The baby has to be moved to the hospital immediately. Since the trip is long, we'll have to try and improve his breathing before we go." He then ordered the nurse to bring in the equipment and asked the Hellers to leave the room.

Symchale received the best of care in the hospital, but he didn't improve and soon lapsed into a coma. Another specialist was called in, to no avail. Mendale and Idisel stayed in the hospital all day, praying at the baby's cribside. Late at night they would return to their hotel room, exhausted and despondent. They slept little, but talked a great deal, and tried to comfort each other.

Then Noah, their partner, came to see them about some urgent matter at the electric plant. But, recognizing the crisis the young parents were facing, he dropped that and suggested to Mendale that they go to pray at the Nozik Synagogue. Mendale loved that particular *shul,* but now he needed some prodding. He agreed finally, and they headed for Twarda Street, where the Nozik Shul was located. On the way, Mendale told Reb Noah about Symchale's deteriorating condition."Ah," Reb Noah said, "the doctors have done all they can for the boy. Now it's time to consult with a man of God. When prayers are over, let us go to see my rebbe."

Mendale did not answer, but he felt sufficiently uplifted and consoled by the prayer service that he agreed to visit the Kozienice Rebbe. However, he warned Reb Noah that he was not a believer in miracle-working rebbes.

"Miracles can only be performed by the Creator, Reb Noah."

When they arrived at the Kozienice Rebbe's house, they were shown into a waiting room full of people of every description and age. Some were dressed expensively and others very humbly. All of them looked worried and sad. After some minutes a thin dark man entered and called out his name, and when he responded, told him to write a note stating what he wanted the rebbe to do.

Mendale wrote the note and handed it over, and the secretary said, "Follow me."

So far it was similar to his encounter with Rebbe Israel at the train station. But then it began to change.

When they entered a long hallway, the man stopped and said, "That will be 500 zlotys, Reb Menachem Mendel."

Mendale took out his wallet and handed him the money, which quickly disappeared into a pouch the secretary was wearing on his shoulder. The man then jotted down the name and amount received in a ledger he was carrying, and then ushered Mendale into the rebbe's study.

The Kozienice Rebbe was seated at a large ornate table. He was a middle-aged man, dressed in a long black velvet robe. The curtains of the room were drawn, and everything looked dark and mysterious. A single light shone on the rebbe's face, making certain features stand out and surrounding it with a halo of light.

"So you're Menachem Mendel," the rebbe said extending his hand. Mendale placed his own hand in the rebbe's, and their eyes met. A kind of hypnotic power seemed to engulf Mendale. He tried to fight it, but was unable to do so. The rebbe finally spoke in a sweet and soothing voice:

"My beloved Hasid, Reb Noah Weintraub, has told me about you. You are a righteous man. You help the poor and the needy, the widow and the orphan. You work for the benefit of our people. You are a loving husband and father, and you obey the commandment to honor your father and mother. Our Heavenly Father will surely reward you for that."

The rebbe now released Mendale's hand, but held him spellbound with his eyes.

Now tell me, Menachem Mendel ben Symcha Shlomo, of blessed memory, what is your petition?"

The secretary laid the note on the table, but the holy man didn't look at it. His eyes were concentrated on Mendale. They looked green at times and seemed to change suddenly to an intense gold.

It seemed to Mendale that he was in a surrealistic dream. He had never believed in the powers of Hasidic rebbes, but he heard himself saying words against his own will:

"Help me, Rebbe. My only son, Symchale, is in the hospital. He is only a baby of sixteen months, and he's dying. He's dearer to me than my own life. Save him, Rebbe. He's a beautiful and innocent soul."

The rebbe now stood up, his gaze still holding Mendale riveted. Then he closed his eyes and began to sway. Mendale felt himself swaying too. The rebbe seemed to be in a trance. After what seemed a long time, the holy man opened his eyes. They seemed to release Mendale now, and he was able to move normally.

"Wake up, Menachem Mendel," the rebbe said, "and go back to your son. He will live. He will get well. The Holy One, blessed be He, has heard my prayer."

Mendale walked out of the rebbe's study in a daze. If Reb Noah hadn't been with him, he later thought, he could not have found his way back to the hospital. He saw himself in the window of a nearby shop and thought his eyes looked glazed and strange. His body felt light, and he seemed to be floating in air.

Idisel was sitting beside the baby's crib. She was crying, and he told her to cheer up. The Kozienicer had promised that Symchale was going to recover. They both looked at the baby and were filled with great hope.

Symchale died the next day.

After the funeral they went home. The ride in the bus had a dreamlike quality. Neither of them talked. They felt empty and forgotten by God.

The girls heard them coming and woke up. Someone switched on the light in the hall, and Mendale and Idisel stood in the doorway.

"Where is our baby?" Surale asked, but even as the words were coming out of her mouth, she saw the expression on their faces and the black armband on her father's jacket, and she understood everything.

Cyla, being older, didn't have to ask. Chanale looked on in bewilderment.

"We had to leave Symchale in Warsaw, my doves," they heard their father say. He was near tears and couldn't go on.

Idisel was numb. She had no more tears left, but she felt pity for her girls:

"Symchale is now in heaven, my dear children," she heard herself saying. "Nothing can hurt him now. He's with all the beautiful angels."

Now they took the girls into their arms and stayed with them until they stopped crying and fell asleep.

Idisel went to the closet where the baby's clothes were put away in neat piles. She picked them up one by one—the little shirts, the sweaters, the night clothes, the socks. Then she put her face against a sweater that had not been laundered since the baby got sick. It still held Symchale's sweet smell. She began to sob, but no tears came. Her body was heaving, her hands trembling. Mendale had lost a son, but she had lost a baby.

"My baby, my baby," she kept repeating, "so cold and alone in his grave."

After the death of his son, Mendale threw himself more and more into his work, and spent a great deal of time on business ventures. The pain in his heart didn't subside even when he said *kaddish*, the special prayer for the dead, twice a day. It only served as a reminder to him of what he had lost.

As a city councilman, he worked harder than ever, taking on the jobs no one wanted and heading difficult committees, which were most time-consuming.

One day, Wielgosek, the mayor, called a joint meeting of the city council, and the freeholders, who represented Stoczek in the county government. When all had assembled, Pan Wielgosek rose from his seat and announced that he was resigning the mayoralty.

There was an outburst of protest, but the mayor silenced them by holding up an official letter from the Ministry of Interior, which pointed out that he was no longer entitled to hold two positions. He was both mayor of Stoczek and principal of the public school.

"Our beloved fatherland needs me most in the field of education," Wielgosek said, and had to stop because all over the room he heard shouting:

"Don't do it". . . "Our city needs you". . . "We'll never be able to replace you."

"Poland has to nurture a young generation of free men. We have to combat ignorance and old prejudices, and overcome both. Under Russia, we Poles weren't allowed to study. Now we have to instill in the youth of today the knowledge that only through education can they continue to be truly free men."

There was much animated and agitated discussion, but the mayor had made up his mind, and in the end he handed his letter of resignation to the secretary, and walked out of the chamber.

Silence. Then someone timidly suggested they take up the question of interim mayor, to hold office until a new man could be elected. Everyone began talking at the same time, names were bandied back and forth. Someone suggested that Michalowski, one of the freeholders, was the logical choice, and many others called out in agreement.

Then another of the freeholders, Jan Buzynski, a tall, corpulent fellow, stood up and said, "Before a new mayor is elected, I think certain steps should be taken. Mayor Wielgosek, with all due respect, represents the point of view of the old Pilsudski regime. We would like to see someone with a more modern outlook. I therefore move that all the freeholders resign, so we can elect a new group, who will better represent us in the county government.

"Wait a minute, Pan Buzynski," someone broke in. "What do you mean by 'a more modern outlook'?"

Buzynski, gazed coldly at his questioner, but his reply was unequivocal: "We look to new leadership to modernize our country along German lines."

"I second the motion," someone shouted.

Mendale was appalled. He had had no idea that there were Nazis right here in little Stoczek. He realized that Jan's strategy was to get rid of the only Jewish freeholder, Nuhem Latowicki, who was also a Zionist.

"Pan Secretary," Mendale said, "I move to postpone this meeting so all of us may have time to decide what to do next."

He got shouted down. Many people were clamoring for the resignation of the freeholders.

Mendale quickly signaled to his Jewish colleagues, and they gathered around him. "If we walk out of here, they will no longer have a quorum, and anything they decide will be illegal." The others agreed, and Mendale addressed the council: "Gentlemen, I respectfully submit that the meeting be adjourned. My colleagues and I are leaving the chamber. Under the rules, no further business can be transacted." He then walked out, followed by his friends.

In spite of this warning, the meeting went on. All the freeholders resigned. The new freeholders who were elected subsequently were of a new breed. Realizing that by law they had to have at least one minority representative, they appointed a shoemaker, Shloma Weinberg, as their token Jew.

Michalowski, who was elected mayor, was quite different from the democratic Pan Wielgosek. The new mayor was a self-seeking individual, pompous and openly disparaging of the Jewish minority.

Mendale knew that there was no appealing to him on the illegal way the freeholders and council had acted. He therefore drafted a letter to the Ministry of Interior, outlining the irregularities.

It took a year for the ministry to act on the case. An investigation was made by them, and a new election was ordered, at which Nuhem Latowicki was reelected to his original seat, as were other freeholders, who considered Wielgosek to be their mentor.

But as things got somewhat better locally, the general situation in the country deteriorated, politically, economically, and socially. Where before people tried to hide their negative feelings about Jews, it now became fashionable to express them publicly, both verbally and through violence. With the death of Pilsudski and the ascendancy of Hitler in Germany, the Republic of Poland was being steadily engulfed by a foul tide of anti-Semitism.

Chapter 33
HARD TIMES

The week before, a great tragedy had befallen the Jews of Minsk-Mazowiecki, a town less than 30 kilometers away—a pogrom. The terrorists had shouted "Jews to Palestine," The community in Stoczek was gripped by fear.

Mendale was distraught by the news. As a man of action, he wanted to do something about this latest outrage. He thought of arming himself and advising others to do the same. Possession of arms was against the law, but the government hadn't stopped the murderers from using arms against the innocent people of Minsk-Mazowiecki. All he could think of at the moment was to call a joint meeting of all Jewish organizations in town.

It was a Thursday evening and the Hellers were at supper, when Sura Celnik, the housekeeper, announced that two men had come to speak to Mendale. He told her to show them in.

Haim Zisia, the butcher, tall and muscular, spoke first:

"Reb Mendale, the rabbi sent us here to discuss something of utmost importance." He glanced sideways at the children, and Mendale took the hint. Idisel and the maid ushered them out.

"This morning, I went out to a farm to buy a cow from a farmer I know. Zbigniew is a good man, and I've known him for many years. As we were closing the deal, he said: "Haim Zisia, I must warn you. They are planning a pogrom in Stoczek this coming Tuesday, during market day."

"The news was not unexpected, but Mendale still felt his heart jump. "Go on," he said.

"Well, I asked him who "they" were, and he answered that it involved people form his village and a few other surrounding villages, under a group of leaders in Stoczek itself. I tried to get him to name some of these leaders, but he either couldn't or wouldn't. He swore me to secrecy not to divulge his name, or they would surely kill him."

Froim Lerman, the baker, then took up the story:

"When Haim Zisia came to me with this news, I asked some of my trusted customers from the villages if it was true that a pogrom was being planned, and they said they had heard about it too. They cursed their fellow villagers for planning such an evil act, but were afraid to name them.

"Haim Zisia and I then went to see the rabbi this afternoon, and he decided to call a meeting of our leaders for eight o'clock this evening. He sent us to get you personally."

Mendale looked closely at the two men, and noticed that each was carrying a knife in his boot. He then went into the bedroom and came out wearing his army belt and pistol. He put on an overcoat to hide the weapon.

Before he left, Mendale turned to Reb Shaul, and asked: "Father-in-law, what do you counsel us to do?

The older man, who'd been listening very attentively to the terrifying news, said:

"My children, if it comes to a fight, there will be bloodshed. Let's try to avoid that. I believe that you should try to alert the authorities, sot that the tragedy can be prevented."

When the three men arrived at the rabbi's house, there were six others there already. Shea Halpern was seated next to the rabbi. Everyone looked worried.

The rabbi began; "Since the death of our beloved leader, Josef Pilsudski, our people have suffered five pogroms in Poland. The pain in my heart is great for the suffering of the Children of Israel. But how are we to put a stop to the massacres?"

Everyone sat quietly thinking, then Latowicki, the freeholder, said; "My dear brothers, we will not stand by and see the innocents slaughtered by these brutal terrorists. We will defend ourselves."

Shea Halpern said, "Defend ourselves with what? They forbid us to carry arms, and yet the assailants have guns."

"We have knives and clubs, and if necessary, we'll defend ourselves with our bare hands." Haim Zisia shouted, "Yes!" and stretched out his powerful arms.

"I say no" the rabbi said loudly. "Esau will not devour Jacob in this town of Stoczek. Let us put our minds together." He looked at Mendale and indeed now they all looked at him.

"It seems to me," he said, "that for all our talk of defending ourselves, we are unarmed. That doesn't mean that we should not fight for out lives, if it comes to t hat. But, my father-in-law advises that we seek the help of the government, in order to prevent violence before it begins."

"Which government?" said Shea Halpern. "You know mayor Michalowski. Some of these terrorists may be his supporters."

"I propose that we send a delegation to the Governor in Lukow, to explain about the impending danger and ask for him help," Mendale said. Meanwhile I will go to the mayor. If we can induce him to put through a call to the governor, that will strengthen our hand, and he doesn't have to act himself."

The men nodded and seemed to take reassurance from the mention of the governor's name. They voted on adoption of Mendale's plan, and it was unanimous in favor.

Early next morning, Mendale went to see Mayor Michalowski. The mayor greeted him jovially. He liked Mendale because he was modern and sophisticated, and had fought in the Great War. "Well, what brings you here so early in the morning, Heller?" he asked.

"Pan Mayor, it's a matter of extreme urgency. Next Tuesday, a group of peasants, led by people from Stoczek, plans a pogrom right here in Stoczek."

"A pogrom in Stoczek? My dear sir, what are you talking about? That's simply preposterous."

"It was probably thought preposterous in Minsk—Mazowiecki, too, Pan Mayor. Before it happened. Our information is very definite."

"Well, that's too bad," Michalowski huffed. "I suppose a few hooligans plan to cause trouble, but they blow off a lot of steam, and then they simmer down. After all, Poland isn't Germany." He started to pack tobacco into his pipe, and puffed to get a light started.

Obviously the mayor determined to pretend that the news was not serious. After all, if Jews were to be the victims, he had nothing to worry about. Perhaps, Mendale thought, the best thing was to give him something to worry about.

"But Pan Mayor," he said, "if there is a pogrom, a lot of town property will be destroyed. Our main revenue comes out of market day. If the market is broken up, there will be no money coming in for months to come."

Now Michalowski put down his pipe, his face a picture. "Maybe you're right, Heller. We can't afford to lose revenue. Well, what do you want to do?"

Mendale told him of the plan. "At ten o'clock Monday morning, we have an appointment with Governor Dr. Szykaly. We request that you put through a call to him at that time to confirm our story."

"And what else?"

"Nothing, Pan Mayor. Except that we ask you not to discuss this matter with anyone else. We must have confidentiality."

"Well, I don't see any problem with that, Heller," the mayor said. "As long as I don't have to deal with this matter personally. Let Szykaly decide."

"Then you will call him, without fail?"

"All right, all right, I will attend to the matter personally on Monday," Michalowski said impatiently.

The entire community spent the Sabbath in prayer and meditation, for the success of the mission to the governor. At dawn on Monday Mendale and Shloma, who had been chosen to accompany him, left for Lukow.

They arrived early and sat in the waiting room for what seemed an eternity. They said little to each other, too nervous about the upcoming meeting. The secretary finally came to call them.

The room they were led into was tremendous and splendid. It was hung with ancient tapestries, depicting scenes of Poland's vanished glory. On the opposite side of the room sat a middle-aged bald man, wearing heavy glasses, Governor Dr. Szykaly. As they approached his desk, he seemed to be studying them carefully. His large green eyes were now fixed sternly on Mendale:

"I hear from my sources that you're from my neck of the woods, Heller," he said to Mendale with a smile.

"Yes, Your Excellency, from the village of Zbora near Lwow," said Mendale, "but I've lived in this area for many years now. This is my home."

"I was born in Lwow and educated there," said the governor. "I must say that the Austrians had an excellent educational system. Unlike the Russians. The illiteracy in this part of the country is positively incredible—a legacy of Russian rule." He broke off and looked at Shloma.

"Pan Weinberg," he said, "you're a native of Stoczek according to my information. What is your opinion of all this?"

"Your excellency, I'm a workingman. I don't have much time to speculate about the things you are discussing. I'm a member of the Bund, and my primary interest is in making conditions better for working people. Aside from that, I don't get mixed up in politics."

"Interesting, Pan Weinberg," Szykaly said, and then added; "well, lets get down to business. What brings the two of you here?"

"As you see, Your Excellency, Weinberg and I are of somewhat different backgrounds, but we have one bond in common—we are both Jews. We were sent here by the Jewish community in Stoczek to appeal to you for yelp. You see, Dr. Szykaly, a lawless element is planning a pogrom in our little town, tomorrow."

The governor looked startled. "In Stoczek? But—no, go on." "We will not allow them to do this to us. If we have to, our people will defend themselves. We refuse to permit a repetition of what happened in the other towns around here. Many lives will be lost, if their plan succeeds, but this time both sides will suffer, not only ours." Mendale stopped.

The governor seemed to be in a state of shock. He rang the bell, and when the secretary came in, he shouted:

"Where is my secret service commissioner? Why wasn't I informed of this? Get him here right away."

"Yes, sir. Right away." The secretary ran out, looking alarmed.

The governor now turned to Mendale "So you plan to offer resistance to these terrorists?"

"Yes, Governor Szykaly," Mendale answered firmly. "We are, by nature and by our most sacred teachings, a peaceful people, but we plan to defend ourselves when attacked. We appeal to Your Excellency to prevent this tragedy."

Dr. Szykaly was about to respond, but the telephone rang. It was Mayor Michalowski. The governor listened attentively and then said:

"My dear mayor, Heller just told me of these unfortunate circumstances. . . . No, we absolutely cannot allow this to happen again. Not in our state. . . . We'll be in touch with you shortly, Mayor Michalowski. Thanks for the information. Good bye." The governor hung up, and seemed totally under control now. The telephone rang again. It was the commissioner, and the governor gave him a series of rapid orders. Then Dr. Szykaly hung up and turned back to his two visitors.

"There will be no pogrom in Stoczek," he said firmly. "The commissioner and his men are on the way, and should be here soon." He then stood up, and continued:

"I have fought for our country's independence, and by my side were people of your religion. They too were patriots. They gave their blood, so Poland would be free. Our constitution guarantees equal rights to all our citizens, and gives them protection under the law. These criminals will not prevail. We Poles will not be compared to the bestial Nazis if I can help it." The governor wiped his brow.

"Pan Heller and Pan Weinberg, I want you to go home now. I promise you that all my agencies, from the secret service to the state police, will be in Stoczek to prevent any illegal activity."

The governor shook hands with them, as they thanked him, and he walked them to the door, saying:

"Go with God, gentlemen. I have a great deal of work to do in the next few hours."

When Mendale and Shloma boarded the train that afternoon, a group of men were already waiting in their compartment: the deputy commissioner of police for the county, and four undercover agents. They introduced themselves and said that they would be traveling with them, and that they had very specific orders from the governor. They were now busily coordinating their activities.

Heller, Weinberg, and the government men got off the train in Siedlce and changed to a bus. As they approached Stoczek, the deputy commissioner asked the bus driver to stop at the mayor's house on the outskirts of town. To Mendale he whispered that fifty additional policemen would arrive during that night to back up the local force.

When Mendale and Shloma got off the bus, they immediately headed for the shul, where the rabbi was deep in prayer. They accompanied him to his house for supper, after which they met with fellow community leaders and reported on the interview with Dr. Szykaly. There was relief on every face when they finished.

Now Yakov Mayer Halpern, the Betar leader, got up to speak: "That's all very well, but we need a contingency in case the governor's strategy fails to abort the pogrom." He pulled a large and efficient-looking Mauser out of his pocket. "I, for one, have a gun."

Mendale reluctantly produced his own Schwartlose automatic, and others pulled out knives, cleavers, and even sticks. In addition, an arsenal would be collected tonight in a shed near the synagogue. At a given signal all able-bodied men would meet there. Everyone had a job to do. There was to be a guard protecting the synagogue and the rabbi.

"But remember, this arsenal is to be used only if the police fail to protect us," the rabbi concluded, and it was agreed.

Mendale got home very late that night and found Idisel and Reb Shaul waiting up for him, worried about his safety. He told them about his mission to the governor and the meeting with the rabbi. "I think we'll be safe," he concluded.

Mendale fell into an exhausted sleep as soon as he got into bed, but Idisel couldn't sleep. She finally got up and checked all the doors and windows, looked in on the sleeping children and then noticed her father in a corner of the dining room. He was in deep meditation, his body swaying gently. He didn't seem to hear her come in. She went back to bed, cuddled up to Mendale, and fell asleep too.

At dawn, the Jewish shopkeepers put up their stands and laid out their wares throughout the main square. Strange policemen appeared at all the entrances to the square, and local men began patrolling between the stands, greeting the shopkeepers politely. Most of the stand owners knew of the threat, and were prepared to defend themselves.

Soon it was light out, and the peasants started entering the square, some in wagons and others on foot. Many were carrying empty sacks. The police knew what those were for, but said nothing. The farmers had planned to fill them with the wares they would steal during the pogrom.

The plain clothes agents circulated through the crowd. When they spotted suspicious-looking people, they turned them over to the local police. Those would be searched and, if found with arms, immediately hauled off to jail. The arrests continued throughout the morning. By noon the jail was full, and the confiscated arms were being sorted out by policemen; pistols, rifles, long knives, and assorted clubs.

In another room, the terrorists were being interrogated. Some of them proclaimed their innocence, but most admitted that they knew about the planned massacre and had been ready to take part. Their leader had escaped into the woods but the police now knew who he was and were fanning out to search.

Mendale's headquarters were at the Halpern house. It was there that he received the news from a group of young Betar boys, on the events in the square. The deputy commissioner came in at three o'clock to report that everything was under control, and that the leaders of the planned pogrom were being hunted in the woods. Leaving Yakov Mayer at the helm, Mendale made his way home through the side streets, accompanied by two state policemen. He saw peasants beginning to return to their villages. Everything seemed orderly.

At home everything was fine. Business had gone on as usual at the mill. Noah was in control, and as far as he knew, nothing extraordinary had happened. Mendale brought the policemen into the kitchen and asked Sura to feed them.

Dinner was served, and everyone was relieved that the threat was over. Mendale told the family about the young boys, some of then no older than ten, who had bravely acted as couriers. He also described the heap of arms the police had confiscated. They finished eating and were about to leave the table when Sura announced that Karol, a farmer who milled his wheat regularly at the mill, was asking to speak to Mendale. The policeman checked Karol for arms, then told him he could come in. "Pan Heller," Karol said, filling the doorway with his powerful frame. " I looked for you all over to warn you, but couldn't find you."

"Come in, Pan Karol," Mendale said. "Don't stay there in the doorway."

"No, my boots are dirty. I'm comfortable right here," the farmer said.

"Well, what's this all about warning me?"

"It's about your engineer, Jaworski, he's your enemy," Karol said. "Early this morning, he told all the farmers who came into the mill that at a given signal the pogrom was to start, and you were going to be the first one to be killed. He picked up one of the huge weights near the scale and showed us how he was going to do it."

Idisel gave a gasp, but Mendale hushed her. " I sneaked out to warn you as soon as I could," the farmer went on, "but couldn't find you anywhere. I just want to tell you that Jaworski is a dangerous man, and you have to keep an eye on him."

"Don't worry, Pan Karol, I'll take care of Jaworski. And for me, thank you for being my friend. One needs a friend in time of trouble." He tried to induce the husky farmer to have a celebratory drink, but Karol refused.

"I can't drink now. I'm going to get my horse and wagon and my flour, and head for church to thank Jesus for saving you from the massacre."

After he had left, Mendale asked the policemen to wait in the dining room while he dealt with his engineer. "If I need you, I'll call," he said and sent word to the mill that he wanted to speak to Jaworski immediately.

Mendale was sitting coolly at his desk, when the engineer appeared. He looked puzzled and ill at ease. Mendale let him stand there for a minute and then said:

"You've been with me for five years now, Jaworski. Do you have any complaints against me or my treatment of you?"

The man looked suspiciously. "I can't say that I have," he said warily, fidgeting from one foot to the other. "You paid me regularly."

"Good wages?"

"Yes."

"Well, I'm hereby reducing your wages by fifty percent," said Mendale. "Times are bad, and our profits are sharply reduced."

Jaworski looked shocked. "You can't do a thing like that, Pan Heller," he protested. "I have a big family and many mouths to feed."

"That's the situation," Mendale said flatly. "If you agree to the reduction, fine, but if it doesn't suit you, you may leave."

The engineer came toward him pale with anger. "Don't give me your double-talk, Jew," he shouted. "I'm quitting your shitty job right now."

"Don't come any closer, you son of a bitch, or I'll break your head." Mendale warned him,

But Jaworski kept coming and swung wildly. Mendale warded off the blow and, hooking a leg behind his opponent, jerked him off his feet. The man crashed to the stone floor, and at the sound of commotion, the policeman rushed into the room and secured him.

"So you were going to kill me today," Mendale said, shooting his cuffs. "If you ever set foot on my property again, I'll shoot you down like a mad dog."

As the police led him through town, some man commented acidly, "There goes another Haman."

By evening, the town was quiet. Soon a delegation of shopkeepers came to see Mendale, to thank him for what he had done. They also brought money and wanted him to give the deputy commissioner 200 zlotys. Mendale declined to have any part in it. "The police had a job to do, and they did it. The law states that they are here to protect all citizens. They don't need a tip."

"Would you then consent to come to a party that we're giving at Hanchi Rubinsztein's bar?" they asked. Mendale agreed to come to the celebration and was the first to offer a toast to those who saved the community from disaster, and to the esteemed governor, Dr. Szykaly.

New laws were constantly being reenacted to stem the deteriorating economic situation. The Jewish community in Stoczek, like those in other small towns, was caught in a squeeze. They were mostly small shopkeepers, artisans, shoemakers, tailors, porters, and middlemen. The poor and hungry were multiplying, as more and more of them were forced to leave their homes and wander about the countryside begging for food and a few groszy, (pennies). Entire families took to the roads, on foot and sometimes in wagons, pulled by mangy horses, who like their owners were perpetually hungry.

Mendale's business was also affected, but now he thought of a way to recoup his losses. He met with his partner Noah and nephew Symcha to discuss the building of a sawmill on the property adjacent to the electric plant. The Stoczek area was surrounded by forests, and there was no sawmill in town. He figured that the plant and machinery would pay for themselves within a period of six months—if all went well—and it would provide work for the unemployed. The sawmill was built rather quickly, and equipped. Labor was plentiful and cheap, because people felt themselves lucky to have even a temporary job. The new mill provided jobs for a number of workers.

The success of Mendale's new business impressed the leaders of the Jewish community, and he was asked to help set up the years' budget.

Until that time, the Jewish community had been autonomous, taking care of its own services, such as welfare for the poor and the sick, and the support of its schools. Now the new law stipulated that the yearly budget would have to be reviewed and approved by the state authorities.

Revenues for Jewish community needs were collected by a special committee, which assessed wealthy individuals in town. Seldom did these citizens refuse to participate, they felt it was their duty to provide the money and time to administer the funds. There was also another source of revenue, taxation on certain community activities, such as ritual slaughter of animals, which provided the kosher meat and poultry for the people.

Mendale and the other budget committee members worked hard on the proposed budget, and after several months' labor, submitted it to the authorities. There was no question in their minds that it would be accepted, yet it was rejected, and in addition, a fine of 200 zlotys was imposed on each member of the committee for "irregularities" in the proposal.

Stunned by the news, the committee wondered what this all portended. A budget commission soon arrived in Stoczek to investigate. They turned in a report to the governor, which stated that the salaries paid out, and expenditures made by the community, proved that the Jews of Stoczek were immensely rich, and they could not allow such a high budget to go through in bad economic times. Furthermore, they proposed an investigation of the Jewish notables, to ascertain if their declared income was not being falsified.

When the committee received a copy of the commission's findings, they were shocked and angry. Had the news of this outrage reached the ears of Dr. Szykaly? They decided to have Mendale draft a letter to the governor.

Mendale made it very clear in his letter that the entire Stoczek community was voicing its protest against this injustice, perpetrated by the budget commission. The people of the town were not asking for government aid for supporting their charities, their schools, or their functionaries. They were providing these services themselves. They had not committed an offense against the law, and yet were being fined and subjected to yet another review of their books. Contrary to the budget commission's report, the Jewish community in town was acting in a most responsible and patriotic way. Mendale concluded the letter by asking Governor Szykaly to intervene on behalf of the people of Stoczek again.

The governor arrived in town the following week with a number of assistants, and met with the Jewish Community Council and the budget committee. By then Mendale and the other members had worked hard to cut out any possible extra spending, and trim off any unnecessary expenditures. The new budget was reduced somewhat, to show that an effort had been made, in views of the criticism.

Dr. Szykaly looked very carefully at the figures and passed the papers on the other officials. They whispered to him concerning their findings for quite a long time. Finally the governor said:

"Things seem to be pretty much in order here. However, I have one question: Is it possible that the rabbi of this small town gets three hundred zlotys a month in salary or is this an error?"

Nuhem Latowicki, the chairman of the committee, stood up and answered: "Yes, Your Excellency. That figure is correct."

The governor shook his head in disbelief. "Do you gentlemen have any idea what my monthly salary, as governor is?" They all shook their heads, and he replied, "Only fifty zlotys more"

Mendale now stood up. "Governor Szykaly, with all due respect to you and your high position, I must state the truth. Our rabbi has had as many years of schooling and preparation in the theological field, as your Excellency has had in secular education. Perhaps this is an important point for you to consider."

Dr. Szykaly began to laugh jovially, and his entourage with him.

"Well, Heller, my friend, send in the new amended budget proposal, and it will be taken care of."

"Sir," Mendale responded, "this budget has to be sent to the office of the lieutenant governor, who doesn't share your sympathy for our problems."

"I know what you mean, Heller," the governor said. "Address a covering letter and revised budget directly to me. I will deal with this matter myself."

Golda came back to Stoczek again, her permanent home now. The options of where to stay were now limited. She could of course, stay in Zakopane, in the mountains where she had her villa, but she was lonely there, and missed her children. America was out of the question, and now she wouldn't be able to go to Germany either for obvious reasons. Golda knew that the mail was being censored by the Nazis.

Reports of their reign of terror were printed in the papers daily. Prominent people were arrested and sent to what the Nazi called "concentration camps." The few individuals who were released told of torture and bestiality by the SS guards and their henchmen, criminal inmates. Jewish businesses were boycotted. Jews were attacked in the streets and beaten up by roaming gangs of ruffians. Their properties were confiscated, the atrocities against them mounting each day.

Earlier that year Willie, one of Shainchi's sons, decided to leave Germany for good. He was a Zionist, en route to Palestine to work on a kibbutz. He stopped off to visit the Polish contingent of the Heller family, and at night, when the younger children were asleep, Willie told the family about the day-to-day horrors of living in Nazi Germany. Golda was torn. She was glad he was out of Nazi Germany, but she wasn't too certain of his safety in Palestine, either.The Arabs there were making life miserable for the settlers, she had heard. But she gave him her blessings and wished him godspeed.

One cold morning, as Golda was looking out the window, she saw a wagon full of beggars approaching her house. It stopped at the gate. Three people got out, and the rest continued on into town. The beggars were heading for the back door, and she hurried there as well.

They were already in the hall when she got there: an old man dressed in a patched coat, with rags tied around his boots, and two women; one middle aged, and the other young, also dressed in rags.

"Dear lady, we're hungry," said the old man sadly. "Anything you can spare will be welcome."

Golda brought them each a large slice of bread and jam, and some money. "May our Heavenly Father repay you for your kindness," said the older of the two as she and the man went on their way. The young woman, however, lingered.

"Please allow me sit down for a moment, dear madam. I'm with child and due any day now." She opened up the loose jacket she was wearing and revealed a big belly. She touched her stomach and said:

"The baby is kicking so hard now. It's trying to get out. It's making me so tired."

"Come into the kitchen, my child," Golda said. Her heart was filled with pity. She took the young woman's hand and led her into the kitchen and sat her down. She heated up some soup and made the young mother eat every drop.

"My name is Hava," the woman said after she had eaten her fill. "Soon after I got pregnant, our house burned down, and my husband lost his job as a tanner. We had to go out begging because we were starving. We joined this group of poor people for protection. One day, about a month ago, as we were spending the night in the woods, my husband disappeared." She began to cry. "I thought he would come back," she said between sobs, "but he had threatened me before that he would run away. He couldn't take this life any more. He always said that he would go to Argentina, where his brother lives, but I didn't believe him. But this time—"

Now she doubled over and cried, "Oh, the pains have started," but then almost immediately she sat up straight again. "No, it has stopped for now." Then she began to beg and plead feverishly, "Don't turn me out into the street. Please, please, I'm an orphan, and have no one to help me in this world, and think my time has now come." She caught her breath and then cried: "Oh, oh, that pain again."

"Don't worry, my child," Golda said. "I wouldn't turn you out. Come with me to the guest house. I'll set you up there, and after your baby is born, we'll see what to do next."

Golda now called in the handyman to start a fire in the stove and clean up the place. She then brought Hava in, fixed her a bed, and handed her a clean nightgown. She tried to help her undress, but Hava declined and said that she was too tired, and would do that later.

Evening came, and Golda sent the handyman to the main house to explain what had happened. "Are the pains starting again?" she asked Hava, as the woman gripped her belly again. Golda looked at her watch and said: "I'll send for the midwife right away."

"No, don't do that yet," Hava said. "The pains stopped now. I just want to rest." She lay down on the bed and closed her eyes.

When she was sure that Hava's pains were no longer coming, Golda decided to go home. She told the woman that the maid would bring her some supper, and after that, the night watchman would be on duty, and would look in on her all night. He would alert Golda if help was needed.

Golda slept fitfully that night. It seemed that someone was calling her. She dreamed that her husband, Symcha was crying, and she had to take care of him, but couldn't reach him.

It was dawn, and she heard Reb Shaul moving about in the next room, getting ready for his morning prayer. She got dressed and went out. She saw the watchman, and he told her that he had checked periodically during the night, but nothing had happened.

Hava was fast asleep, when Golda came in, her big belling sticking up under the covers. She didn't wake her, but got busy and lighted the fire in the stove. She began cooking some oatmeal she had brought with her. She set out bread, and butter, and milk, and waited for the woman to wake up.

While Hava was eating her breakfast, she told Golda that the pains had stopped altogether, and it seemed that it had been a false alarm.

Hava stayed in the guest house for three weeks. The women in the neighborhood came to see her and said that first babies sometimes came as much as a month late. Golda catered to Hava in every way possible. On the Sabbath the young woman would eat with the Hellers. In the afternoon, she would sit with the children and listen to Golda read the *Tsena-u-Rena*. Her pretty face lighting up with pleasure. She was like a little child, asking all kinds of questions.

Now Golda began to worry. The young woman was a month overdue, and no baby in sight. She suggested that they call the doctor, but Hava wouldn't hear of it.

"You have been so kind to me, Frau Heller," she said. "I don't want you to spend more money on me."

When Paya, Sura's mother came to do the wash that week, Golda asked her advice. "To tell you the truth, Frau Heller," she said, "I'm suspicious of this young woman. I wasn't going to say anything, but now that you're asking me, I'll tell you. She certainly doesn't look to me to be in the ninth month. She walks too briskly. The whole thing is very strange."

Golda decided then and there to call the doctor, this time without consulting the young woman. The doctor arrived and went in to examine

Hava, while Golda waited outside. Suddenly she heard the young woman scream:

"Don't you touch me. You get out of here, or I'll knock you down." The doctor came running out of the room, holding on to his black bag.

"This is unheard of," he said breathlessly. "That woman isn't pregnant at all, Frau Heller. It's all padding. She has perpetrated a most ridiculous hoax on you."

Now Hava came running out of the room, dressed and carrying a small bundle. As she passed Golda she shouted: "He's lying, Frau Heller. I'm not staying here another minute."

Golda and the doctor watched in amazement as Hava disappeared quickly down the road.

One day when Mendale arrived early for a City Council meeting, Mayor Michalowski seemed terribly upset.

"Come in, my boy," he said. "I'm glad that the others haven't arrived as yet. I have to talk to you about this business of Zelig Rogalski. The subject has been brought to my attention again. When is this unpleasant matter going to be resolved?"

Mendale had to think for a moment what this was all about. Oh, right, Zelig had been renting a store in the Town Hall building, from which he had sold gasoline, kerosene, naphtha, and other petroleum products. His small business, like many others in town, had collapsed in the general depression, and for months now, he hadn't paid his rent. Mendale knew that in order to dispossess him, the town council would have to bring suit against him in court. He didn't want to suggest that to the mayor, because he felt sorry for Zelig.

"Mayor Michalowski," he said finally, "to sue this man would cost money, and our treasury is depleted, as you well know."

"We know that he's closed the store," the mayor said, agitated, "so what's he doing with it? We've asked him time and again to vacate the premises, and each time he has refused." Michalowski stood up. His corpulent frame shaking with anger. "If this man doesn't get out of our building right away, I will take my revenge on all of you people in this town."

Mendale winced. Michalowski wasn't as nasty as he sounded right now. The mayor didn't particularly like Jews, but lately, he had tried to be fair, and had personally treated him with kindness, often stating that he forgot that Mendale was a Jew. This insult was supposed to be a supreme compliment, but most Jews were used to it.

Heller remembered also that the previous winter, a severe one, he had persuaded Michalowski to provide 110 square meters of cut wood from the national forest, to be distributed to the poor. Michalowski had known, that very few Christians would benefit from the charity, for most Christians owned land around town, including wood lots, whereas Jews did not—another legacy of the long Russian occupation. Yet he had agreed, and Mendale had been grateful to him for showing such compassion and understanding.

He decided now to swallow his anger and, try to straighten out the problem at hand.

"Pan Mayor," Mendale finally said, "allow me to speak to Zelig. His behavior has been inexcusable, and I promise I'll have an answer for you at our next meeting."

Michalowski seemed pleased. "All right, Heller, I depend on you to take care of this matter."

At the first opportunity, Mendale went to see Zelig Rogalski, and told him about his encounter with the mayor. "Reb Zelig," he said, "you'll have to move out to avert more trouble. Besides, it's unfair of you to keep the store and not pay the rent."

Now Zelig was upset. "Why are you mixing into this business, Reb Mendale?"

"Look, Reb Zelig, the mayor good as promised to take revenge on all of us if you don't give up the store, " Mendale answered, bluntly. "So far he hasn't been bad to us. He tries to be fair. . . "

Zelig had heard enough. "All right, all right," he shouted. "I've had enough of this preaching. Go back to the cripple, and tell him he should drop dead. I don't have money to pay the rent. Does he want my children to starve?"

"Nobody wants that, Reb Zelig, but if you persist, we'll have to evict you. I wouldn't want to be a party to that. It's a very unpleasant business."

Zelig showed Mendale to the door, and said: "Good-bye Heller. I'm not afraid of Michalowski's threats. I know that the town treasury doesn't have enough money to prosecute me, so they can't evict me." Then he whispered into Mendale's ear:

"Just tell the old son of a bitch Essau to drop dead. And may he rot in hell. That's my answer to him."

At the next meeting the mayor asked Heller what he had accomplished with Rogalski.

"Pan Mayor, Mendale said, "I spoke to Zelig. The situation is complicated. He's a poor man with six mouths to feed and deeply in debt. I checked, and it's true that his store is closed. But he keeps his merchandise in it and goes out to the villages to peddle a bit here and a bit there, trying to stay afloat . . ." Mendale stopped, waiting for Michalowski's reaction.

"Well, go on, what was Rogalski's answer?"

"He said that he can't possibly give up the store now, because he and his family would starve if he did," Mendale said uncomfortably.

Michalowski was now livid with rage. "You people, you're so underhanded and dishonest," he shouted. "One of us Christians, if he got angry at somebody, might kill him, but he would never swindle him like you Jews do."

Mendale wanted to knock the man down, but restrained himself with a great effort.

"I get your point, Pan Michalowski, and I'd like to reiterate publicly, that our people don't believe in killing," he managed to say. "The feelings you expressed just now make me realize more than ever, that our morality is indeed different than yours."

Mendale then walked out of the meeting and resolved to have as few dealings with the mayor in the future as possible.

Chapter 34
TIME TO JOURNEY AGAIN

Mayor Michalowski's tantrum struck hard at Mendale. What the mayor had expressed in anger, Heller felt, would soon be put into action, not only in Stoczek but all over Poland. Now he had to concentrate all his efforts and ingenuity in getting to the Land of Israel.

The English, who held the mandate for Palestine, had restricted Jewish immigration to that country after the riots of 1929. Although the mandate called for the reestablishment of a Jewish national home in Palestine, the British were now, years later, hedging and stalling, giving as a reason the opposition of the Arabs to the creation of such an entity.

Mendale wrote a number of letters to the British consul in Warsaw, requesting an appointment. After some weeks, he received the appointment, and his interview went well. He returned home in a hopeful mood. But not for long. Soon inquiries were made in Stoczek concerning the would-be immigrant, and he was refused a visa. Mendale tried to get another appointment with the consul to plead his case, but his assistant said emphatically:

"We know you're a Zionist, and a leader in your community. Right now we don't need more trouble in Palestine. We've got our hands full, keeping you and the Arabs apart," and the Englishman hung up on him.

Mendale had been a member of the General Zionist Organization for some time, but now he decided to join the Mizrachi. He had known some of the leaders of this organization in Altona after the war. That city had been the center of the movement for many years. Now, so many years later, he felt the need for a greater spiritual base in his striving for Zion. Since the death of his son, his religious consciousness was more profound. Others in Stoczek were of the same mind, sharing a common goal of reaching the Land of Israel, where they would achieve personal fulfillment in the spiritual revival of the nation, based on the Torah.

Soon after he joined the Mizrachi, he got word that the British were admitting a new category of people to Palestine: rabbis. He decided to become a rabbi, even if only temporarily. He made some contacts at the Yeshiva in Lublin, and after a special examination, received an official certificate of ordination. He grew a beard and dressed like a rabbi, and had pictures taken of himself looking the part. He made a new application to leave the country through the Mizrachi Organization in Warsaw. Then came months of waiting for a reply. He was refused again. This time no explanation was given.

Mendale didn't despair. He continued for ways to get out. At night he had recurring dreams about another war, and he saw himself in the trenches fighting again. There were dead people all around him, but he survived and was running toward Idisel and his children to save them from danger. His dream always ended there. He would wake up each time with greater resolve to get out of Poland.

He knew instinctively that a war, of more terrible proportions than the last one, would soon come.

One day he got word from a member of the political committee of the Mizrachi in Warsaw that a new British consul had arrived in Poland. It was possible now to apply for a visa as a "capitalist." This meant depositing a large amount of money with the consulate. Mendale's hopes were again revived. He went to Warsaw and filled out a new application. Within a few months he was called for an interview.

"Mr. Heller, what do you propose to do in Palestine?" asked the consul, a thin man with gray impersonal eyes.

"I hope to use my capital to establish a business there, sir." he answered. He knew that he had to be concise and careful in answering the questions put to him. He was going to tell this Englishman exactly what the man wanted to hear.

"Do you realize, Mr. Heller, that you may fail in what you propose?" the consul said. "Times are very hard in Palestine, and we do not like to encourage people to think that they will be entering Paradise." The man looked sternly at Mendale, and continued: "Does this information discourage you, Mr. Heller?"

"No, sir," Mendale answered. "I have a talent for business and have been successful in most of my undertakings. I'm confident that my luck will hold out in Palestine as well."

"Do you believe in armed resistance to the British authorities?" the consul asked, as he looked down at a paper in front of him.

"By no means, sir. I do not believe that anything can be gained by brute force. I fought in the World War. It proved nothing, as far as I'm concerned."

"We have a dossier on you," the consul continued, "and it states here that you're a militant Zionist. We must suspect that you may harbor terrorist ideas." The man stood up now, and looked down on Mendale, trying to intimidate him.

Mendale wanted to say, Jews have always been the *victims* of terrorist ideas, not the *promoters* of them. But he kept his tongue and said evenly, "If you'll check on that information, sir, you'll find that I belong to Mizrachi. We are a peaceful group. Our aim has always been to uplift our people spiritually, according to the precepts of the Bible. We do not engage in terrorist acts and reject the use of force to solve problems."

"I, too, am a believer in the Bible, and the prophecy that the Promised Land will one day belong to your people," the consul said. "However, I'm also a pragmatist. Unlike many in the foreign service, I do not favor the Arabs. They are a feudal and barbaric people, constantly fighting their Jihad (Holy War). They are polygamists, and treat their women like slaves. They are simply uncivilized." The consul stopped and looked at Mendale inquiringly. "Do you agree with this assessment of the Arabs?"

"I try not to prejudge the Arab people and their customs. It's true that in recent years they have massacred our people in Palestine. However, there was a period in history when we and they lived in harmony in Spain, and together we formed and produced a great cultural revival. Now the Arabs possess many lands in Asia and Africa. We want only our small country back, where we can be free men, and guide our own destiny with the help of the Almighty." Mendale stopped, then added: "I'm sorry. I didn't mean to make a speech."

"That's quite all light, Mr. Heller," the consul said. "This has been an interesting revelation to me. We should not be taking sides in these delicate matters." He stood up again and said, "Now to the subject of your visa, Mr. Heller. I will personally review your case, and will make inquiries as to your financial position. Is there anything else you want to say on your behalf?"

"Yes, I do, sir," Mendale answered. "I want to appeal to you to grant me a visa. At the present time, indignities are being perpetrated against my people in this country and I'm afraid they are going to get worse. I'm willing to suffer hardships in Palestine to regain my pride as a man."

"Assuming that your information checks out," the consul said, "I see no reason why we would refuse you a visa." The man shook hands with Mendale and added: "You should hear from within a short time. If our answer is favorable, you will have to deposit the money required immediately."

Mendale returned home with great hopes. In his mind's eye he could see himself in the Land of Israel, working hard physically but a free man at last. The dream would soon become reality.

He now took the next step and applied to the Ministry of Interior for permission to leave the country. Soon after, he received an answer that he must pay all his taxes before he would be allowed to leave. The Internal Revenue Commission then sent him his estimated tax, and when he received it, Mendale was stunned. The commission had decided to tax him beyond his limits to pay. This was obviously an anti-Semitic act on their part, to defraud him of all of his money. He decided to fight fire with fire. He immediately filed a petition, requesting that his estimated tax be reviewed. He stated that the sum the commission requested was totally unfair and would leave him penniless and unable to emigrate to Palestine. He got no reply.

Mendale knew that there would be inquiries as to his financial status. Government questions of this type had often come to him concerning other citizens of the community, or they were directed to Shea Halpern. He went to see his friend then and told him about his problem.

"Reb Shea, if the ministry inquires about my financial status, tell them that although my income is good, I have a number of debts and I'm in real financial trouble. Maybe that will get them off my back."

His friend readily agreed to help, and when, a few weeks later, a confidential letter arrived from an independent law firm in Warsaw, asking about Mendale's financial status, Reb Shea answered exactly as his friend had told him. He added that Heller was on the verge of bankruptcy.

Within days Mendale received a rejection form the British Consulate. The inquiry had been made by them and not the ministry. The letter included a copy of the findings concerning Heller's financial status signed by Halpern. There was also a note from the consul. He wrote that he was particularly disappointed in Mendale's fraudulent statements concerning his finances and added that, as long as he was British Consul in Warsaw, he would never issue Heller a visa for Palestine.

Mendale had difficulty dealing with this setback. He was in a state of shock for days. The only way left for him now was to go illegally, as others were going. A new plan would have to be devised, and that would take a great deal of effort, time, and money.

But once he made his decision, he began to work toward it in secret. There was no use brooding about lost opportunities and mistakes. Life had to go on. . . .

In the spring of 1936, a young and very handsome couple came to Stoczek and rented an apartment in the Halpern house. Dr. Vovek Honikman was a medical doctor, and Hadasa, his wife, a dentist. Both of them came from very wealthy families in a nearby town of Ciechanow.

They had no children, but received a Scotch terrier as a gift from Vovek's mother. Special foods were prepared daily for Morus, the little dog. He was pampered and dressed in very elegant outfits and dog collars.

In a town where dogs were not particularly catered to, Morus was the subject of many jokes. Some people were downright angry: "Why don't they adopt a poor child and feed and clothe it, instead of fussing over that useless dog?" they'd fume.

The Hellers and Honikmans became friends. One Sunday afternoon at the Hellers' house, they were discussing Mendale's latest attempt to leave Poland, and Vovek said carelessly, "Give up your business of trying to go to Palestine. Stay here. Poland is your real home."

Mendale was surprised and a bit annoyed. "Vovek, you are really naïve," he said.

"Naïve?"

"Don't you see what's happening right in front of your nose? Last September, Hitler instituted the Nuremburg Laws, a throwback to the Dark Ages. But no one in this so-called 'civilized' world seems to give a damn. The Jews in that country have lost their citizenship, their rights to hold jobs, the right to be human beings."

"But that's Germany," the doctor said. "Poles are different."

"Oh, are they? How far from Germany are we? We now have our home-grown Nazis. They're ready to do the same thing right here." Mendale stopped for a moment. "This country is falling apart. Another war will soon come, and we will be the first victims of it."

"Oh, come on, Mendale, you sound like a prophet of doom," Vovek said. "England and France would never allow Poland to be attacked. Besides, it's rumored that Hitler is afraid of us. Our government seems to be dusting off the old Pilsudski plan for a preemptive strike against Germany. Hitler isn't ready to move against us yet."

"Yes, and how long will it be before he is?"

"Now, Mendale, let's not get emotional," Vovek said. "Let's look at this problem dispassionately. You and I and our families have prospered in Poland. It is our country and has been for a thousand years. We are inextricably bound to it. Maybe it's our own fault that some of us haven't assimilated into the main culture, and still dress in Hasidic clothes and speak Yiddish. But given time, I hope that this will change too. Right now we must try to make progress in that direction."

"Vovek, you're again forgetting Germany. No one was more acculturated than the German Jews, but look what Hitler is doing to them."

"Are you implying that we will lose our rights totally in Poland, the way they did there? Preposterous," Vovek insisted.

"All I know is that with that madman running Germany, there will be a war soon. I vowed to do everything in my power not to be here when it comes. Vovek, I have loved this country, but now I reject it because it has rejected me. I know who I am. I'm a Jew, not a Pole, and I belong in the land of my ancestors, ours alone."

Idisel and Hadasa had listened to the conversation between their husbands, but they became bored and decided to take a walk in the woods. They took Surale along to take care of the dog.

"Surale, walk ahead of us, and take Morus with you," Idisel said as they entered the woods. Hadasa put the leash on the dog and handed it to the girl.

"Isn't it scandalous," Hadasa whispered to Idisel, "the story in the paper about Wally Simpson and the King of England?"

"Do you think the king will marry that woman?" Idisel answered her. "She's been divorced twice. She's a commoner and an American. The English will never stand for that."

"But wouldn't it be romantic if he did marry her? It's strange. She isn't good looking at all."

"She must have charm we're not aware of," Idisel said. "And besides that, she's extremely elegant."

The two women began to whisper inaudibly, walking very slowly now. Morus ran ahead, and Surale let herself be pulled along by him. The path became wide now, and the trees seemed to form a roof overhead. The sun was setting, and it sparkled between the trees.

They turned to go back at the fork in the road and saw their husbands walking toward them. "Well, I have a good and handsome man of my own," said Idisel, "even though he's not a king." They both giggled. Then Hadasa said, "So do I."

Yakov Meyer Halpern was now the assistant to Mayor Michalowski, but his real love was his work for the Betar. As the leader of that organization in Stoczek, he had attended the Second World Conference of Betar in Cracow. Delegates from many countries were there. All the young men and women had assembled to hear their leader, Jabotinsky, propose the codification of the Betar ideology, called "The Oath." It was a most inspiring experience for Yakov Meyer, and he learned a great deal about the new activities of the organization.

On his return to Stoczek, he called a meeting of the organization to inform the membership about the momentous events at the conference. He had also met with Mendale and found him to be most sympathetic to the Betar cause. He invited him to be the main speaker.

The young men and women, dressed in their uniforms, assembled at the Halpern house. Yakov Meyer asked everyone to stand at attention, and administered the oath. As he read the stirring words, sentence by sentence, the members repeated them with pride:

"I devote my life to the rebirth of the Jewish State, with a Jewish majority. . . ." The oath completed, they sang "Hatikvah."

Yakov Meyer now asked them to be seated, and began reporting on the atmosphere and substance of the conference.

Jabotinsky had again stressed the need for continued training in self-defense. In view of the events in Germany, Italy, and other countries in Europe, Jewish youth had to be particularly vigilant. In time of need, the members of Betar had the duty to defend not only themselves, but all their people. Although they may at times have to resort to violence, they must always keep in mind that physical force was not their aim. They had to maintain a sense of "respect, self-esteem, politeness, and faithfulness," as envisioned in the Philosophy of Jabotinsky.

Now Yakov Meyer called on Moshe Wodinski to give a report on the progress being made in pioneer training. Unlike Yakov Meyer, Moshe came from a humble family, but he was a born leader. He and his girlfriend Ester Perkal, had just completed a two-year training course on a farm in a "work brigade."

"It was rigorous training and required a great deal of stamina," he concluded, "but we try to simulate the kind of life we will have to deal with in the Land of Israel. That includes learning to handle small arms, street-fighting techniques, boxing, and military tactics. Ester and I will be leaving, but we want every one of you to join us in our own land soon. To that end we will dedicate all our efforts." There was a great burst of applause, and Moshe added in Hebrew: "And now, I give you my future bride, Esterl. She has something to tell the young women of our organization."

Ester, a pretty blond, got up to speak and present the feminine point of view. Farming, she said, wasn't easy for a town girl, but she had learned to like it. There was something beautiful about being close to nature and living off the land.

"We will make the desert bloom again," she said, "and our land will be ready for future generations to enjoy—no longer exiles, but a free people in our own land. Like our men we women must learn self-defense. In the pogroms, women were raped, their men killed, and their children—you know what happened. We the women of Betar will defend the honor of our people, and if necessary, we will give up our lives to that purpose."

Now Yakov Meyer began to tell about a new plan, which Jabotinsky had proposed, for the emigration of 1.5 million Jews from Eastern Europe to Palestine. If the plan succeeded, it would need international cooperation. All the Jewish leaders and newspapers had to play a role in this great endeavor. Their brothers in England and America would have to join the effort. Jabotinsky had issued an appeal to the various European governments to help him carry out this plan and propose it to the League of Nations. If that organization approved, the tremendous task could begin.

At this point, Yakov Meyer introduced Mendale, who spoke in favor of Jabotinsky's plan. "Brothers," Mendale began. "Although I'm not a member of your organization, I agree completely with your leader, Ze'ev Jabotinsky, that we must act now to save the Jews of Europe, before it is too late.

"Yakov Meyer has informed me of the details of the plan. I was also fortunate to be able to read an article by Jabotinsky in the 'Haynt' (Warsaw Yiddish paper), about the reactions to his proposal. There is violent opposition to the plan from many Jewish sources," he said. "The loudest protest is being voiced by people who consider themselves Jews only by religion, not nationality. They claim that such action will only reenforce anti-Semitic elements, who insist that we don't belong in Europe, anyway.

"These foolish people should stay where they are and face the consequences of their beliefs. But we, the majority, want to go to our own land. We have a right to do so, and they have an obligation to help us. Some of these men are politically powerful, in a position to move the important people in their own countries to accept Jabotinsky's plan.

"If the democratic nations do not back us up, we must begin a mass clandestine exodus from the lands where we are oppressed.

"On the positive side, we have received news that the leadership of your party, is at present negotiating with Polish government circles to back up this plan at the League of Nations. It makes sense for them to help us. They don't want us here, so it would be to their advantage if they helped convince the League to move the British Mandatory Power to allow our people from Poland to enter Palestine without any restrictions.

"We are at a crossroads in our history. We have to prepare ourselves to leave this unhappy land, no matter what the nations decide."

Mendale sat down, and Yakov Meyer brought the meeting to a close: "We can't leave this gathering without expressing our deep concern for our brothers during the recent riots in the Land of Israel. Many of our people lost their lives, and we shall endeavor never to allow this to happen again. For this purpose, a special brigade has been formed in Palestine to stand ready in case of future terror. We pledge eternal vigilance to our people."

Yakov Meyer got engaged soon after. His bride was from Sokolow, a nearby town. Sara was the daughter of a wealthy clothing manufacturer, who had spent many years in the United States. Her father had learned American mass production methods and utilized them when he returned to Poland.

It was a wedding of the established aristocracy, and the newly rich, but everyone was fond of Sara. She was a dark skinned brunette, graceful and intelligent with a mind of her own.

Yakov Meyer and Sara's wedding was celebrated in Sokolow, with great pomp and luxury. The young couple were given an apartment at the Halpern house, and within a year became parents of a little girl, whom they named Tamara. She was a miniature of Sara, playful and intelligent, with a ready smile and a happy disposition.

Mendale was going to Warsaw on a business trip, and decided to take Surale along. She would return the following day with Sara, who was visiting Warsaw to do some shopping. Mendale had to stay in the capital for a few more days, to finish his business transactions.

By the time the bus left the city, it was dark out. They traveled along narrow country roads, and passed through many villages and towns. Lights were now visible in the windows of the houses along the way. Surale, sitting with Sara Halpern in her comfortable seat, spoke in hushed whispers, as some of the travelers were sleeping, lulled by the movement of the bus.

Suddenly they heard a commotion. They looked around and saw a big man trying to push a short, bearded man off his seat. The bully was a swine dealer, whom Sara Halpern recognized immediately.

"Dirty Jew," he shouted. "Get the hell off my seat. I don't want you sitting next to me." The short man moved hastily to the back of the bus, but the swine dealer followed him down the aisle, bellowing: "Are there any more dirty onion eaters here? Get out, you traitors, and go to Palestine, or I'll finish you off right now."

As he got closer to where Sara Halpern and Surale were sitting, they could see the half-empty whiskey bottle in his pocket. He stopped at the seat just in back of them, near an old man dressed in traditional clothes.

"Hey, you, dirty Jew," he yelled. "Didn't you hear what I just said?" He began pulling the old man out of his seat.

Sara Halpern could stand it no longer. "Leave the poor man alone," she yelled. "Can't you see he's old? Shame on you, a strong man, picking on an old man like that."

The drunk looked surprised, but let go of his victim, "Well, well," he said, looking down at her menacingly. "Look who's talking now, the pretty Jew bitch. If you're not careful, Jew girl, something very bad might happen to you."

He bent down and tried to grab her breast. Her elbow hit him right in the groin, and before he could straighten up, she stood up and shouted:

"Driver, help! Stop this bus right now. If this beast hurts someone, you'll be responsible."

The bus stopped with a jolt, and the driver came back to Sara Halpern. The bully was still bent over, groaning and a bit in shock.

"Pani Halpern, what's going on here?"

"If this man tries to put his hands on me again, or mistreats any human being on this bus," Sara Halpern said, "I'll report you to Mayor Michalowski for neglect of duty."

"Pani Halpern, I'm terribly sorry. I didn't hear the commotion, and my assistant here had dozed off."

The driver turned to the swine dealer. "Come on, man, you can't behave like a savage in a public conveyance." Then he turned to his assistant and nodded at him, and they grabbed the bully between them and threw him out of the bus. The driver now closed the door, and announced loudly, "Ladies and gentlemen, we're sorry for the commotion. The man was drunk. We don't allow this kind of behavior on our bus. You all know me. My name is Majdczyna. You see this hat I'm wearing? It's my souvenir for fighting with Pilsudski. He taught us to be fair to everybody. No one gets abused on my bus, not even a Jew."

Majdczyna seemed satisfied with his own little speech, and added: "Now let's get moving. I have a job to do, and a schedule to meet."

Sara Halpern said nothing more to the driver, and the bus continued on its way a bit faster than before. She hugged Surale and asked her if she had been afraid during the commotion. "Yes," the girl answered her. There was a terrible turmoil inside her. Why did these things happen to her people? Was there no justice in the world? Would she be that brave if the time came for her to act?

Aron's second oldest son, Srul, came to Stoczek for a visit. He had been drafted into the army and was wearing his soldier's uniform. He looked very handsome, with his flaming red hair and jovial manner.

He had come for Rosh Hashanah, the New Year holiday, but his real purpose was to discuss with his Uncle Mendale his desire to go to the Land of Israel.

"I've had it," he said. "I'm not going to continue quoting the old clichés, but as soon as I take off this uniform—and I only have a few more weeks to serve—I'm getting out of here, and heading for Palestine. There is no future for me or any of us here."

"How do you plan to go about it, Srul?"

"Illegally," he answered promptly. "I'm going to skip the unpleasant formalities and simply go."

They spent much of the night on the details of his plan. When Mendale was satisfied that the strategy was good, he asked his nephew:

"And how can I help you?"

For the first time, Srul looked a bit sheepish. "The only thing I need from you," he said, "is money. If you'll finance this trip, Uncle Mendale, one day I'll repay you."

"Done," Mendale said. "And as for repayment, you can start worrying about that once you are settled."

The next evening, the entire family attended Rosh Hashanah services at the synagogue. The cantor, who worked all week as a *shohet* (ritual slaughterer), was dressed in a white robe while he conducted his choir, five boys of different ages, the youngest being only four.

A few months later, the Hellers received a letter from Tel Aviv. Srul was now safe in Palestine. In veiled language, he sent a message that he had joined the Haganah. He hoped that his uncle and the family would soon follow him to their homeland.

Chapter 35
IN SEARCH OF AN EDUCATION

Mendale was now actively pursuing the idea of going to Palestine illegally, as his nephew had done. He had an important contact in Kielce and stayed with Aron while they were negotiating the conditions of the trip.

Much had happened since he'd been in Kielce last. The depression had hit very hard in the area, and the brewery was in financial trouble. To add to these difficulties, Aron and his partner, Mayer Kaufman, were quarreling—an unpleasant situation made even more awkward by the romance that had sprung up between Aron's son and Mayer's daughter.

As their parents argued, Symcha and Hindzia grew closer. Their parents refused to acknowledge their relationship. Hindzia was repeatedly warned by her father and mother to have nothing to do with Symcha, and when they spoke to Mendale about this situation, he advised them to wait. Besides, Hindzia would shortly receive her *matura* (equivalent to a junior college certificate) and if she were to go on to study at the University of Warsaw, as she planned to do, they could continue their relationship without interference. Symcha was negotiating for a trucking partnership and eventually would be in Warsaw almost every day.

Hindzia's application to the School of Medicine at Warsaw University, was rejected because of the exclusionary Jewish quota. She was, however, accepted at Charles University in Prague.

A new life opened for the young woman. She missed Symcha, but she was thrilled to be living and studying in the beautiful and exciting capital city. Political freedom existed here for all nationalities, and was extended to foreign students in its universities. How different this was from struggling Poland.

The tone for this type of free society was set by the Czech President, Thomas Masaryk. He and his American born wife, fostered a new spirit in the reborn nation, based on the American pattern of pluralism.

Masaryk, professor, philosopher, and statesman, believed that it was impossible to be a true Christian and an anti-Semite as well. Therefore, he embarked on a mission to eradicate this plague, by educating his people.

Soon Hindzia's fellow student from Kielce, Dora, also came to Prague to study, entranced with the atmosphere of freedom. Away from home and their conventional families, the girls reveled the possibility to debate and to meet with students of different political persuasions. The two thrived on it.

Hindzia corresponded regularly with Symcha at first, but soon her life was so demanding that she found little time for long letters. Everything in Poland seemed to recede to second place in her mind. She was going to be a doctor, and her mind was full of ideas for helping people.

She was brought back to reality when Symcha's brother, Chaim, arrived in Prague. He told her that nothing had changed between their parents, it was comforting to her that they were far away, and she didn't have to listen to their arguments. Her feelings for Symcha hadn't changed, but she felt more detached from him than ever.

The German University, where Chaim was now studying engineering, was an outstanding university, the home, a number of years before, of the great Albert Einstein. Chaim had no difficulty in fitting in to life in his school. He made friends easily, and his brilliant mind was stimulated by the demanding classes he attended.

Hindzia, Dora, and Chaim often met in the cafés frequented by students. Together they explored this lovely city of magnificent old castles, palaces, cathedrals, bridges, flower-bedecked squares, heroic statues.

The upcoming Berlin Olympics of 1936 were being discussed by all the students. But only among Jews did it have political significance.

The Jews of Czechoslovakia had their own athletic clubs, and the stars of these associations were top-ranked in several fields. Their swimming and water-polo teams were considered world class contenders. But did they want to compete in Berlin?

On the eve of the Olympics, the Jewish champions of Czechoslovakia met and decided to refuse participation in the Games. Hitler was sparing no expense in putting up a great show, but he could afford it because he had robbed g Jews of their property. To the Jews of Czechoslovakia, it was a matter of honor not to grace that country with their presence.

Hindzia, Dora, and Chaim met in their favorite café one sunny Sunday afternoon when the conversation drifted to the painful upcoming Olympics. "I think that the champions made a mistake, " Chaim said. "They should have voted to go, just to destroy the myth that 'Aryans' are the best athletes in the world."

"I disagree," Hindzia said emphatically. "If I were Czech and an eligible athlete, I'd refuse to go too. The Nazis can fool the British and the Americans with their big show, but they can't fool us."

"All the so-called democracies should be boycotting the games too," Dora said. "Let's face it, the other countries haven't got the guts to stand up against Hitler. I'm sick of the entire bunch."

"Dora," Hindzia said soothingly, "Democracies move more slowly than dictatorships. Things aren't that bad."

Dora was not placated. "Perhaps this is the beginning of the end of capitalism," she added. "A new dawn is coming to our troubled world."

"What dawn?" Chaim scoffed. "This socialist talk is just utopian nonsense. Besides, a nation that produced Goethe and Schiller can't be fooled too much longer by Hitler. One of my friends at the university, a German, told me that many Germans hate the little dictator and call him "the little evil Austrian housepainter." They'll soon get rid of him."

"No more!" cried Hindzia, holding her ears. "I came for a rest from serious discussions!"

"Right," Chaim said jovially, raising his cup of coffee. "Here's to us, the youth of Poland. May we prosper and continue debating."

They lifted their cups in unison. But in back of their minds they were worried about the future—their own and the world's.

Chipale, or Cyla, as she was now called, was eleven. It was time for Mendale's oldest daughter to enter *gymnazjum* (academic secondary school). Pan Wielgosek, the principal, suggested that Cyla apply to the public *gymnazjum* in the nearby town of Siedlce. Her grades were excellent, and he would recommend her.

The family debated what to do. Idisel was worried that Cyla was too young to be away from home and thought that she should finish the last year in Stoczek. Besides, Cyla would certainly miss her friends.

She had organized a group of girls, who called themselves the Company. Their original purpose had been social, but eventually they decided to collect money for the poor and to help reclaim land in Palestine. To get the money, they presented plays, which were written, produced and directed, by Cyla. The parents of the Company members helped only with the costumes, many of crepe paper. These performances were astonishingly successful, and netted the girls a sizable amount to contribute to Palestine and much public applause.

Cyla didn't really want to leave the Company, but she felt privileged to be able to go to *gymnazjum*. It meant that she would now be a member of "the educated," a small select group in Poland.

Mendale consulted with his mentor, Shea Halpern, and he was enthusiastic about the Siedlce school. His younger daughter, Hudka, was a graduate of the *gymnazjum*, so he knew that their standards were high, and the curriculum excellent.

But before a final decision was made, Hania, Aron's oldest daughter, arrived for a visit and convinced Mendale and Idisel that Cyla would be better off at the private girls' *gymnazjum* in Kielce. She herself, Hindzia, and Dora, had all studied there, and the standards were much higher than in the public secondary school. Best of all, Cyla would live with Aron's family.

So, it was settled. Mendale took Cyla to his brother's house in Kielce at the beginning of the school year, the girl was fitted for her school uniform, and the proper accessories were purchased, as well as school supplies.

It was an exciting time for Cyla—her first step in entering an elite group of Polish society, "the intelligentsia."

Hindzia was about to begin her third year of medicine in Prague when she received a telegram that her mother had died suddenly. She returned home to Kielce immediately.

In addition to the terrible shock of losing her mother, she suffered another cruel disappointment. Her father made it clear that she couldn't go back to school. She would have to take charge of the household and try to be a mother to her two younger sisters and brother.

At night, when the others were asleep, she lay awake brooding over her shattered hopes. But she couldn't blame her father. Who else could take over the responsibilities of her mother?

Symcha understood her feelings, and was there to give her moral support. Their love rekindled and was stronger than ever. She realized that they were destined to be together always. She had loved him from the time she was fourteen.

But as the months went by, her responsibilities grew. Her father retreated into drinking, but she could do nothing about it.

One day, a fire broke out in the apartment, caused by an explosion somewhere in the brewery. The fire destroyed both the Kaufman and Heller apartments. The Hellers now moved into a small house on the property, where the brewer had previously lived. The Kaufmans decided to stay on in their apartment, and rebuild.

When things became somewhat more settled, and her brother and sister left home to study and work in Warsaw, Hindzia decided that it was time for her to have a life of her own. She and Symcha wanted to get married. Uncle Mendale was, as always, the one they asked for help.

Mendale had come to Kielce to visit with Cyla, and the young couple arranged to meet him at a café.

"Uncle Mendale, you're the only person who has some influence with our fathers," Symcha began. "We want you to make them see that we are in love and have the right to marry."

"We don't want to run away and do it without their consent," Hindzia added. "Will you help us?"

Mendale sighed. This was a sticky business, and he knew he could end up alienating both families. But he had to agree to try. "I can't promise that it will work."

Next day, Mendale approached Mayer with the problem. The man, who hitherto had been friendly to him, got very angry: "Don't talk to me about this ridiculous proposal. I will never consent. She better forget about him."

"Reb Mayer, Hindzia and Symcha love each other very deeply," Mendale told him calmly. "In this world of increasing hatred and cruelty, love is a rare and precious thing. You should be glad that they have each other."

"Don't be naïve, Mendale. It's just an infatuation. Hindzia never went with anyone else. How would she even know what love is?"

"She hasn't looked at another man since she was fourteen. Denying it isn't going to change anything."

"And neither is this conversation going to change anything," Mayer said, and tried to leave the room.

Mendale stopped him. "Pan Kaufman, I know that you and my brother Aron don't get along, but that shouldn't cloud your sense of justice. Tell me sincerely, what do you have against my brother Aron's son?"

Mayer was silent for a moment. Then he burst out: "Aside from being *his* son, he's simply not good enough for my Hindzia. They have absolutely nothing in common. She lives in a world of ideas, and what is he? A trucker, that's all. Besides, he's impulsive like his father and irresponsible." He ran down. Then he added: "Look, Mendale, you want to help, but you'll only make trouble if you continue. I will never give my consent to the marriage." This time Mayer walked away from him.

Mendale had failed with Mayer. Would he succeed in convincing his own brother? Aron was very hostile at first, but Mendale finally said to him:

"Your son and this girl have been in love for ten years. They never considered marrying anyone else. It's classic Romeo and Juliet stuff. Do you remember what happened to the star-crossed lovers?"

Aron didn't answer at first, but Mendale could see that he had touched some chord in his brother. Aron stood thinking for what seemed like a long time, and then he finally said:

"If it weren't for you, Mendale, I would never consent to this marriage, but I guess I shouldn't stand in their way any longer, since they both want it so much. He's my son. I can't keep fighting him all the time."

Mendale made all the arrangements for the wedding, but neither Aron nor Mayer was present. It was January 19, a cold and snowy day, but the bride was radiant in a pink blouse and gray skirt, and the red-headed groom charmed everyone with his ready smile. Idisel and Mendale gave the bride away, and when the young couple stood under the bridal canopy, there was joy and satisfaction in their eyes. Their love had finally conquered all obstacles.

They rented a small but elegant apartment in town, and soon Cyla went to stay with them. Their happiness was marred by another tragedy. Hindzia's brilliant brother, Yosio, who had recently finished his engineering studies at the University of Warsaw, drowned while swimming in the Vistula. No one could explain what had happened to him, an outstanding swimmer. He had gone swimming alone, and his lifeless body was found a few days later.

For Hindzia, it was a devastating blow. She had been very close to her brother, and his death, so close after her mother's, was difficult to bear. If she hadn't had Symcha to comfort and support her, she thought she would have died of grief.

Chapter 36
FREE AT LAST

By 1937 war had become a reality in Europe. Two years before, Mussolini sent his Fascist army into Abyssinia (Ethiopia). The Emperor of that country, Haile Selassie, personally led his troops against the Italians, and was overcome by their superior forces. He now pleaded in the League of Nations, in a most moving speech, to impose sanctions against Italy and force it to stop the war. He was totally ignored.

In Spain a bloody civil war was raging. Franco's forces had attacked the Republic. A merciless totalitarian regime was established in the areas which Franco had conquered. Germany had sent its airforce, the Luftwafe, to help the new dictator in Spain. It seemed that Hitler, imitating Mussolini, was rehearsing for a war on a much larger scale.

Soon many idealistic young people from all over Europe and America came to fight on the side of the Spanish Republic, in the International Brigade. Russia, too, sent arms and military advisors to try and stop Franco.

In *Mein Kampf,* Hitler had written about uniting all Germanic or Aryan people into one nation. He called the concept the *"Anschluss"* (Annexation). Now he cast his eye on Austria, his native land. The Nazis infiltrated the country to lead their local sympathizers. They unleashed a reign of terror in Austria. There were bombings, murders, and massive demonstrations for propaganda purposes. Hitler's plan was to soften up Austria for a successful invasion.

Mendale observed all these events with great concern. The world seemed to be on the brink of total war. He redoubled his efforts to leave Poland illegally. The opportunity finally came in the spring of 1937, but he couldn't make use of it. He was told that he could go, but his family would have to stay behind. He couldn't leave Idisel and the children and had to refuse the offer. He continued exploring ways to leave the country together with his family, but he couldn't even get a visitor's visa from the British Consulate in Warsaw, where he was considered an undesirable because of his Zionist activities.

Just when he began to feel totally despondent, he received a letter from his brother Max in New York. Max and his family and also his brother Morris were coming to Poland. They would be there in June and would spend the summer visiting different members of the family. They would avoid a German ship and travel by the French Line, driving from Le Havre to Hamburg first, to visit Shainchi and her family, then on to Poland.

Max expressed some concern at the events that had overtaken Europe, but didn't really seem to know the extent of the tragedy. People in the United States, where Hitler and Mussolini were regarded as jokes, believed that the stories they read in the papers were grossly exaggerated. Well, his brother would soon see for himself.

Mendale and his family were waiting on the road near Stoczek. Soon a Buick came into view with three small American flags attached to the fender. The brothers jumped out of the car, and they hugged Mendale, Idisel, and the girls. Now Max introduced his American wife, Ruth, and his children, Gloria and Stanley.

Morris told the children to pile into the car, while his two brothers and sister-in-law walked. They passed the town square and stopped to greet the Halperns, who were waiting on their porch. People on the street greeted them and waved. The American car, proceeding very slowly through town, was a wonder to everyone. Children ran out of the *heder* to follow the vehicle, to touch it and be part of the excitement. By the time the Hellers reached their house, it seemed that everyone in town had greeted them.

The following day, the brothers went swimming in the river. It was the first opportunity they had to be together alone, and as they sat under the trees after the swim, Max finally said:

"How peaceful this place is. I had forgotten how beautiful the Polish countryside can be in the summer."

"Yes, it's lovely here," Morris agreed. "Quite different from what it feels like to be in Germany." He told about instances he had witnessed of brutality. The Nazis patrolled the streets, looking for Jews to torture, and the secret police were everywhere.

"I saw a Nazi on a busy street in Hamburg, torturing an old man,"

Max said. "The people passing either pretended not to see or egged the brute on. I tried to stop him, but he just laughed and said that the man was only a Jew. He asked me for my identification, and when he realized that I was an American citizen, he told the old man that he could go. He said he hoped that I wouldn't spread any bad propaganda about Germany when I get back to the States. He was only disciplining the man because he was 'breaking the law'." Max took a puff of his cigarette and then continued:

"The experience unnerved me so, that when I got back to Shainchi's house, I told her and Nehemiah to get out of Germany immediately.

"Nehemiah feels that things might still improve in Germany," Max said, "but I, personally, think that time is running out for the Jews there, and wish that someone could convince him to leave now."

"Well, at least you seem to understand why I'm trying so desperately to leave," Mendale said. "And the British have just issued a new 'White Paper' which limits immigration to the Land of Israel.

"Recently, our minister of foreign affairs proposed that the League of Nations place some European colonies under a Polish mandate, so they could send all the Polish Jews there. Can you imagine how they would administer such a mandate?"

"They would probably do a worse job than the English in Palestine," Morris said. "At least the British have democracy at home."

"Yes, and at the universities," Mendale said, "our young people are being attacked and even killed by the other students. This terrorist bunch is clamoring for a seating ghetto in classes. Can you imagine? In the cities they're boycotting Jewish stores—in fact, there's been some of that right here in Stoczek."

"Peace in this country is an illusion. While the Nazi menace threatens to make an end to independent Poland, the government is busy baiting us. Instead of building up Polish defenses against Hitler, they're trying to join him against us." He stopped for a while, out of breath, and then continued: "I've got to get us out of here before it's too late."

"It can be done, Mendale," Max said quietly. "As our brother, we can send you an affidavit to come to America. Although the quota from Poland is very small, there's a special clause in the immigration laws that provides for the reunification of families—outside of the quota. Morris and I would take full responsibility for your support. That seems to be the chief concern of the authorities, because of the massive unemployment in the States. I'm sure that you'd receive an American visa within a short time."

"I don't want to go to America. I want to go to the Land of Israel."

"Be practical," Morris said impatiently. "You've been trying for years to get to Palestine. After five years in the States, you'll become an American citizen, and then nothing can stop you from going where you want."

"Let me think about this for a while," Mendale said. But as he pondered, his feelings slowly changed, and the old excitement stirred. A roundabout route, yes, but the longest way around is often the shortest way home. "If I agree—I'm not saying I will—I'd like to assure you that you will not be burdened by me and my family."

Max laughed: "That's the last thing that worries us! You have more money than any of us."

"Look," Morris added, "we'll go to see the American consul in Warsaw before we leave the country and get the details straight and—"

"And when we get back to New York," Max broke in, "we'll start working on the documents for your immigration."

After a few weeks stay in Stoczek, the family went to Aron's house in Kielce. Shainchi arrived from Germany with her youngest two girls, and Laichia came from Rozwadow with her entire family. Golda had all of them with her now. She and her children had not been together like this since Max left for America before the Great War.

Aron seemed pleased to hear that Mendale and his family were going to America, but he declined to accompany them. "I'm too old," he said. "Mendale is still a relatively young man. I'll take my chances here."

From Kielce the family went to Zakopane in the Tatra range of the Carpathians, where Golda had her summer villa, "Eliaszowka." The mountain resort would be the last stop for Max and Morris before their return to the United States. The American contingent stayed at a luxurious "Three Roses" hotel, while the rest of the family stayed with Golda. There were almost daily excursions into the mountains, led by a young relative who lived there and was an avid mountain climber and skier. They climbed the Morskie Oko (The Eye of the Sea), a beautiful transparent lake high up in the mountains. They rode the cable car to the highest points and admired the views. They took pictures to commemorate the family reunion.

And then the Americans were gone, leaving behind them precious memories and new hope for Mendale and his family.

It was the winter of 1938, and the situation in Europe was deteriorating. On February 20, Hitler made one of his mad speeches, which was broadcast all over Europe. Austria, he argued in his high-pitched shrill voice, must become an integral part of Greater Germany.

Within a few days, Nazi terror in Austria escalated into a frenzy. In Graz, a wild mob of 20,000 Nazis invaded the town square, tore down the Austrian flag, and raised the swastika. Economic chaos followed as people withdrew their money from the banks and tried to flee. Arturo Toscanini, the famous conductor, canceled a concert he was to give at Salzburg. Chancellor Kurt Schuschnigg's appeals to the League of Nations fell on deaf ears.

On March 12, the Nazis marched into Austria, and unleashed fresh terror. Jews, of course, were the primary victims. Sadistic stormtroopers forced men and women to scrub the sidewalks and gutters on their hands and knees, beating them if they stopped. People were picked off the street or in their homes and jailed. Apartments were looted of all valuables. Some fled, giving up all their possessions in exchange for freedom. Desperate people jumped from their windows into the Danube or committed suicide in other ways, to escape the hands of the Nazis.

And just at this tragic time for Austrian Jews, Mendale received a call to report to the American Consulate in Warsaw. There he was told that the papers had arrived from his brothers in America, and that now there were certain steps to take in order to receive his visa. This would have to include an exit permit from the Polish authorities, stating, among other things, that his property taxes had been fully paid up.

As Mendale left the office, he had to make his way through hordes of people in the lobby. Some were standing on lines, others sitting down, and the crush was so great that it was difficult to get to the front door.

"Pan Heller," Mendale heard someone shout in the crowd. It was Pan

Levin, an old acquaintance, who owned an industrial machinery store in Warsaw.

They shook hands, and the older man said excitedly: "I've been hounding this place for months, to file my application to go to the United States, and no one wants to talk to me. Have you had better luck?"

"I'm sorry about your situation, Pan Levin," Mendale said. He was almost ashamed to admit his own good fortune. "This is the sad state that the nations have reduced us to, to beg and plead to be admitted."

"But what about you, Pan Heller?"

Reluctantly, Mendale told him about his brothers and the papers he had just received. Seeing the misery of the other man, he hated every word he had to say, especially since Pan Levin's face lifted up with pleasure for him.

"I'm on my way back to my store," Levin said. "Come with me, Pan Heller, so we can talk freely. I must hear all about how you managed this."

Mendale agreed, and soon they reached Pan Levin's place of business. "I'm not ashamed to tell you, Pan Heller," said the older man, ushering Mendale into his office, "that I'm filled with envy at your good luck. I've tried to emigrate to America for the past five years, and so far I've failed miserably."

"Well, I'm in luck in that my brothers emigrated in the days before the laws were tightened, back in the 1920s. Otherwise, I'd be in the same boat."

"But now the situation is desperate, Pan Heller. The Anschluss has changed the entire picture. I've lived through too many political upheavals not to realize the great danger we're in."

For a few minutes the two men sat there despondently. Suddenly Pan Levin's mood seemed to change. He gave a mad little laugh and said, half jokingly, "Pan Heller, give me your visa, and I'll give you my entire business, my apartment, and everything I own in this city."

"I wish I could do that, my friend. I wish I could smuggle you out as a member of my family. But I can't."

"My lawyer tells me that I could apply for a visitor's visa to the States for myself and my family," Levin now continued. "Next year they're planning to have a World's Fair in New York. Once there, we could 'get lost,' so to speak, and find a way to stay. But the plan is no good. I'd have to leave everything here, and what would we live on? But if I start selling off my properties, the Americans will never give me a visa."

"But if that's the only way to get out, try it, my friend," Mendale responded. "Sell some of your lesser properties, and send the money to Switzerland. You're smart enough to know that there are ways to do that."

Mendale got up. "Good luck," he said to the man as he shook his hand. "Keep trying. Here's my brother's address in New York. If all goes well, I will see you there soon."

Now Mendale began his visits to the different ministries to get things started for his official emigration. His last chore was to visit the shipping office to make ticket reservations from Gdynia to New York. He found that the first available space was for August 15, on the Polish ship *Batory*, and made reservations to leave on that day.

It was only a few days before the Hellers' departure date. Reb Shaul sat at the table studying. He was surrounded by a number of books in which he had been researching a particular question concerning the coming of the Messiah. Weary, he fell asleep, his head dropping gently onto his large Talmud.

He'd just been cross-referencing his own studies with Isaac Abrabanel's commentaries on the subject. In his dream, Reb Shaul was transported to Spain, where the great scholar had lived and been an advisor to Ferdinand and Isabella. Reb Shaul heard the monarchs pronounce the Edict of Expulsion and Don Isaac plead with them to revoke it, and allow the Jews to stay in Spain.

Suddenly Reb Shaul woke up. He felt agitated and depressed. What was the meaning of this dream? Were the Jewish people to suffer again like they did in 1492?

His thoughts turned to his children. What was the reason that Mendale was struggling so hard to leave Poland? Did his son-in-law have a premonition of doom? He decided to broach the subject with his son-in-law.

"Mendale," he said to him that evening, "it seems to be the will of the Creator that you shouldn't leave. Otherwise, why has He put so many difficulties in your way? Why don't you remain in Poland until you can go directly to the Land of Israel?"

"I know you mean well, father-in-law," the younger man answered. "But please try to understand that something compelled me not to give up. I'm a driven man. I *must* get out of Poland. I *must* go toward the light. I see a dark cloud gathering over this unhappy land." Mendale stopped, expecting a to protest. When he didn't, Mendale went on in a lighter tone: "And see—now I have been assured of an American visa. Isn't that a sign that the Almighty wants us to go?"

"Well, Mendale, I see that I can't stop you," Reb Shaul said sadly. "It's difficult for us, mere humans, to figure out what the Holy One, blessed be His Name, has in store for us. I trust in Him, and I know that He will protect you, Idisel, and the children. My prayers will always be with you."

What really bothered Mendale was that they were not being allowed to take the old man with them. At the American Consulate, Mendale had been told that once he got his first papers (applying for citizenship), he would be able to start the process of getting his father-in-law to America too. But that would take time. His vision of approaching doom was very real. Would it hold off long enough for all these wearisome formalities to complete themselves?

His heart ached especially for Idisel. The idea of leaving Reb Shaul had upset her from the very beginning. She was convinced that once she left Poland, she would never see him again. He half-expected her to refuse to go, but she was too dutiful a wife for that.

At night, she cried because she felt so helpless, and Mendale would console her as best he could, reminding her how lucky they were to be going at all. Lucky, yes, of course, and they were both grateful to the Almighty for this miraculous chance. But he knew Idisel didn't feel lucky.

"As soon as we get to America, we'll find a way to bring your father over, to hurry up the process a little," he said gently. He reminded her of her cousin Ana, rich and influential, who lived on Fifth Avenue. "We'll ask for her help, and then before you know it, he will be with us again." It was the best reassurance he could give her.

The wicker trunks full of bedding, winter clothing, dishes, and other household items stood in lined up in the dining room. The following day the Hellers would leave Stoczek forever. Everyone felt anxious and depressed as they walked to the synagogue that evening.

After prayers, the rabbi spoke: "As you all know, my brothers, we are losing our Reb Mendale. We here in the community will miss him terribly. Who will stand up for us now before those in power?" The rabbi turned to Mendale: "You, my son, spoke to them with a voice of courage, as Aaron spoke before Pharaoh. May you continue to work on behalf of our oppressed brothers in exile. And may our Heavenly Father bless you and strengthen you in every path you take."

The rabbi's voice shook with emotion, as he placed his hands on Mendale's head and pronounced the customary blessing. Soon Mendale was surrounded by the people, each vying to shake his hand. Greeting his friends, he made his way through the crowd to the *bimah* (dais), where the rabbi was standing. He began to speak:

"Honored Rabbi, beloved father-in-law, and friends: It is my destiny, and the Creator's will, that I embark on this journey. I will be traveling in a roundabout way, but the road I take will lead me in a short time to the land of our fathers. There I hope to live and die.

"I will never forget any of you. I know each one of you by name. Before I leave, I want each of you to strive with all your power to get to the Land of Israel. It doesn't matter what political conviction you have. That is where we belong. I hope to see you there one day soon. Until then, long live our people, Israel."

It was still dark when the family got up the next morning. Reb Shaul was praying softly in the next room. They could hear his melodic voice, somewhat muted but always comforting. Soon they got ready and left the house.

A delegation stood waiting at the bus and a little girl, prompted by her mother, presented a bouquet of flowers. "Good luck. . . good luck!" people cried as the bus door opened. "Don't forget us. We'll never forget you. . . ."

They boarded the bus. It was starting to get light, and the town square was flooded with a shaft of bright sunlight. People began to move about, opening shutters, and going about their business. The cobblestones shone, and the old houses seemed very small and alone around the square.

As the bus took off, the people looked smaller, and so did the buildings. Soon they disappeared from view, and the bus passed the Halpern house, the church, and then drove down the hill toward the water mill. They were on their way.

After some hours of travel, they reached Warsaw, they passed the suburb of Praga, and continued on to the heart of the city. From the bus station they drove to the house of some friends, where they were going to stay for a few days.

The following day Mendale and Idisel had an appointment to pick up their exit visas. After that they would go to the American Consulate for their entry visas. They were to leave the next day for the port of Gdynia.

As Mendale presented his identification to the clerk, a small muscular man grabbed his arm.

"Are you Emanuel Heller?" he demanded. Puzzled, Mendale said he was, and the little man told him he was under arrest.

"Arrest? There must be some mistake here."

The man flashed a badge and continued to tug at Mendale's arm.

Flabbergasted, Mendale gaped at the man. "I demand to know why you're arresting me, officer."

"You'll get your answer in jail. Come along now, and don't struggle."

Thoroughly confused, Mendale pulled himself together the best he could. "Idisel, follow us," he whispered, "and see where he's taking me, then get Aron on the phone immediately. He will find a way to get me out." Then the police agent took him away, and she followed close behind them.

Aron arrived in Warsaw within hours and contacted the proper authorities. He was informed that Mendale had been denounced for trying to leave the country while a law case was pending against him.

A man had been injured at Mendale's sawmill and had lost three fingers on his right hand. The man attempted to blackmail Heller & Weintraub by demanding a large sum of money in compensation, and when they tried to bargain him down, he sued. The verdict of the judge was that the employee was negligent, but in view of his disability, the partners were to give him a reasonable sum as severance pay.

The worker had evidently not been satisfied with this verdict of the court and had chosen this particular time to get even with Mendale—by trying to prevent him from leaving the country.

Aron, now a partner in the sawmill, took over his brother's liability and promised to abide by the higher court's decision. In return, Mendale was released.

But he had been detained just long enough for the *Batory* to sail without the Hellers, and now new accommodations had to be found before his exit visa ran out. That left Mendale a deadline of only one week.

It was Friday, and he went early in the morning to the shipping office. The place was crowded as usual, and he had to stand on a long line. But once he reached the head of the line, the clerk was very attentive.

When Mendale inquired about immediate passage, he said courteously, "Pan Heller, we put you on a waiting list as soon as you informed us that you were unable to leave on the *Batory*. Now let me see." He checked on various schedules. "The *Pilsudski*, the sister ship of the *Batory*, is sailing to New York on Monday. If I can get you on her, the accommodations will be exactly the same." But his eyes trailed down a long passenger list, and he shook his head. "I'm sorry. It's fully booked, and there have been absolutely no cancellations."

"What's to be done?" Mendale inquired. "I'm in a desperate situation. My visa expires on Wednesday."

"Give me a minute, and I may be able to work something out for you," the clerk said. He began rummaging through the schedules again. "This is unconventional, Pan Heller, but I can get you on a freighter to Southampton, sailing Tuesday. From there we can eventually get you connections to New York. It may not be very comfortable, but it seems to be the only alternative. Shall I try?"

"Please do," Mendale said.

The clerk called Southampton. After a while he hung up the receiver and said, "I'm sorry, but I'm unable to confirm passage from Southampton to New York. That means you'll have to stay in England for a few days until you make connections and even for such a brief stay, you'll have to get permission from the British Consulate here."

Mendale's heart sank. How much chance was there of that? But between a small chance and none, there was little choice. "I guess we have no other alternative," he said.

"Then do you want me to go ahead and book the tickets on the freighter?"

"Yes, please."

The clerk went to work and soon handed Mendale the tickets and the schedule for Southampton. Mendale paid him and thanked him for his help.

From the window, he went across the hall and sat down. He was very tired, and now he had a new ordeal to face: He had to go to the British again. And what happens if they refuse him? He covered his face with his hands and sat there for what seemed an eternity.

Was this what Reb Shaul meant by "It seems to be the will of the Creator that you shouldn't leave"? Perhaps he was fated to remain in exile with his fellow Jews and share the doom he felt hanging over them.

Suddenly he heard the clerk's voice: "Pan Heller, Pan Emanuel Heller, please come forward."

Mendale dragged himself to his feet and went to the window.

"I'm so glad you're still here. I just received a telegram, stating that a train from Lvov to Gdynia was derailed, injuring a number of passengers. Many of them were to leave on the *Pilsudski*, but it's obvious that they can't make it. They're in the hospital."

Mendale couldn't believe it. It was horrible to benefit from other people's misfortunes, but he was too desperate to worry about that now. "You mean there will be room for us?"

"Yes, indeed, sir."

Mendale exchanged the tickets and paid the additional money. Silently, he uttered a prayer to the Almighty, whose will it apparently was that the Hellers should escape to America.

Before being allowed aboard the ship in Gdynia, the Hellers were thoroughly examined, even the children subjected to a body search. From there, they were conducted to a large hall, where all of them had to submit to a health inspection. This was an American requirement, to prevent the importing of infectious disease. Some would-be passengers were turned away at the last minute, the Hellers noticed. But they passed.

The *Pilsudski* glistened in the sun as they boarded her. The red and white Polish flag rolled and swayed in the gentle breeze. An orchestra was playing popular Gershwin tunes in the ballroom, and some people were dancing and enjoying cocktails.

The family put their things away in their cabins and went out on deck. A band had assembled at the pier. Everyone on deck was handed gaily colored streamers.

As the ship began to move, the passengers threw the streamers, which unrolled and floated off toward the crowd on the pier. The orchestra struck up the Polish national anthem, the ship's officers stood at attention on the upper deck, and many people joined in the singing.

Mendale and Idisel stood silent, looking on. They were leaving a land where their ancestors had lived for a thousand years and going into an unknown future—in a new country whose language they couldn't even speak.

"I thought that I would be ecstatic at this moment," Mendale whispered, "but I feel terribly sad." He put his arm around his wife, and he felt her tremble a bit.

"I have a premonition that we'll never see our country of birth again. I just feel it," she said sadly.

Only the girls were truly happy, dazzled by the farewell ceremony and excited about traveling across the great Atlantic Ocean in a big ship.

The music on the shore now faded, as they sailed due north on a calm blue-green Baltic. Next stop was Copenhagen, Denmark, and then across the North Sea and the Atlantic to America.

Notes concerning the fate of the individuals in this book.

Shaul Hakohen Rosenmann—Martyred by the Nazis and by their Ukrainian collaborators in Skole, September 1942. He was forced to dig his own grave, and then buried alive.

Aron Heller—although he was offered a position in the underground, he refused because they would not take Ester. He was arrested as the leader of the Jewish community in Stoczek, and tortured and killed in the infamous Pawiak prison by the Nazis.

Chaim Heller, his son, was murdered by the Nazis when he attempted to pass as a *folksdeutsher*. A small box with his ashes was received by his parents before Aron was arrested.

Wladyslaw Wielgosek, the former mayor and patriotic Pole, was killed in the Pawiak with Aron.

Shea Halpern—died of a heart attack after hearing the story from Shainchi and Nehemia about their expulsion from Germany and the brutal behavior of the nazis as they forced the Polish born Jews across the German Polish border. (Zbazyn Incident—October 28, 1938)

The Rabbi of Stoczek—Eluzerel Goldberg died of a heart attack before the expulsion to Treblinka when he had to witness the cruelty of the Nazis against his people.

The following people were martyred with most of the Jews of Stoczek:

Ester Heller
Shainchi and Nehemia Weissman
Busia Halpern
Yakov Mayer Halpern, her son and leader of the Betar.
Sara Halpern, his wife, and Tamara their child.
Mayer and Paya Celnik, Sura Celnik, and her two sisters.

Some of the people in this book fled to the Soviet Union, where they perished in the Gulag.

Golda Heller died of hunger and disease.

Avrumchi Silber, her son-in-law, defied the Communists with prayer, and died of exhaustion and hunger.

Avrum Celnik—one of the twins, just a boy, disappeared after being arrested.

> "Oh earth, cover not thou my blood . . . .
> behold, my witness is in heaven."
>
> Job, Chapter 16